GW00647851

A
Botanist's Garden

JOHN RAVEN

A
Botanist's Garden

SILENT BOOKS

This edition published in Great Britain 1992 by
Silent Books
Swavesey
Cambridge CB4 5RA

First edition published 1971

ISBN 1 85183 034 0

Typeset and printed in Great Britain by
Redwood Press Ltd, Melksham, Wiltshire

In memory of
EMMELINE HUGH SMITH
and gratitude to
DICK CHAPMAN

Contents

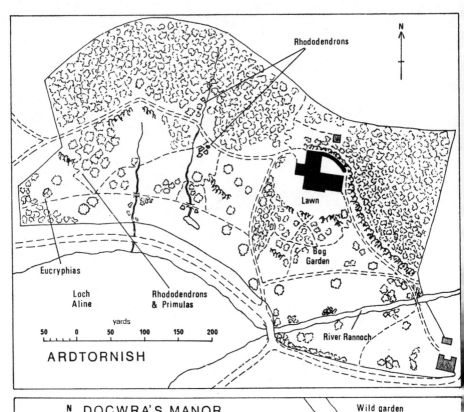

Rhododendrons

N

Rhododendrons

Lawn

Bog
Garden

Eucryphias

Loch
Aline

Rhododendrons
& Primulas

yards

50   0   50   100   150   200

ARDTORNISH

River Rannoch

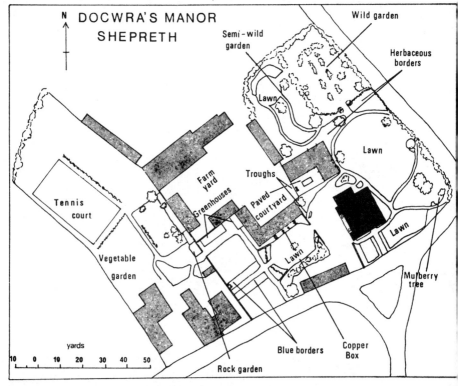

N   **DOCWRA'S MANOR
SHEPRETH**

Wild garden

Semi-wild
garden

Herbaceous
borders

Lawn

Lawn

Farm
yard

Troughs

Greenhouses

Paved
courtyard

Tennis
court

Lawn

Lawn

Vegetable
garden

Mulberry
tree

Blue borders

Copper
Box

yards

10   0   10   20   30   40   50

Rock garden

Foreword 1992

GARDENING books are legion; but every now and again one among them becomes especially treasured, either because there is something particularly engaging about the personality of the author and his or her way of writing, or because the book offers information that is very much out of the ordinary or uniquely useful. John Raven's *A Botanist's Garden* is one such treasure, and on both counts.

John was a distinguished classical scholar with a main interest in Plato. His writing strikes me as having a distinctly Socratic flavour: the artfully leisured development of an argument, the unexpected pounce on a conclusion, the gentle half-disguised humour that pervades the whole. His education in Greek and Latin also made him particularly alive to the derivations and meanings of the scientific names of plants, and his disquisitions on these are always a delight.

When he was not being a professional classic, John's chief interest (apart from his family) was field-botany, with the stress on field. I have known many botanists but none other quite equalled John in his extraordinary ability to spot a rare plant in the field or to pinpoint, often from a distance, precisely the habitat in which it would be found. Add to this an eye for character in a plant, for what makes it aesthetically pleasing, and a sure taste about just where to place it in a garden. Then again there is something engaging about his strong likes and dislikes. Among the likes were green-flowered plants – Hellebores, Spurges and Wormwoods; among the dislikes almost all the other members of the family Compositae, although John had made himself something of an expert on the extremely difficult genus *Hieracium*, the Hawkweeds.

John's early botanising had occasionally made some connection with gardens, particularly those of his father, the distinguished naturalist Canon Charles Raven; but the real impetus to active gardening derived from his marriage in 1954 to Faith Hugh Smith. Her parents' rhododendron-filled garden in the Scottish Highlands had made of Faith an enthusiastic gardener, though one highly suspicious of academic 'Botany'. This garden Faith inherited on her mother's death. As a newly-married couple the Ravens bought Docwras Manor, with its mainly chalk garden on the borders of Cambridgeshire and Hertfordshire; and it was largely on Faith's initiative that they embarked on a series of excursions, principally to Greece and Italy, in search of garden-worthy plants. The planning and planting of Docwras was a joint venture.

The two gardens are described in the Introduction, with fuller details in the following chapters. Since John's death Faith has continued to care for and develop them, and both are now open to the public, so that the conclusions of the book can be checked on the ground.

A Botanist's Garden is, then, for anyone with a taste for and taste in gardening, a good read; and it introduces the reader to a host of little-known or undeservedly neglected plants and exactly describes the horticultural conditions in which they will show themselves at their best. These have seemed to be good reasons for reprinting the book twenty-one years after it was first published and twelve years after the death of its author.

The lapse of time does mean, however, that some up-dating has to be done. To begin with there is the phenomenon, so vexing to gardeners, of changed botanical names. These may come about in three different ways. First, taxonomic experts may decide that a plant has been assigned to a genus to which it is not very well matched and that it would fit better in another (e.g. Hollyhock transferred from *Althaea* to *Alcea*); or that a large and multifarious genus is better understood if divided into smaller units (vide *Lithospermum* or *Polygonum*). In the second place, there is an international agreement among botanists that, to avoid endless confusion, each plant should be universally known by one name only and that this should be the earliest to have been validly published for it. In itself this rule would seem to be eminently sensible; but it happens not infrequently that a researcher will unearth a name that is earlier than the one currently in use and, by the rule, must be substituted for it. (Gardeners may sometimes suspect that the research has been undertaken merely to make mischief or a name for the researcher, but such a danger is in future likely to be circumvented by a new rule that may allow a name hallowed by long and widespread usage to be preserved despite the discovery of another that antedates it). The third kind of change is much less troublesome. The practical decision has recently been taken to distinguish garden varieties or 'cultivars' from true species or subspecies by printing the names of the former in roman with an initial capital (Fanal or Variegatum) rather than in the lower case italics (*variegatum*) that are de rigueur for the natural taxa.

In this edition all plant names, except a very few that have proved elusive, have been brought into line with *The Plant Finder* 1991 and/or *Flora Europaea*. Apart from these alterations – and they are many – it has been necessary to notice one major shift in the climate of botanical opinion that has affected the book. When the Ravens were quartering Europe for unfamiliar species or particularly beautiful forms to be introduced into British gardens, the concept of conservation had hardly taken hold, and they followed, in a mild way, the great tradition of British plant-collectors. The reader should not, however, be shocked by John's account of his activities. His generation had moved a long way on from Reginald Farrer's biscuit-tins full of rare alpines left roasting on the railway station of Torre Pellice. John was in fact a very scrupulous collector, choosing to take seeds or cuttings by preference and uprooting plants only where they were abundant and no other means of propagation was available. It should in any case be borne in mind that to prune, thin or even divide plants may be as beneficial to their health in the field as in the garden. The changes in attitude and practice have also rendered obsolete John's remarks on how to obtain a licence to import plants. The remarks have been left in the text as a curious memorial to times past. Such licences are indeed still available, now for a very substantial fee, from the Ministry of Agriculture, Fisheries and Food, but are intended for cultivated plants and the bulk importer. The amateur will probably be satisfied with a concession that permits the bringing in, without licence, of a small quantity of wild plants provided that they are neither on the list of those that might introduce disease (e.g. species of *Rosa*) nor on that of internationally protected species (e.g. all *Cyclamen*, which before protection suffered wholesale depredation in Turkey). It should also be remembered that most European countries have each their own list of protected species that must not be collected.

Finally, the illustrations that appeared in the first edition have been dropped from this. The prime reason was that the plates from which they were originally printed have been lost, and to re-collect or replace the photographs would be both troublesome and expensive. More important, the omission of the pictures makes it possible to offer the book at a much lower price.

The adjustments that have had to be made to John Raven's book do not affect the warmth, the breadth of intimate knowledge, or the accuracy of *A Botanist's Garden*. May it continue to inspire and delight new readers.

CAMBRIDGE 1991   R. W. DAVID

Preface to the first edition (1971)

SINCE this book is not wholly a work of fiction I have naturally incurred many debts in writing it. My indebtedness to other publications, and especially to the Royal Horticultural Society's *Dictionary of Gardening*, Clapham, Tutin and Warburg's *Flora of the British Isles* and the two volumes so far published of the *Flora Europaea*, will be obvious throughout and is always, I hope and think, duly acknowledged. My gratitude to the many friends and relations who have, in one way or another, helped and encouraged me is not so easy to assess or express and I can hardly hope to name them all. I can only assure those who have suffered from my preoccupation, notably my wife and family, and those others who have assisted me with professional advice and information, particularly Max Walters, Peter Yeo, Dick David and Harold Fletcher, that I am genuinely and deeply appreciative. The errors are all my own.

I was lucky enough to find two kind ladies, one Rosie Lane, in our home village of Shepreth, the other, Joan Hopkins, in the neighbouring village of Barrington, who are not only skilled and experienced typists but who also proved to possess the much rarer gift of being able to decipher my handwriting. It was very kind of them indeed to devote so much of their little leisure to rendering my hasty scribble, and often under pressure of time, at least superficially presentable. And I have been unbelievably blessed in my publishers. Not only were Sir William Collins himself and his scientific editor, Michael Walter, generous (or foolhardy) enough to accept my book within little over an hour of their first glimpse of it, but the latter has ever since, through all those difficult negotiations that are inevitable between publisher and author, extended to me every sort of kindness and help.

My last acknowledgments are the most difficult if only because they are the most intimate. My mother-in-law, Emmeline Hugh Smith, in whose house at Langham in Rutland a considerable chunk of the book was written, showed a characteristically lively interest in its progress, and her sudden death just before the task was completed robbed me, as it robbed countless others, of a very dear friend of boundless wisdom, sympathy, generosity and humour. My wife's first cousin, Nancy Hugh Smith, a regular visitor, though by no means so regular as we should wish, to both our English and our Scottish house, has read sundry chapters, in the haphazard order in which they were written, and has never failed to come up with valuable constructive suggestions. One of them, attributable no less to her keen sense of smell than to her botanical and horticultural prowess, is gratefully if anonymously acknowledged in the text. My one-time colleague at King's College, Cambridge, Kenneth Harrison, who also spent part of his Christmas vacation 1969 at Langham and who read a few excerpts from what I was then and there writing, was the first to hazard a guess that a book upon which I had embarked solely for my own entertainment and for the good of my health might conceivably one day interest a publisher. And last but by no means least, my very good friend Dick Chapman of Barrington, who also, along with his house-mate Ben Duncan, is mentioned anonymously at least once in the following pages, not only volunteered to read my first faltering beginnings, which had him frankly but politely baffled, but thereafter, incredibly, kept offering himself for further punishment. More than any other single factor his unfailing encouragement brought to completion an undertaking which would otherwise have been abandoned almost before it was begun.

13

Introduction

I, John Raven, wrote this book; my wife Faith took almost all the colour photographs [omitted from this edition: see Foreword]. It is therefore a joint production. But when the first person is used in the plural it means the two of us collectively, when in the singular it refers to me and me alone.

Two important points need to be made at the outset, the first of which concerns the title. As any perceptive reader will soon enough detect, neither of us is, or ever has been, a professional in either botany or horticulture. Faith draws a very sharp distinction, repeatedly demonstrated to her to be wholly indefensible, between botany, which she professes to detest, and horticulture, to which she enthusiastically devotes what little spare time she has. I, on the other hand, failing to distinguish between the two hobbies, still owe a primary allegiance to field botany. But even so, the title of the book, eventually chosen as the best of a bad lot because it had occurred independently to both the publishers and me, is grossly misleading.

The second point concerns the manner in which the book was written. Several years ago a publisher invited us to write a specialised horticultural treatise on any one of certain genera, such as Bergenia and Hosta, which seemed to be gaining or regaining favour in British gardens. After a little thought we soon decisively declined. But the suggestion went on ineffectually hovering at the back of my mind until, in the late autumn of 1969, I decided the time had come to do something about it. By that time, however, the proposed nature of the book had been subconsciously so altered that it had become, as a rapid glance at almost any of its pages will show, at least as much a field botanist's as a gardener's effusion. And moreover, no sooner had I begun to write than I succumbed to a mysterious illness, and when, two months later, the root of the trouble was shown to be an unusually large gastric ulcer, I was confined to bed for several weeks and strictly forbidden to do any of my normal work. As the result, presumably, of these unusual circumstances, I seem to have become unduly long-winded. My original intention had been to go through, in the order in which they are treated in Clapham, Tutin and Warburg's classic *Flora of the British Isles*, all those botanical families which have at least one representative in our flora and to say something about every genus in these families, whether represented in Britain or not, which seems to me to deserve a place in British gardens. But by the time I had finished ten chapters, the book had already assumed such proportions that I reluctantly decided to stop at the end of the dicotyledons and to defer my treatment of the monocotyledons, which embrace, besides rushes, sedges and grasses, such glamorous genera as Iris, Crocus, Narcissus and Tulipa, Allium, Lilium and even Hosta, to a second volume. And there are at least two factors which obviously militate against the production of that second volume. In the first place it is unlikely in the extreme that, once this first volume has seen the light of day, there will be sufficient demand for a repeat performance to justify the necessary expenditure of time and money. And in the second place I gravely doubt whether, even if I am spared, I shall ever again enjoy (and I use the word advisedly) so long a period of enforced leisure.

Any book remotely connected with horticulture, except of course a dictionary or encyclopaedia, must perforce be both selective and subjective, and this particular book lays no claim to be less so than the majority of others. Some readers, for instance, may think it strange that, having little use for Asters or Chrysanthemums in general and for Michaelmas Daisies in particular, I should have almost confined my treatment of that vast family, the *Compositae*, to the genus Artemisia, or that I scarcely mention any cruciferous plant other than sea kale and its noble relative *Crambe cordifolia* and one or two species of Draba. The simple explanation for such eccentricities of choice is that, without consulting Faith, I have usually selected families or genera the foliage of which, in variety of both form and colour, strikes me as a more durable embellishment to an ordinary garden than their often all too ephemeral flowers. And if again my choice of representatives of a genus strikes any particular reader as tiresomely arbitrary, that is only because I have seen fit to exemplify the genus in question with as wide a range as possible.

We are lucky enough to have some say in the planting and maintenance of two gardens as different in every respect as any two gardens in Britain could be. The garden at our permanent home at Shepreth is relatively small, apart from a few places where we have deliberately created minor undulations absolutely level, exceptionally well drained and, being near the heart of the area with the lowest rainfall in Britain, very dry indeed. Since it lies directly between the chalk downs of southern Cambridgeshire and those of north Essex and Hertfordshire, it is slightly alkaline: its pH ranges, according to an analysis of four samples from different parts of the garden, from 7.5 to 7.8. It is also very irregular in shape, being comprised of the ground immediately surrounding an old manor house and its outlying barns, and so prompts the suggestion, on which we have acted by planting two dividing hedges, that it might easily be split up into a number of small gardens each with its own character. And finally it has the enormous advantage, to offset in part the heavy frosts to which the whole district is liable, of being sheltered, chiefly by old brick walls, from almost every quarter.

Most private gardens in England, even when seen only from a car or a train, reveal at a glance the owner's horticultural taste and preferences. Our own garden, though in no sense a specialist's, might perhaps strike a casual visitor as in a few respects unusual. We grow no annuals whatever except those few, such as love-in-the-mist, which with no human aid happily perpetuate themselves; and likewise, except in a few wooden tubs, we grow not a single bedding-out plant. Again, we have no rock garden but cultivate our alpines and miniature trees and ferns exclusively in two enormous stone troughs, both incidentally filled with lime-free soil fetched from Norfolk, pH 6.1, to enable us to grow such calcifuges as miniature Rhododendrons, and eleven old stone sinks, all but two of them containing our own local soil mixed with a little sand, peat and stone chippings. And finally we may conceivably betray to the more percipient observer a preference for a few particular genera such as species roses and shrubby Potentillas, Clematis species, Artemisia, Eryngium, Euphorbia, Cistus and rock-roses. But for all that the garden at Shepreth is intended to be simply a garden as varied as could reasonably be.

By way of contrast the garden at Ardtornish, in the remotest Scottish Highlands, has only lately become ours; for almost forty years before that my mother-in-law had lavished on it a great deal of thought and skill. In the twenties it was laid out in park style by a gardener who later achieved eminence as designer of municipal parks and gardens, and in those far-off days of plutocratic prosperity it provided employment for a force of no less than twelve gardeners. To-day, when not even one man can devote his whole time to it, it has been perforce, but advisedly, allowed to return largely to nature. By way of contrast again with the Shepreth garden, it is alleged on the highest authority that the walk around its encircling deer fence is about one and a half miles. Again, it slopes steeply down to the very edge of one of the sea lochs off the Sound of Mull, and is diversified by numerous natural cliffs and outcrops of rock, as well as by two or three tiny burns, which, over the ages, have hollowed out for themselves their own little valleys. Its soil iş uniformly acid: its pH, on the basis of two samples only, varies between 4.9 at the bottom and 5.6 at the top. Apart from a separate and large walled kitchen garden it is all of one piece. And finally, though perilously exposed to the south-west wind, a few parts of it at least have been proved by experience to be exempt from the heaviest frosts. The same casual visitor might perhaps notice, as he walked up the steep and winding drive, a few such relatively unfamiliar shrubs as *Tricuspidaria lanceolata*, alias *Crinodendron hookerianum, Hoberia lyallii* and *Eucryphia* × *nymansensis* Nymansay, not to mention various unusual trees. But the overall impression with which he would undoubtedly leave the garden would be one of the great variety of ericaceous plants, notably species of Rhododendron and Azalea, and of Primulas. The treasures of the garden, in fact – and especially a group of three *Eucryphia glutinosa*, formerly *pinnatifolia*, which are allegedly, with the disputed exception of those at Poltalloch, the finest in Scotland, and a magnificent *Embothrium coccineum* var. *longifolium*, which may or may not be a synonym of *E. lanceolatum* – are such as could not conceivably be grown in south Cambridgeshire unless in an artificial peat bed in a glass house.

Since our marriage sixteen years ago, and in my own case long before that, we have had a passion for stocking our own gardens, so far as possible, with plants we have ourselves collected occasionally in Britain but almost always abroad, in their natural stâtions. Of course, we **never** dig a plant up unless it is at least locally abundant. We have had the greatest success with bulbs, corms, seeds and, rarely, young seedlings. Few of the alpine or herbaceous plants which we have been reduced to digging up in maturity have successfully established themselves. This passion for collecting plants is, I know, shared by a large number of those gardeners in this country who have an occasional opportunity of going abroad, and my heart bleeds for the great majority of them who seem to think that it is an illicit occupation and go to any lengths, such as gum-boots or sponge bags, to smuggle their loot through the customs. All you need do is to apply for a Plant Import Licence to the Plant Health Department of the Ministry of Agriculture, Fisheries and Food at Great Westminster House, Horseferry Road, London, S.W.1. [Times and regulations have changed: see Foreword.] Tell them the date of your departure from Britain, the countries you hope to visit, the approximate date of your return and the address to which you intend to introduce the plants, and nine times out of ten the licence will reach you by return of post. With it will come a list of plants which it is forbidden to import, arranged both by families and countries and consisting mainly of various fir and fruit trees. Personally I have never been under the slightest temptation to import any of them, and least of all a potato. When you brandish the precious document in front of the Customs Officer he is so nonplussed, never apparently having seen the like before, that he forgets to ask any embarrassing questions. On your return home you are under an obligation to send a full list of what you have imported to the Plant Health Department, who will by then presumably have had the permit back from the puzzled Customs Officer and be bursting with curiosity. But they are evidently tolerant of their weaker brethren, who cannot be expected to name any alien plant, and seem quite satisfied with such returns as 'twenty-two assorted bulbs, the roots of three different herbs.' They prudently safeguard their own and the national interest by reserving the right to come and inspect your trophies at their appointed destination at any time within the following three weeks. In our case this dire threat has never come to fulfilment.

This recital of our respective eccentricities, to which should be added that for more than twenty years I have been a full-time Lecturer in Classics at Cambridge, goes some way towards explaining any peculiarities that the book may betray. Though I have tried to avoid rigidity, most of the chapters seem to begin with a brief survey of the more striking British native species in the family or genus under discussion, go on to say something of the more exciting species that may be collected in southern Europe, and end with a summary selection and description of the best non-European species, hybrids and garden varieties. I hope that I have not too often lapsed into irrelavance, but if I have, that is doubtless attributable to my classical education.

Next, as befits my profession, a short lecture to the uninitiated. In the plant kingdom, as in most others, there is a hierarchy: division, class, order, family, genus, species, subspecies and variety. The first three are of little concern to a practical gardener, except perhaps when he succeeds in germinating spores or seeds. The names of families, such as *Ranunculaceae*, tend to end in that suffix – *aceae*. Generic names, such as Ranunculus, should always have a capital letter and, in common with all Latin plant names that have not become fully anglicised, should properly be in italics. Specific names, even when they are palpably derived from a man's name, as in the case of *Paeonia mlokosewitschii*, should never in any circumstances, according to the latest international rules of botanical nomenclature, be given a capital. Thus to write, as almost every writer on botany does, of Japonica is to infringe the regulations in two respects. Tiresome as these rules indisputably are, I shall do my best to obey them.

And so, finally, to what is probably the most vexed question of them all concerning plant names: Latin or English? In the only other botanical or horticultural publication longer than an occasional article in which I ever had a share, namely *Mountain Flowers* in the New Naturalist series, the editors insisted on the use, whenever possible, of the popular English name. But such a practice can become at the best of times misleading, at the worst utterly useless. As everybody knows, for example, the familiar bluebell means one thing and one thing only to an Englishman and quite another to a Scot, while I have yet to hear anybody refer to that local and beautiful unbellifer *Meum athamanticum* by any of the three alluring choices offered by Bentham and Hooker, 'Spignel, Meu, Baldmoney.' Nor unfortunately is the case for Latin names altogether unassailable since, for a variety of reasons, some good and some bad, they are repeatedly being changed. The scarce British native wintergreen, for instance, which I was brought up on Bentham and Hooker to call *Pyrola secunda*, has since then, with its second, or specific, name unaltered, become successively first *Ramischia* and then *Orthilia*; while anybody who remembers what the generic name may now be of the aforementioned plant inaccurately but almost universally known to gardeners as Japonica is a better man than I am. In the present book I have therefore struck what I hope is an acceptable compromise. Where, as in the cases of bracken or caper spurge, no shadow of doubt attaches to the English name, I have often seen fit to employ simply that; where, as is frequently the case, the popular English name is either ambiguous or even non-existent, I have naturally had recourse to the Latin name; often, to avoid any possible confusion, I have used both. I can only hope that by the time the book eventually appears in print not too many of the current botanical names, which I have checked as thoroughly as I can in the latest literature, will already have been superseded.

CHAPTER I

Ferns

THE fernery, beloved of the Victorians, is almost as much a thing of the past as the Victorian bustle. Few except botanical gardens now boast a systematic collection of ferns set aside in a special bed, or sometimes even a separate corner of the garden. True, many gardens in Britain, especially in the north and west, contain several species of native ferns, put there usually by nature, both on old walls and in shady or boggy corners, and the addition is usually a welcome one. And true again, there is in many an English garden, at the foot of a north- or east-facing wall, a narrow border, as dry as dust, which is inhospitable to almost everything except ferns but in which many of them thrive happily. The garden at Ardtornish falls emphatically into the former category; without even going out to count them I can think of at least ten native species which grow there unprompted and unaided by man. The garden at Shepreth, on the other hand, falls equally emphatically into the other category and contains by nature, even on the old walls with which it is so plentifully endowed, not a single species of fern. But it does possess, at the foot of an old barn and measuring some thirty feet in length by three in breadth, exactly such a border as I have just described. Here, over the past sixteen years since we bought the house, we have introduced about twenty species of fern, and have intermingled them, in what many visitors to the garden notice as an unusually attractive harmony, with the tall and beautiful, albeit very common British sedge, *Carex pendula*, which sows itself freely in the gravel path beside, but which can be controlled with the utmost ease and is anyhow surprisingly often accepted by other gardeners as a welcome present. Other accidental introductions which have come into the same border with the roots of the commoner British ferns include meadowsweet, which flourishes beside a leaky old barrel put there to catch the rainfall from the barn roof, wood-sorrel and sanicle, which came in with the beech fern or the oak fern that we brought down from Ardtornish, and, from the same source but less happily, because it spreads fast and far by fragile white underground stolons, enchanter's nightshade. Some of the ferns, notably the beech and the oak, *Adiantum pedatum*, and a very rare one that we found in local abundance in the hills behind Cannes, *Asplenium jabandiezii*, have not unreasonably so much resented the change of environment that they have with varying rapidity died on us. But sufficient of the rest remain and spread to stock other unpromising patches, not only of our own garden, but of other people's as well.

The only British fern that is at all costs to be avoided in the garden is bracken. Although Reginald Kaye, in his recent and invaluable book on Hardy Ferns, considers two varieties of it 'well worth growing where there is room,' he freely admits that bracken is general is not a plant for the garden 'on account of its extremely invasive habits.' The reasons for this invasiveness are twofold. First, I have been told by a well-known botanist who lives in the outer parts of London S.W. – and his statement is amply borne out by the abundance of bracken on basement walls in so self-consciously immaculate a district as that, for instance, of Harley Street – that at the right season the air of London is so full of spore carried in on the prevailing south-west wind that you need only turn two or three jam jars upside down on the soil to be sure of at least one bracken sporeling. And second, there is the characteristic specifically attributed to bracken by Clapham, Tutin and Warburg, 'Rhizome underground, creeping for long distances.' Again I have it on the highest authority, though this time a different one, that a mature bracken plant stretched horizontally for at least fifty yards. Hence, as many a farmer knows, once bracken gets a hold it is not easily extirpated.

Bracken apart, then, there are still some forty species of British native ferns, not to mention the countless named varieties described by Mr Kaye, every one of them worth a place in the garden. In defiance of all scientific principles, and conceivably thereby justifying the writing of this chapter so soon after the publication of Mr Kaye's book, I shall divide them, for the benefit of the gardener rather than the botanist, into five groups; the very large, the large, the medium-sized, the small and the very small. Size is, after all, as many a catalogue in these enlightened days recognises, one of the most important of all criteria by which the average gardener decides what plants to choose.

In the first of the five groups, that of the very large, there is unfortunately only one candidate, but that one, the royal fern or *Osmunda regalis*, is widely regarded by gardeners as the noblest of all British plants. It seems to have a natural preference in the British Isles for the west, but for all that it is to be seen growing as a native within a few yards of the East Anglian coast. Its vital requirements are, in fact, simple enough: it demands a damp but well drained situation; it prefers a peaty soil, apparently the more acid the better; it grows on limestone only where the calcium has been leached out by the elements; and it cannot abide chalk. For these reasons, though not apparently native within six or seven miles, it thrives like a weed in the garden at Ardtornish, but could only be induced by the most laborious and time-consuming artifice to survive at all at Shepreth. We find life too short, and our gardens too large, to attempt to grow any plants that will not live without excessive mollycoddling.

The second group, that of the large ferns, ranging in height from eighteen inches to three feet, presents the greatest difficulty for the gardener because, unless he aspires to a complete collection, there is really no visual effect to be gained by the attempt to grow them all. Once again, strictly scientific distinctions are of little relevance in the garden. One species of *Oreopteris*, for example, the so-called mountain fern, *O. limbosperma*, bears so close a superficial resemblance to the male fern, *Dryopteris filix-mas*, and its two closest relatives, that I always, if usually needlessly, look at the arrangement of its sori before reaching a definite verdict. And similarly there is little to choose for garden merit between the lady fern and one or two of the buckler ferns. My own primary criteria would be, first, gracefulness, and second, tidiness of habit. If I were confined to, say, six species, I should, I think, choose on the first score the lady fern, *Athyrium filix-femina*, and the common and hay-scented buckler ferns, *Dryopteris dilatata* and *D. aemula*; and on the second score *Dryopteris affinis*, which, with the dense orange-brown scales on its leaf-stalk, its relatively upright habit, and the tendency of its fronds to remain green throughout the winter, is far superior to the male fern itself; next *Polystichum aculeatum*, the hard shield fern; and finally the lemon-scented fern already referred to, *Oreopteris limbosperma*.

The group of medium-sized British ferns – those, that is, which commonly exceed a foot in length of frond but never attain as much as two feet – contains at the most four species, all of them so distinctive as to cause not the slightest difficulty to either botanist or gardener. Indeed two of the four, namely hartstongue and polypody, seem virtually uniquitous in Britain and tolerate even the most intolerable conditions in the garden. And what is more, each of them has a large number of varieties, well established in cultivation and described, and some of them illustrated, in Mr Kaye's book, which are probably as long-suffering as the types from which they originally sprang. Hard fern, on the other hand, though it is superabundant in many districts, including the neighbourhood of Ardtonish, seems a good deal harder to please, and the same is doubtless true of its varieties. Like most British ferns, it is much more frequent and luxuriant in the humid atmosphere of the west than in the relative aridity of the east; but in this particular case that is by no means the whole explanation. Like *Osmunda*, it cannot abide chalk, and can only be induced in Shepreth to eke out a meagre existence by the artificial means of planting it in almost pure peat. And last in this small group, if indeed it can be properly classed as medium-sized at all, comes the aptly named holly fern, *Polystichum lonchitis*. Although I know at least one locality where it abounds at an altitude of less than a thousand feet, holly fern is in Great Britain essentially a plant of mountain cliffs and screes, and its natural place in a garden is therefore the rockery rather than the fern border. But to offset this restriction it has the great advantage, to judge at least from our own experience of it in cultivation, of almost total indifference both to height above sea-level and, despite the repeated (and actually true) statement that it is by nature a plant of basic hills, to the soil in which it is asked to grow.

The next group, that of small ferns native in Britain, consists of nine species in all, each once again, except perhaps two pairs, with its own distinctive character. Limestone polypody or *Gymnocarpium robertianum* is, in the words of McClintock and Fitter's *Pocket Guide to Wild Flowers*, 'the lime-loving counterpart of the oak fern' (*G. dryopteris*), 'with tougher, dull green, mealy-looking, less extremely 3-lobed leaves.' Those therefore who, like ourselves at Shepreth, are unable to grow the oak fern proper have a substitute, admittedly somewhat less attractive, available to them. And similarly the very rare *Cystopteris dickieana*, though classified by Clapham, Tutin and Warburg as a distinct species, is superficially not at all unlike certain forms of the relatively common bladder fern, *C. fragilis*. For the rest, however, few plants could be easier to recognise. The Killarney fern, *Trichomanes speciosum*, always very local in Great Britain, has unfortunately by now been reduced to extreme scarcity by the cupidity of collectors. But demanding as it does, like the filmy ferns to which it is closely akin, if not the constant spray of a waterfall, at least a permanently humid atmosphere, it can never have been easy to cultivate unless perhaps under the kind of glass hemisphere with which the Victorians apparently delighted to adorn their dining-room tables. Similarly, maidenhair fern, *Adiantum capillus-veneris*, though it grows just above sea-level as far northward as Westmorland and Donegal, is too intolerant of frost to survive out of doors in any but the mildest districts in Britain. Even parsley fern is choosy and grows naturally in this country, though there it is often locally dominant, only on the screes of acid hills; while both the beech and the oak ferns demand a combination of peat, shade and moisture which is by no means everywhere easy to provide. Of this whole group, in fact, only the bladder ferns, *Cystopteris fragilis* and *C. dickieana*, seem easily satisfied. Contrariwise *C. montana*, which is often said to bear a superficial resemblance to the oak fern but which is to my mind the most beautiful of all British ferns, is, despite its inclusion in Mr Kaye's 'List of Ferns for Rock Garden and Dry Wall,' so specialised in its habitat, damp shaded ledges high on mica-schist mountains, as almost (but not quite, as Mr Kaye himself has proved) to defy cultivation altogether. The final group, which contains no less than seven species of Asplenium, is on that account appreciably larger than the last two. The filmy ferns, *Hymenophyllum tunbrigense* and *H. wilsonii*, for the reason already given, call for very special treatment, while the two species of Woodsia, *W. ilvensis* and *W. alpina,* both exceedingly rare in Britain but both figuring in the same list of Mr Kaye's, are so similar that if you are lucky enough to grow either you may as well rest content with that. Rusty-back, or *Ceterach officinarum,* on the other hand, though it reveals in Britain the same marked preference for the west as so many other ferns, is much more accommodating. Indeed two years ago, under the mistaken impression that it was a slightly different species, I brought back from Corfu three roots of Ceterach, planted two in sinks containing our ordinary Shepreth soil and the third in a trough filled with lime-free soil from a Rhododendron-growing district of Norfolk, and was surprised to find that all three flourished alike. As for the species of Asplenium in Britain, they are for the most part as distinctive as plants could be. The only pairs that could occasion any doubt whatever are the black and the lanceolate, that is, *A. adiantum-nigrum* and *A. billotii* (formerly *obovatum*), the common and the green, *A. trichomanes* and *A. viride.* The former pair could sometimes admittedly give even the expert momentary pause, because there are variable forms of *A. adiantum-nigrum* two of which are even classified by Clapham, Tutin and Warburg as separable subspecies. But in the latter case a mere glance at the colour of the mid-rib, not to mention the more delicate deckling of the margins of the pinnae, should be sufficient to enable even the professed ignoramus to distinguish the local *Asplenium viride* from the almost uniquitous *A. trichomanes.* And for the rest there is no problem. The most distinctive of them all is the forked spleenwort, *A. septentrionale,* which I recently saw growing in the hills above Orta in north Italy cheek by jowl with *A. trichomanes,* but with no trace, alas, of the hybrid between them, a plant that I have only once seen wild in the British Isles, variously called *A. × breynii, A. × alternifolium* and *A. germanicum.* As its English name suggests, its individual fronds are like nothing so much as forked lightning. But, by the same token, anybody who had ever condescended to look at wall-rue, *A. ruta-muraria,* could only thereafter confuse it with one other native British plant, namely that significantly called alpine meadow-rue, *Thalictrum alpinum.* And that, with the exception of the beautiful *Asplenium marinum,* which is virtually impossible to cultivate inland, is the last of the British spleenworts, and therewith the last fern native in these islands, which I propose to mention. Though none of them except the very commonest should ever in any circumstances be uprooted from their native British stations, those common ones alone, with their numerous varieties in commerce, should provide all but the most specialised of gardeners with all that they could need.

Nevertheless, the impression must not be given that all ferns, even when they are native to the British Isles, can be trusted to look after themselves. Not so long ago we suffered under that delusion at Shepreth and, as I have already recited, we paid quite dearly for it. The smaller ferns in particular, being in the main accustomed to plenty of bare space and fresh air, so resent the overcrowding of a fern border that they are best planted, if not in a wall or on a natural outcrop of rock, then in a crevice in the rockery or in a sink. Even the fern border itself, for all but the commonest and most accommodating species, imposes a few simple demands: ideally it requires not only protection from the fiercest wind and heat but also sharp drainage and a decent modicum of humus in the soil. And even when all this is provided, there will still remain some species, whether calcicolous or calcifuge, that are not easily satisfied. Like the majority of other plants, most ferns have their own particular fads and fancies; and who are we to blame them on that account?

Of the countless species and varieties of fern which are not native to the British isles, every gardener who grows any ferns at all will have his own favourites; but his special predilection for them will probably rest more on practical than purely aesthetic grounds. Take, for instance, the widespread European *Matteucia struthiopteris* or the North American and Asiatic *Onoclea sensibilis*. Although both are perfectly hardy, and indeed locally naturalised, in the British Isles, and although both, along with *Osmunda regalis*, look contented enough in the swampy ground near the pond in the Cambridge Botanic Garden, any attempt to grow them in a garden as thirsty and lacking in humus as ours at Shepreth would betray an optimism verging on lunacy. Even *Adiantum venustum* from Kashmir, with which I have lately replaced our defunct specimen of *A. pedatum*, is already looking so sickly in our fern border that I begin to doubt whether we can anywhere, unless possibly at Ardtornish, provide accommodation worthy of any allegedly hardy member of this delicately graceful genus. Indeed, the only non-British ferns which seem to be tolerably happy so far in our dry and chalky soil are the little *Lomaria alpina* from Antarctic America, which Mr Kaye (rightly or wrongly, and in either case in opposition to Mr G. S. Thomas in his article on 'Ground Cover Plants' in the R.H.S. Journal of May 1967) distinguishes from *Blechnum penna-marina* from New Zealand, and the aforementioned *Asplenium jabandiezii*, the very rare and deminutive species which I long ago collected in the hills behind Cannes and of which I have recently recovered an offset from the plant I originally gave to the Botanic Garden. And I strongly suspect that the reason why these two, along with our specimens of *Ceterach officinarum* from Corfu and *Asplenium septentrionale* from near Lake Orta, are still surviving is simply that last autumn I decided to devote one of my north-facing sinks to miniature ferns and accordingly added a liberal admixture of peat and leaf-mould to the typical sample of our local soil that it already contained.

Would that I could dwell for longer on those foreign ferns which are willing to adapt themselves to our very different environment; but, though we are still far from abandoning hopeful experiment, there the story so far rests. Even so, however, that is not quite the end of the matter. There still remain the almost countless varieties, authoritatively but not necessarily exhaustively listed in Mr Kaye's book, of our own natives, and though I have never been lucky enough to come across any in the wild, I can claim a nodding acquaintance with a good many of them in cultivation and have even successfully introduced a few of the more elegant into our Shepreth garden. Personally, even if here I differ from Faith, I tend to regard the majority of varieties, if not as deformities, at best as undesirable declensions from the norm. The numerous frilled, fringed and crested varieties of the common harts-tongue, for example, seem to me, in a desperate attempt to be distinctive and original, to have sacrificed the indisputable claim of the type to real beauty, the simplicity and purity of its lines. In the case of the common polypody, *Polypodium vulgare*, which is perhaps the most undistinguished of all British ferns, there is so much less to sacrifice that it could not unreasonably be maintained that its deeply pinnatifid sister at least, *P. australe*, is so successful in its quest for novelty as to have achieved a marked improvement. And the same could perhaps be said, though this time with no disparagement of the type, of *Dryopteris affinis* Cristata The King. But there is to my mind only one species among all our native ferns in which two or three varieties mark an unquestionable improvement on the type, and they have the further inestimable advantage of being not only preternaturally accommodating but also exceptionally easy to propagate. The species in question, the soft shield fern or *Polystichum setiferum*, is widespread in the south and west of England and over much of Wales and Ireland.

Opinions are divided on the relative merits of the two varieties which make the most delicate of all contributions to our fern border. My own preference is for the one described by Mr Kaye, and indeed illustrated in an excellent black-and-white photograph of the young fronds unfurling, under the name of *Polystichum setiferum acutilobum*, which, unless I am much mistaken, I originally had from Hillier's as the synonymous *P. s. proliferum*. But the other, *P. s. plumoso-divisolobum*, which is again illustrated in Mr Kaye's book and also figures in Hillier's list, usually evokes even louder admiration from our friends and visitors. The former has the advantage, in my eyes at least, that its individual pinnae, themselves exquisitely bipinnate, are so spaced as to be seen even at a distance in splendid isolation from the rest, while those of the latter, if even more perfectly chiselled, so overlap as to present a continuous surface of green broken only by the somewhat bluer shade around the midrib of the pinnae and by the shadow of one pinna on the next. Since neither needs a lot of room and they vie with one another in ease of temperament, any gardener worth his salt (or at any rate mine) will look for a shady site where he can grow them close together. And if space permits, he might be well advised to follow our example and plant between the two, for the sake of the stark contrast in styles of elegance which the fern kingdom embraces, a root of the ordinary common or garden hartstongue.

Both of these varieties are endowed with the felicitous habit of producing in the axils of the pinnae, on the prostrate and part-withered second-year fronds, more or less numerous and diminutively leafy bulbils. These bulbils, if carefully picked off the rachis and shallowly planted in a pan of damp lime-free soil, will, with surprising alacrity, develop into mature and similarly prolific plants. Many are the young plants of these two ferns that we have already given away, even while our own stock is steadily increasing. I can think of no characteristic in any plant of comparable grace and elegance more endearing than the prodigality with which these two provide an unfailing source of effortless and almost invariably welcome presents.

CHAPTER 2

Ranunculaceae and Paeoniaceae

OF all European families of plants there can be none more diverse in its manifestations, nor any probably more popular in the average garden, than the *Ranunculaceae*. For the benefit of the uninitiated here is the definition of the family as a whole given in Volume I of *Flora Europaea*: 'Herbs or rarely woody climbers. Leaves alternate, exstipulate, rarely opposite or stipulate. Flowers usually hermaphrodite and actinomorphic, hypogynous. Perianth petaloid or sepaloid, whorled. Honey-leaves (petaloid structures bearing nectaries) often present, funnel-shaped or petaloid. Stamens numerous, usually spirally arranged, extrorse. Carpels 1-many, usually free and spirally arranged. Fruit usually of 1 or more follicles or a head of achenes.'

Even when, however, you have read this luminous paragraph, and noted in the process how frequently the words 'rarely,' 'usually' and even 'or' occur, you may still admire the ingenuity, be it nature's or man's, which has made it possible to group under this one definition plants as various as buttercups and anemones, hellebores, Clematis, Thalictrum, Aquilegia, monkshood and Delphinium. Since in our very limited horticultural library we possess one book, entitled simply *Anemones*, by Roy Genders, and another, equally simply, *Clematis*, by Christopher Lloyd, it may well seem the act of a lunatic to attempt to cover so vast and diversified a family in a single chapter.

The order, which will not, I fear, be very orderly, in which I propose to take this vast and polymorphic family is, first, the native species of Europe (including the British Isles), and secondly the garden varieties, the hybrids and the more exotic species.

Not only in Europe as a whole but in England in particular the family of *Ranunculaceae* is nobly represented, and many of the English representatives deserve cultivation in their own right. To follow the *Flora Europaea* once again and adopt what is evidently now the standard order of genera within the family, we ourselves grow in shady and inhospitable corners of the garden at Shepreth both species of British hellebore, *H.*

foetidus and *H. viridis*, not to mention what appears in infancy to be the spontaneous hybrid between the two. In one of our very few damp patches, once more beside a leaky rain pipe, *Trollius europaeus*, the lovely native globe flower, fares well enough. The marsh marigold thrives in a deliberately created swamp in the corner of a small rectangular formal pool, with much the finest of British buttercups, *Ranunculus lingua*, towering above it; while *Pulsatilla vulgaris*, the Pasque flower, raised from seed gathered on a nearby down, flourishes equally happily on the dry and sun-baked border of the same little courtyard. We fail to grow old man's beard, *Clematis vitalba*, among our many other species of Clematis only because we have never had the initiative to plant it at the foot of an old tree. And finally *Thalictrum flavum*, a regular inhabitant of fenland ditches throughout much of the British Isles, grows with apparent indifference, alongside its subspecies *T. glaucum* from the Spanish peninsula, in the invariable aridity of our herbaceous border. Needless to add, creeping buttercup and lesser celandine await no invitation.

The most popular of the garden hellebores is without a doubt *H. niger*, the Christmas rose, and particularly in these days its large-flowered form known in commerce as Potter's Wheel. But for some reason, perhaps simply because we have not yet found the right place for it or else have insufficient leaf-mould for its taste, it always seems to do better for other people than it will for us. Far more successful in this climate are the numerous varieties of *H. orientalis*, ranging in colour from deep plum through palest pink and white to almost pure primrose. These all sow themselves freely in a barren bed at the foot of an old Judas tree and tend as they do so to produce yet different shades of colour. But to me a true hellebore should bear flowers of a true green, a particular weakness of mine in any genus, and for that reason my favourites among those we grow, apart from the two British natives and the true *H. orientalis* [now considered to be a form of *H. cyclophyllus*] from Corfu, which is even now in mid-November in full flower in the garden, are *H. cyclophyllus*, which abounds in the deciduous woods of Thrace and throws up fresh beech-green leaves with its flowers every spring and, above all, *H. argutifolius*, which, though it shares with *H. foetidus* a certain tendency to flower itself to death, shares also the recompensing habits of sowing itself profusely and of hybridising with the same near relative.

We cannot be bothered much with the Nigellas since they are all annuals, whereas the winter aconite, *Eranthis hyemalis*, once introduced, calls for no bother at all. As for the Delphiniums, whether annual, biennial or perennial, they are in these days, however splendid an adornment of any garden, so specialised a subject as to call emphatically for special discussion. We grow, of course, a considerable number of hybrids but, as in the case of hybrid roses or hybrid Clematis with their fancy names, I never shall remember which is which. When we reach Anemone, Pulsatilla, species Clematis, Ranunculus, Aquilegia and Thalictrum I feel on safer ground.

Of all the plants which we have ever imported the anemones have been the most obliging. Apart from the large pale blue wood anemone, which is, I believe, originally a native British sport, *A. ranunculoides* and *A. apennina*, both from the hills of central Italy, and *A. blanda*, from Mount Parnassus, all alike spread themselves freely in the shadiest and least arid corner of our garden, while *A. hortensis*, which we brought, in a staggering range of colour from claret through purple and mauve to salmon, from olive groves bordering the golf course at Biot in the Alpes Maritimes, and which strongly resented the dry sun-baked border in which we first put it, flowers brilliantly in the same half-shaded spot. Even *A. coronaria* and *A. pavonina* happily adapt themselves from low down near the coasts of Attica or the Greek islands, with the solitary proviso that they are given plenty of sunlight and air, to the rigours of our Cambridgeshire climate. Indeed, our only failures to date are first the white *A. trifolia*, collected with *Erythronium dens-canis* in the moist woods at Asolo (to both of which we vouchsafed small chance of survival by planting them among the ferns in our hungry and thirsty fern border but for which we are amply compensated by the vigorous survival of an exceptionally pure colour form of *Hepatica nobilis* from the same source) and second the yellow *A. palmata* from the Algarve, which succumbed to its first Cambridgeshire winter but which would almost certainly survive the soft climate of the far west of Britain.

The Pulsatillas, with the exception already mentioned of *P. vulgaris*, have proved less amenable, doubtless because, being for the most part in our experience plants of the higher mountains, they call in winter for the comparative security from damp afforded them by the alpine house, the erection of which we are still awaiting. We very recently imported a root of *P. vernalis*, the most bewitching of them all, and seed of *P. alpina* subsp. *apiifolia*, from Cervinia, at the head of the valley leading up from the south to the Matterhorn, but it is still too early to say with what success. I certainly would not ensure the survival of the former, which I have optimistically planted in one of the two north-facing sinks that we reserve for alpine plants which we ourselves have imported; but I have higher hopes of the latter surviving in the open ground. And the same general caveat is unfortunately necessary of most of the more alluring European species of Ranunculus. This time the exception is *R. asiaticus*, of which I successfully imported corms of the white variety from Crete in 1938 and of the blood-red from Rhodes as lately as 1967. The former endured and flowered freely for several years in the open ground of a Cambridge garden, but was eventually killed by an exceptionally severe spell of frost; the latter still survives and flowers at Shepreth. Both varieties have such flagrant glamour that, even by our present ruthless standards, they may well merit a particular measure of protection. But alas, the even more elegant alpine species, notably *R. glacialis* and its allies, are still awaiting at Shepreth the same special provision as the alpine Pulsatillas.

Anemone and Ranunculus are, wherever possible, better imported than purchased: it is a great advantage to be able to choose your own colours and to know precisely what you are introducing into your gardens. But we cannot say the same of Clematis species. The only three that we have so far imported from Europe are, in the form of wild seed heads, *C. orientalis* from the Thracian coast, which has done surprisingly well, and *C. flammula* from northern Italy, and, in the form of three or four seedlings from near La Mortola, *C. cirrhosa* subsp. *balearica*, which, however, has only once in a dozen years condescended to flower for us. The rest of our considerable collection we have unashamedly bought. The herbaceous species, with the exception of the handsome hybrid *C.* × *durandii*, are barely worth the expense. The leaves of *C. heracleifolia* are, as its name suggests, too coarse to atone for its unspectacular flowers, while the best form of *C. recta*, variety Purpurea, is not sufficiently showy, even with its purplish stems and leaves, to hold its own in the average garden. But the climbing species are an altogether different matter. My own favourite is undoubtedly the true *C. alpina*, which, given a north-facing wall and plenty of rubble around its roots, ramps contentedly here and flowers freely every year; though perhaps the deeper colours of the semi-double *C. macropetala* and Markham's pink sport of it arouse greater general admiration. *C. viticella* in all its forms, especially perhaps Alba Luxurians and the hybrid Royal Velours, which with us makes a spectacular mixture on a shady old wooden wall with *Hydrangea petiolaris* and *C.* × *jackmannii* Superba, is abundantly worth growing even in a small garden. The hybrid *C.* × *jouiniana*, rampageous as it is, looks particularly effective when trailing over a copper-leaved hazel or *Cotinus coggygria*, as would the pale yellow *C. rehderiana* over any dark evergreen. The remaining larger flowered yellow species, *C. tangutica* and Ludlow and Sherriff's feathery variety, if it is such, of *C. tibetana*,[1] are, we have found, especially well set off by the mellowest of old red brick walls. The fragrant white evergreen *C. armandii* climbs up a low wall and over an almond tree. *C. campaniflora*

---

[1] [G. Grey-Wilson in *Kew Bulletin* **4(1)**: 33-60 has now sorted out these yellow clematis. The true *C. orientalis* is the only species in the west, while the asiatic forms that are cultivated mostly belong to *C. tibetana* subsp. *vernayi*.]

and *C. texensis*, the latter of which I have very lately acquired from the Plantsmen in its pure scarlet form, have yet to flower for us. But even without these, and leaving out of account all the glamorous hybrids of the *lanuginosa* and *patens* sections which we do grow, we seem already to have plenty to keep us busy and happy.

The only British native columbine, *Aquilegia vulgaris*, can hardly, either in colour or shape of flower, hold its own with most of its relatives. Both *A. alpina*, none too easy in cultivation, and *A. pyrenaica*, unscrupulously but successfully sown in Caenlochan Glen, are infinitely more desirable, while *A. kitaibelii*, so locally abundant in river valleys in north-east Italy, is well worth growing if only for the almost chocolate colour of its flowers. Unfortunately the numerous smaller species have so far unfailingly defeated us; they do not seem to tolerate the conditions afforded by a sink, while in an open border they are too easily and rapidly overwhelmed. They are, in fact, presumably the ideal inhabitants of either the rock garden or the moraine that we do not yet possess. The Thalictrums are a different proposition; here there are three native British species, all of which are well worth growing, if you can, in your garden. *T. flavum* I have already mentioned; the aggregate *T. minus*, in any of its subspecies, deserves a place, perhaps in the fern border, for the gracefulness of its leaves rather than its flowers; while *T. alpinum*, again for the same reason and because of its rich colouring towards autumn, would amply pay for any space granted it in a damp sink or trough reserved primarily for ferns. And as for foreign species, they likewise usually earn inclusion in any garden. *T. delavayi* and its closest relations, as grown for instance by Mr Jack Drake at Inshriach, unhappily take none too kindly to our dry chalky Shepreth soil, though of course they would thrive at Ardtornish. But their place is adequately filled not only by *T. glaucum*, alias *speciosissimum*, but also by both the mauve and the rarer white form of *T. aquilegifolium*, the latter of which we originally imported from north-east Italy and find sowing itself, like many another plant, with a careless abandon.

Already, in dealing with Thalictrum, I have strayed from my predetermined order, because, from the gardener's rather than the field botanist's point of view, the European and the Asiatic species, being predominantly for the herbaceous border, are to all intents and purposes interchangeable. And the same is true both of Delphinium and Aconitum. Both of these have European representatives, those of Delphinium mostly annual, but it will make better sense after all to take them later with their non-European congeners.

Until very lately the paeonies were grouped under the *Ranunculaceae*, and it is here, if anywhere, that I should try to deal with them. No book on either botany or horticulture can afford to ignore them. Again

33

Britain has one representative, even if only of monastic origin, the gaudy and very prolific single red *P. mascula*. But again, with the exceptions of the many tree paeonies, *P. delavayi*, its subspecies *lutea*, *P. suffruticosa* and their gorgeous hybrids, and of my own personal favourite, the pale yellow *P. mlokosewitschii*, Europe can yield almost all that the heart could desire. *P. rhodia* is the equal of any other single white and, to enhance its desirability in the eyes of the expert, to judge at least from our own experience after importing it, is none too easy to please; *P. mascula* and its subspecies *P. arietina* apart, *P. tenuifolia*, *P. peregrina*, *P. officinalis*, its subspecies *humilis*, and *P. broteroi* between them ought to satisfy anybody who likes his paeonies red; while as to pink paeonies, there is first and foremost the native of the Balearic Isles, *P. cambessedesii*, after which I can only advise anybody as interested as I am to have recourse to the Chinese *P. veitchii* subsp. *woodwardii*. Paeonies in general have two notorious disadvantages: they dislike being moved and, unless they are planted surprisingly shallow, they are for the most part obdurately reluctant to flower. But give them what they want and they will at every stage, from unfolding leaf to ripe seed, repay you as richly and variously as any other family in the whole garden.

So much for the countless species (wherever possible, for the sake of those who share my taste for collecting seed, not only European but actually British) of this vast and polymorphic family. And now for the much more problematic business of their literally unnumerable hybrids and what are so elegantly called cultivars. Here at least we can legitimately desert the strict and apparently wholly unrealistic botanical order and begin with a genus which is, even to a botanist, unique in the family, because it alone contains woody plants, the genus Clematis. In my earlier treatment of the species Clematis I deliberately omitted the most familiar and popular of them all, and I omitted it for precisely that reason. Of course, among the others, we grow the relatively large white-flowered Himalayan species, which, with its various and to my mind less desirable pink varieties, is perhaps the most valuable of the whole tribe, *Clematis montana*. For years before we came to Shepreth an ancient and prodigiously floriferous plant of it had been smothering a large part of the north-facing wall of the high old barn by the drive gate. And several years ago we moved two of its self-sown seedlings on to even less promising north-facing walls of the house, one of them for the purpose specifically mentioned in the catalogue of Treasures of Tenbury (from whom, incidentally, we buy almost all our Clematis and who have never yet sold us a pup) that of 'concealing twentieth-century eyesores.' At the back of our house, on the part that dates from Elizabethan or even earlier times, there was built, out of the local brand of hideous yellow brick, an enormous great chimney, the highest part of the whole house, to extract the smoke and fumes from a recently installed boiler. Unfortunately the boiler proved extremely efficient and since, even now that we are actively contemplating going over to oil, the chimney is therefore indispensable, we have used it as the base of our television aerial. The seedling of *C. montana* which we optimistically planted in the bone-dry dust and rubble at its foot has not only in a few years completely concealed the twentieth-century eyesore, the only one on our property, but from time to time has to be drastically cut back to prevent it creeping through the tiles of the ancient roof far above and getting hopelessly entwined with the aerial.

So to the countless hybrids, the problematical choice between which, based presumably on a combination of vigour and colour, can only depend on each individual gardener's requirements and preferences. For all practical purposes these fall, with very few exceptions beyond those I have already mentioned, into five groups, respectively the forms of *Clamatis* × *jackmannii,* and the hybrids of *C. viticella, C. texensis* and, perhaps the most popular, *C. lanuginosa* and *C. patens.* Of the first group our own selection, apart from *C.* × *jackmannii* Superba, which I have already mentioned and which we slightly prefer, on account of its enormous flowers, to the type, comprises three in all, and all three grow on walls of various heights behind the rose garden. The aptly named Perle d'Azur, the colour of which is unique in the group, sprawls vigorously over the low wall, not more than three feet high and backed and easily overtopped, for contrast of colour, by the brown-spotted orange lily, *L. pardalinum,* behind the smaller of our two rose beds; the shell-pink Hagley Hybrid twines its way through the apricot climbing rose Meg on the higher south-facing wall at the back of the other rose bed; and finally Elsa Späth, a much deeper blue than Perle d'Azur, grows immediately behind the Rosemary Rose and mid-way between the purple-leaved peach and one of our several tall bushes of *Rosa glanca,* at the back of the short stretch of mixed bed, partitioned off by very low brick walls and flanked on either side by predominantly silver plants, which we call the Copper Box.

The varieties of *Clamatis viticella,* as opposed to its hybrids, I have already to the best of my ability and on the basis of first-hand experience covered. All of them, whatever their colour, have delicate and some-times pendant flowers, whereas the hybrids are virtually indistinguish-able from those of the *jackmannii* group. This is, as a matter of fact, less surprising than it may at first sound, since *C.* × *jackmannii* itself, which, according to Mr Christopher Lloyd's excellent and authoritative book entitled simply *Clematis,* 'was first exhibited in 1863 and caused a sensation,' is of course of hybrid origin. Of these *viticella* hybrids we ourselves grow, with the commonest of native honeysuckles and the old climbing rose Glorie de Dijon, on the high east-facing wall of one of our barns, and which is indistinguishable from a red variety of *C.* × *jackmannii*, is probably Ville de Lyon but may quite possibly be Ernest Markham; many years ago we transplanted it from Ardtornish where, like most Clematis, it was obviously feeling the lack of lime, and by that time had already forgotten which of the two it was. Unfortunately the other of the two, the pearly-white pink-barred Huldine, which we intended, along with the single white climbing rose Silver Moon, to scramble up our old and leaning mulberry, must have so resented its situation that it promptly and otherwise unaccountably perished.

The *texensis* hybrids have, at least until very lately and, so far as I know, still, been grossly neglected in this country; neither Notcutt's nor Hillier's, for instance, in their otherwise well-selected lists, include a single one of them. Their relatively small tubular or campanulate flowers, which, in the case of Etoile Rose, are nodding and therefore best seen from below, are admittedly less spectacular than those of the other groups of hybrids; but, given the right setting, they are every bit as desirable as any of the rest. It may perhaps be that they are slightly more tricky in cultivation than the others; like their scarlet-flowered parent from Texas, they die right back to the ground in winter and sometimes, for no apparent reason, fail to reappear. And it is an undeniable drawback that their colour ranges only from pink to ruby. But for all that we for our part would not at any price be without them. Our own favourite used to be Gravetye Beauty, the darkest of them all, which we trained each year over one of the very low walls dividing the Boxes in the rose garden, but which suddenly died on us in the way I have described.[1] And since then its place in our affections, though not in the garden, has been taken by the silver-edged Etoile Rose, which clambers up the wall of the ancient barn on the north side of the aforementioned paved courtyard with the lily pond.

Before we come to the two most popular groups, I must just say a word, because it is trained over the other of the two low walls between the Boxes, about the only large-flowered hybrid I know that does not belong to any of the five classes listed just now. The Duchess of Edinburgh is a hybrid of *C. florida* (whose variety *bicolor*, alias *C. sieboldii*, is just about the best of the whole tribe) and is in my view, by Clematis standards anyhow, frankly ugly. Its fat white flowers are fully double, which alone, in this particular genus, is enough to damn it, and in any garden where climbing space is limited it is to be resolutely shunned.

[1] Even more mysteriously it has, in 1970, returned to healthy and vigorous life. I can only conclude that in 1969 its shoots remained concealed in the mass of vegetation around its base.

The hybrids of *C. patens* and *C. lanuginosa*, which are virtually impossible to distinguish one from the other but which, between them, contain the majority of the popular favourites, are to be collectively distinguished from the rest by the simple fact that, with one or two exceptions from the *jackmannii* group, they are appreciably the earliest to come into flower. Like any other gardener we naturally have our favourites, all of them too familiar to need any description or discussion, notably Nelly Moser, Lasurstern and (if it really belongs here, which is apparently denied by Hillier's, who label it J for *jackmannii*) President or The President among the *patens* group, and, of the offspring of *C. lanuginosa*, Marie Boisselot, alias Madame Le Coultre, and W. E. Gladstone. But here, more perhaps than anywhere in this whole book, any advice on selection would be gratuitous.

So much for Clematis. And now, even though, as I said earlier, the paeonies have lately been excluded from the *Ranunculaceae* and set up in a separate family of their own, a word or two about the only other woody plants that fall within the scope of this chapter, the tree paeonies as opposed to their herbaceous relations. Such a contrast may seem, and of course botanically is, an artificial one, but the fact remains that the two groups, even if they can be grown together to excellent effect, can equally be put to quite different purposes in the garden. Everybody who has the space should, in my view, grow the three kinds of tree paeony from which the many spectacular hybrids have been raised, namely *delavayi,* its subspecies *lutea* and *suffruticosa*. Some may feel that however statuesque a plant *P. delavayi* may be, its flowers are too small in proportion and too dusky in colour to justify its inclusion. In that case they had better try the kingcup-flowered subspecies *lutea* instead, or subspecies *ludlowii,* the flowers of which, if not actually larger, are certainly more conspicuous because, instead of nodding, they are held more or less upright. As for the hybrid between *delavayi* and *lutea*, which can range in colour, through vivid scarlet, between the two extremes, it is in my opinion, if you are lucky enough to lay hands on a good colour, superior to either of its parents. There is in fact no problem about these three. But *P. suffruticosa,* far the most beautiful, unless I am much mistaken, of all the true species, is an altogether different matter. I believe I have seen it twice in my life, once in a private garden which I happened to pass in Suffolk, where I was fool enough not to stop and ask where it came from, and once under a wall near the office in Notcutt's nursery. The plant in question is broad and intensely floriferous and its numerous petals are pure white with a crimson blotch at the base. I naturally wrote to Notcutt's later, with a description like the above of what I wanted. What reached us was the wishy-washy mauvy-pink tree paeony known as Moutan. I know the two are supposed to be synonymous, but I refuse to believe it, and I still have no idea where, if anywhere, the true species, which I covet more than any plant I have ever seen, is to be obtained. On the other hand, the numerous hybrids between its alleged varieties and *P. lutea*, which are undeniably very lovely, are easily enough procured, notably from those specialists in paeonies, Kelway's of Langport.

So we come to the varieties and hybrids whose origin, to me at least, is more obscure; and we may as well start, since they are fewer in all and more straightforward than the rest, with those last mentioned. But before we start at all it may be as well to say that here again, as in the case of hybrid Clematis, every man to his own taste. All tree paeonies need plenty of space so that their total beauty, of leaf as well as of flower, can be fully appreciated; and so, in my view, they are best planted, perhaps in a bed below a wall, as specimen shrubs. They are at any rate almost the only plants in our garden that we do not allow to grow into or through their neighbours. And though all of them are absolutely hardy, they are, owing to their early growth, best afforded some protection from spring frosts. Above all they should not be planted where the morning sunshine falls on them before the frost has thawed off. And finally, all of them are content to grow in any ordinary garden soil, whether alkaline, neutral or acid, though, as Kelway's say, 'the one that perhaps suits best is well drained sandy loam.' Of the group under discussion all have enormous flowers, some double and some single, and most are in some shade of yellow. The two most notable exceptions are Madame Louis Henry, which is predominantly rich pink but shaded with salmon, and Satin Rouge, which is in shades of red fading from ruby to brick. Of the yellow varieties the two with which I am most familiar are surprisingly both double, the sulphur Chromatella and the bright yellow, pink-edged Souvenir du Maxime Cornu. But, as I say, the choice here is easy and depends only on the exact shade you want, which you can find accurately described in Kelway's catalogue, and whether you like your paeonies single or double.

Although I suppose what matters in the present context is their existence rather than their precise origin, the many members of the *suffruticosa* group have always puzzled and narked me. In particular, I cannot make out whether, as the majority of catalogues seem to maintain, the paeony called Moutan (or alternatively *Moutan*, moutan or *moutan*) is actually synonymous with *P. suffruticosa* itself or whether, as I believe and have some slight support for believing, it is rather one of its many hybrids or varieties. But be that as it may, Moutan is in our opinion just about the least desirable of this whole gorgeous galaxy. As in a great many other genera, we prefer the white tree paeonies, notably Mrs William Kelway, to the sumptuously coloured. But we do readily enough condescend to grow, in addition to the two yellow *lutea* forms to which I have already referred, a fair selection of the latter, such as the rose-pink Duchess of Kent and Souvenir d'Etienne Mechin and the scarlet King George V. And when they are in flower, I am so dazzled by their extravagant beauty that I temporarily stop worrying about whether they are really hybrids of *P. suffruticosa* (and, if so, what is their other parent) or merely varieties, and where in their ranks the mysterious Moutan (*Moutan*, moutan or *moutan*) properly belongs. Unfortunately this last, which is, I repeat, just about the worst of the lot, seems to do better than the rest, with which, although we obey all the planting instructions, especially making sure that the graft is well below the soil, we are, for some inexplicable reason other than *Botrytis paeoniae*, not conspicuously successful.

Now that we have deserted botany for practical gardening, the rest of the *Ranunculaceae*, illegitimately including the herbaceous paeonies, can be divided into two vast groups, according as to whether their natural place in the garden is the rockery, which means in our case primarily sinks and troughs, or the herbaceous and mixed borders. And on the former group I have little more to say, because I am convinced that the true species are almost invariably superior to the varieties and hybrids. This applies particularly to the two genera Anemone and Ranunculus, the double forms of which, much more easily obtained from nurserymen than the species, strike me as fat and blowsy. Of the countless varieties and hybrids in the genus Anemone, which for present purposes may be taken to include both Pulsatilla and Hepatica, I have no hesitation in saying that the loveliest in our garden are those which one or other of us has, over the past thirty years or more, collected in southern Europe. But there is no denying that each of the three most popular strains in commerce in this country contains some beautiful things. The St Brigid strain, which springs from *A. coronaria*, comes, like its progenitor, in a huge range of colour, but suffers severely in my eyes from the fact that, unlike its progenitor, whose broad sepals normally number only from five to eight, it is semi-double, its very numerous sepals greatly reduced in breadth and arranged in at least three tiers. The St Bavo strain, the origin of which is unknown to me but which looks very like the known hybrid between *Anemone pavonina* and *A. hortensis*, is less varied in colour, being mainly in shades of pink or red, but has the advantage of being always single. And finally the de Caen strain, which is as varied in colour as the St Brigid and, like the St Bavo, always single, has the slight disadvantage that, whereas the species, whatever their colour, are normally monochrome and the better for that, its flowers have a black centre, usually surrounded with a white or pink ring. As for Ranunculus, there is, I think, only one species in our garden that has not either put itself there or been introduced by us, and we certainly grow no hybrids or double varieties. The exception, R. *gramineus*, was given us by a friend. It is about nine inches high and its flowers, which are large and lemon-yellow, are indistinguishable from the not uncommon pale form of our ordinary native buttercup. But its leaves are grassy, which is exactly what its specific name suggests, and most attractively glaucous.

I have deliberately so far omitted one species of Anemone which we grow because it affords a natural transition from the rock garden to the herbaceous border. The beautiful white *Anemone sylvestris*, a European species which spreads as far east as Turkestan, and which we have never collected for ourselves but found already in possession of a corner of the garden, varies in height from six to eighteen inches and presumably therefore belongs to the rock garden. But the point is that, though its leaves are more delicately dissected, its flowers are very like a miniature version of those of the white variety of its bigger and much more familiar brother, *A. hupehensis*, better known as *A. japonica*.[1] And *A. hupehensis*, the type of which has mauve flowers and of which the equally familiar pink form is another variety known as *elegans*, belongs emphatically to the herbaceous or mixed border. It is in fact, among the plants commonly grown in British gardens, the only species of either Anemone or Ranunculus of which that can be said.

I have nothing to add about hellebores, which belong neither to the rock garden nor the herbaceous border. We ourselves grow them almost exclusively either in shady mixed borders, where the chief among their companions are old-fashioned roses, lilies and sundry onions, in our semi-wild garden, or else, again in a shady border beneath the north-east corner of the house, where their principal associates are columbines, virtually by themselves. I have once seen, at Sissinghurst, a species with grey-blue flowers which I immediately decided must be added to our collection, but when I asked Miss Sackville West what its name was and where she got it, her tentative answers to both questions rapidly proved to be apocryphal. Much as I covet the plant, I still await reliable replies to the same two questions,[2] neither of which is answered in the *Dictionary of Gardening*. But for the rest, I have already mentioned, in the part of this chapter devoted to natural species and their natural hybrids, all that we grow or want to grow. And very much the same is true of the genus Aquilegia, some species of which belong to the

[1] [*A. japonica* is now called *A. × hybrida* and is the hybrid between *A. hupehensis* and *A. vitifolia*.]

[2] I have now had the answer to the first question: the plant is *H. × torquatus*.

rock garden and some to the mixed rather than the herbaceous border. The modern long-spurred varieties are indubitably more beautiful than all the species except *A. alpina* and *A. pyrenaica*, but, since they all alike fare better in shade or half-shade, they are difficult to accommodate in the average herbaceous border. Our own favourite among the taller columbines is not, as a matter of fact, one of the long-spurred hybrids, all of which derive ultimately from *A. longissima*, a native of the states from Texas to Mexico, but an all-white form of our own native *A. vulgaris* which is variously called, among other things, *A. vulgaris* Nivea, *A. nivea* and, most frequently in catalogues, *A.* Munstead White.

And that leaves only Thalictrum, Aconitum, Delphinium and Paeonia. Alone of the four, Thalictrum is, nomenclature apart, straight-forward enough. The best of those that are commonly grown in herbaceous borders, the *T. dipterocarpum* of catalogues, is probably synonymous, whence in small part my warning about nomenclature, with *T. delavayi*; *T. minus*, of course, which surprisingly includes *T. majus* as a local race, is in this respect even worse. But be that as it may, the lovely *T. delavayi* and its closest relatives are not at all happy in the dry, sun-baked and alkaline herbaceous borders which are all that we have hitherto offered them. Maybe they would do better in the shadier and marginally less alkaline mixed borders in the semi-wild garden.

The genus Aconitum, that of the monkshoods, is a great deal larger and more varied than the average British garden, including the nursery gardens, might suggest. It includes, for instance, one rock garden plant, the pale blue Siberian *A. biflorum*, which is only some six inches tall, and one climber, the violet *A. hemsleyanum* from China. The great majority of the remaining species fall into one or other of three large groups. The *napellus* group, which is the largest and much the most familiar, contains our own native *A. anglicum*. The most obvious distinguishing characteristics of the group as a whole are that its leaves are usually finely dissected and that its flowers are for the most part purplish but occasionally white. The best of them, which I know only in its native habitat, is *A. neomontanum* of the European Alps. The salient characteristics of the *cammarum* group, on the other hand, which does not appear to be in commerce in this country, are that its leaves have relatively short lobes and a larger undivided area than in the *napellus* group, and that its flowers, to quote from the *Dictionary of Gardening*, have 'helmet tall and arching, at least twice as high as wide, and erect petals with backward directed spurs.' And finally, *A. vulparia* and its allies can be immediately and easily distinguished from the other two groups by the simple fact that their flowers are always yellow or yellowish. Personally I have not much use for the blue, mauve or purple monkshoods, such as the popular Spark's variety of *A. napellus*, or even the blue and white form listed by Waterers as *A. bicolor*, because, whatever the precise shade, their colour always strikes me as dingy and lifeless compared, say, with that of the Veronicas or Delphiniums. But *A. vulparia*, another European species which extends this time as far east as China, is an altogether different matter. Unfortunately it too is, in this country, far from easy to procure. But I have lately discovered, and obtained a plant of it thence, a source from which it may be had, namely the nurseries started by Miss Davenport Jones and still called after her at Hawkhurst in Kent. I have planted it as one of the few yellow flowers, such as the sulphur *Eremurus stenophyllus*, which punctuate and illumine our twin blue borders. Of the variety *atrovirens* of *A. anthora*, a native of the Pyrenees of whose existence I have only today learnt from the *Dictionary of Gardening*, I know nothing whatever; but, from the fact that its flowers are described as orange-yellow, it sounds highly desirable. And finally, it is perhaps worth mentioning that the name Aconitum, along with many another modern botanical name, goes right back to Theophrastus, the pupil and successor of Aristotle as head of the Lyceum and, at Aristotle's suggestion, the pioneer of scientific botany in Europe, who lived in the fourth century B.C.

The genus Delphinium, which I earlier dismissed so summarily because its most familiar European species are either annual or biennial, now, in the context of the herbaceous border, calls for more extended treatment. The garden larkspurs derive from one or other of two annual or biennial species, *D. ajacis* and *D. consolida* [now transferred to the genus *Consolida* as *C. ambigua* and *C. regalis*], both of which are European, the former naturalised in Britain and the latter reputedly native, and both of which have a large number of colour varieties. Though the normal deep blue form of *D. consolida* is immeasurably more beautiful than any garden larkspur, we have, as I explained in the Introduction, little use for any annual or biennial that will not of its own accord perpetuate itself. The majority of perennial Delphiniums come from either North America or Asia and are as hardy as they can be, but there are also a few from tropical Africa, such as *D. candidum* and *D. macrocentron*, which in this country can only be grown in a greenhouse. It is a curious fact that the two beautiful red perennials, *D. nudicaule*, of which there are suitably named varieties in orange, apricot, yellow and dull purple, and the scarlet *D. cardinale*, should both come from California, while the hybrid between the former and the blue Pyrenean *D. elatum*, first raised in Holland and named *D. × ruysii*, is the pink perennial of the Belladonna type known to nurserymen as Pink Sensation. And so we come, last of all this time, to the European perennials, of which there are actually several, but few, if any, in regular cultivation in this country. There is another Pyrenean species, also blue, known as *D. verdunense*. Indeed, they are all blue, though one, *D. peregrinum*, has in nature a rare white variety, while another, the Mediterranean *D. staphisagria*, has a greenish tinge and again rare natural varieties in pale blue and white. One Persian species, *D. zalil*, which is synonymous with the more significant *sulphureum*, has yellow flowers which are locally used for dyeing silk. And finally, the two perennial species which have given rise to most of the garden forms are the ultra-hardy purplish-blue *D. formosum* from the Caucasus and Asia Minor, which has named varieties in pale blue and white, and the Chinese *D. grandiflorum*, which again has several varieties, including a white one known surprisingly as var. *album* and numerous others with names such as Azure Fairy or Blue Gem. If you want to know which of the multitude to order, you need only consult Blackmore and Langdon's catalogue. As I said just now, all but the Africans are perfectly hardy, but they are all liable to one particularly unsightly disease. To quote once again from the *Dictionary of Gardening*, 'the common trouble with Delphiniums is Powdery Mildew, due to *Erysiphe polygoni*, which makes powdery white areas on the leaves and stems, and if severe may cripple the flower spikes to some extent. Severe mildew attacks, even after first flowering, cripple the foliage and reduce the vigour of the plant for next spring, a fact of importance to nurserymen. This mildew is controlled by spraying with lime-sulphur, 1 part to 60 parts water, as soon as it is suspected, if not before.' And that is enough about Delphiniums.

So we come, finally, to the herbaceous paeonies, on which, having dealt earlier with the European species, I have not a great deal to add. There are, as a matter of fact, several species that I have not yet mentioned, two of which we grow at Shepreth, while a third is not only European but known to me in its native habitat. In the spring of 1938 I went on an expedition, in part archaeological and in part botanical, to the isle of Crete. It was then that I collected the exquisite white form of *Ranunculus asiaticus* mentioned earlier in this chapter, which is abundant on the road-sides along the north side of the island, and also, on the level upland plain of Omaló, very high up in the middle of the White Mountains, where it was growing in abundance, the excessively rare *Tulipa bakeri*, which is still thriving and proliferating prodigiously by its underground stolons in the National Tulip Collection at Cambridge. Close to the latter, in a little stunted fir wood surrounding a shrine, and high above the head of the great gorge of Samariá, second in depth of all the gorges of Europe, I came across a fine colony of the single white *Paeonia clusii*, once *P. cretica*, the segments of the leaves of which are finer and much more acute than those of *P.*

43

rhodia. It was in full flower and, in the sunlight following a night of torrential rain, made one of the most beautiful botanical pictures I have ever set eyes on. Unfortunately, as I was carrying all my own gear on my back and it already weighed the better part of half a hundredweight, I lacked the willpower to add it to my collection. And I have never seen it in a British garden, let alone been able to procure it, since that long distant date. Two other single white species we do however grow with spectacular success, *P. emodi*, which hails from north-west India, and the variety of the Siberian and Mongolian *P. lactiflora*, which is known in commerce either as *P. whitleyi major*, under which name it is obtainable from Kelway's, or as The Bride. These two, in company with the double white garden varieties called Baroness Schroeder and Duchesse de Nemours, themselves two more of the numerous offspring of *P. lactiflora* known to nurserymen as Chinese Paeonies, very effectively flank our magnificent specimen of the single white shrub rose Nevada of which more anon. Besides the Caucasian *P. mlokosewitschii*, my own favourite among all the herbaceous paeonies, there is one more single yellow species, of which I regret to say that I know nothing whatever but which is obtainable this time from Hillier's, another Caucasian called *P. wittmanniana*. As to the pink species, I have already mentioned my two favourites, *P. cambessedesii*, from the Balearic Isles, and *P. woodwardii*, which is actually a subspecies of the magenta *P. veitchii*. Of the red European species the only two, so far as I know, which are in commerce are *P. peregrina*, alias *lobata*, under the names of Fire King and Sunbeam, and the pink variety of *P. arietina* known as Rosy Gem. And for a dark maroon and a purple species we have to turn to America, *P. brownii* of the north-west and *P. californica* respectively, the latter of which is sometimes regarded as only a subspecies of the former.

Enough about the species. And now for the garden varieties, which derive in part from the European *P. officinalis*, in part from the rose-purple Siberian and Chinese *P. obovata*, two white varieties of which var. *alba* and var. *willmottiae* are in specialists' cultivation in this country, and in the main, as I have just suggested, from *P. lactiflora*. The first group comprises the old-fashioned fully double varieties, red, pink and white, which in these days have been largely superseded but which are still to be seen, happily, in many a country cottage garden. We ourselves have only one of them, the red form, which is the least good of the three, known as Old Double Crimson. We found it already in occupation of the least inviting corner of what is now our herbaceous border, where we were more than content to leave it and associate it with oriental poppies of various colours and red and pink Pyrethrums. The second group, though, as I say, sporadically cultivated in this country, does not appear to be on the market. And finally the *lactiflora* group, which is by far the largest, is itself divided by Kelway's into three subdivisions, the single flowered, the double and the so-called 'Imperial' Paeonies. In the first subdivision, apart from the afore-mentioned white *P.* Whitleyi major, the best are perhaps the very dark blackish-red Wilbur Wright, the intense maroon Lord Kitchener, and the two pure pink varieties called Rose of Delight and Strephon. Among the double forms those which we have ourselves selected, with our habitual preference in paeonies, are all but one white or nearly white, namely the aforementioned Baroness Schroeder and Duchesse de Nemours, James Kelway, Primavère, Laura Dessert, which, as Kelway's say, is 'the yellowest herbaceous Paeony,' and the apple-blossom-pink Sarah Bernhardt. The third subdivision is again described by Kelway's as follows: 'These possess a different style of beauty from other Paeonies of the *lactiflora* section. All have stout, shell-like guard petals forming a wide saucer filled half-way to the brim with golden, rosy, cream, white or parti-coloured narrow petaloids lying in a tightly packed rosette formation, or with silk floss-like filaments. Some remind one of rare water lilies. They are just as hardy and easy to grow and require the same treatment as other herbaceous Paeonies.' Of these we have as yet introduced only one, which however elicits as much admiration as any paeony in our garden, the large pale pink Bowl of Beauty, the upright petaloids of which are creamy-white. But, to display once again our usual predilection, the 'milk-white' Kelway's White Lady, with its 'cream centre,' and the 'pure, glistening white' Queen Alexandra, 'with lemon or canary-yellow central petaloids,' sound particularly seductive items in the Kelway catalogue.

A few final disconnected observations on the family *Paeoniaceae* and I shall at last have finished. First, with regard to their number, there are, despite the countless garden varieties, only thirty-three species known in the world. Second, concerning their hardihood, the tree paeony in particular is, once more according to Kelway's, 'subject to more than 40 degrees Fahrenheit below zero in its native country,' followed by a hot summer, and is therefore by no means ill adapted to our reputedly temperate climate. Third, on the question of their situation in the garden, all paeonies prefer half-shade, and the hybrids and varieties of *P. suffruticosa* do best with a northern exposure. Fourth, the occasional reluctance of the herbaceous varieties to flower is attributable almost always to their crowns having been planted more than the recommended two inches below the surface of the settled soil. In the fifth place, the easy and virtually infallible way to propagate the species, such as *P. mascula* and *P. mlokosewitschii*, which, at Shepreth or in my mother-in-law's garden in Rutland at least, very readily sow themselves, is by seed; whereas, of course, the only way to reproduce the garden varieties true to type is by division, which is obviously, for reasons given earlier, much less conducive to rapid success. Last but one, as I mentioned in passing on the topic of the tree paeonies, all the family is liable to the disease of botrytis, primarily if not exclusively connected in the mind of the average amateur gardener with lilies or lettuces, for the treatment of which, once more in the words of the *Dictionary of Gardening*, 'it is essential to cut off affected shoots below ground-level and burn them as soon as the disease is noticed, and if necessary further spray the clumps with Bordeaux mixture.' And last of all, but deserving a paragraph all to itself, comes the family's name.

Like Aconitum, the name Paeonia first appears in extant European literature in the pages of Theophrastus. But it reappears, together with many other modern botanical names, in the Herbal of Dioscorides. Dioscorides was a physician attached, in the ancient equivalent of the R.A.M.C., to the armies of the notorious Roman emperor Nero and, as such, he perforce travelled at least as far as India. On his travels he evidently collected plants for medicinal purposes and tried them out on his unfortunate patients, while in his hours of leisure he must have composed his herbal. This curious work happens, by the purest accident, to be the earliest European publication of its kind to have survived; but it undoubtedly owes a large debt to several earlier Greek herbals, notably one by Cratevas, which have all alike perished. Although until very lately it was the medical bible of, for instance, the monks of Mount Athos, it is for the most part a nauseating mixture of obscenity and superstition. But in the midst of all the magical mumbo-jumbo there is an occasional paragraph which points unmistakably to a modicum of empirical observation. Thus, to give the obvious illustration, he describes in some detail the extraction and decoction from *Mandragora autumnalis* or *M. officinarum*, alias mandrake (a Greek species of the same family as contains the true deadly nightshade, the potato and the tobacco plant), of a drug which he tells us, when mixed with white wine and administered to the patient, puts him into so deep a sleep that he is unconscious of the pain, and so remains for three or four hours. So, almost exactly nineteen hundred years before the elaborate celebration of the first centenary of the discovery of anaesthetics, Dioscorides anticipated the modern use of the extract from another plant of the same family, the preliminary anaesthetic popularly known as Twilight Sleep. A thousand pities that this is the only example I can cite off the cuff from Dioscorides or, if it comes to that, from any other European literary herbalist in antiquity, of the origins of medical science. For after the Renaissance such was the influence of Dioscorides throughout the whole of civilised Europe that the first occupant of the chair of Botany at the University of Bologna, Luca Ghini, was seriously referred to by an English friend and fellow-botanist as 'reader in Dioscorides in Bonony.' I will not dilate on the uses to which Dioscorides put paeony, the name of which is itself allegedly derived from Paeon, the first Greek physician to use it for medicinal purposes, or even worse, another member of the *Ranunculaceae*, hellebore.

CHAPTER 3

A First Miscellany

TWENTY-TWO whole families intervene, in the flora of these islands alone, between the *Ranunculaceae* and *Paeoniaceae* and the next family to which I propose to devote a chapter to itself, that of the *Geraniaceae*. Fortunately, however, less than half this number are of any real relevance to normal British horticulture, and those that are not I shall, with no further apology, pass over in anonymity. Even those that are, poor dears (and a few of them really do contain some of my pet plants), will have to put up with even shorter and more selective shrift than my usual. As the British flora embraces a hundred and thirty nine different families, if we continued on the present scale this book would run to five volumes and even fewer people would read it than will as it is now.

Since the *Berberidaceae* follow in our flora immediately after the Paeony family, we begin with a bang. They actually comprise twelve genera, but I am only interested in three of that dozen, namely Berberis itself, Mahonia and Epimedium, of each of which there happens to be a single representative either native or naturalised in Britain. I suppose I owe to my classical education my considerable interest in botanical names, which usually convey a clearer mental picture to me than they seem to to the average gardener, and of the diverse origins of which these three afford an illuminating example. Epimedium is the oldest of the three, being an ancient Greek plant name which first appears in extant literature in the Herbal of Dioscorides. Berberis comes from the Arabian *berberys*, the name given to the actual berries. And the name Mahonia was bestowed, according to the *Dictionary of Gardening*, which I am in no position to question on this particular matter, 'in honour of Bernard M'Mahon, 1775–1816, American horticulturist.' I am glad that even a botanist had not the heart to call a plant M'Mahonia – or rather, since the double capital would obviously infringe the rules, M'mahonia – even though *okellyi* is still admitted as the subspecific name of a native Irish orchid.

But to business. The simplest distinction between Berberis and Mahonia is that the leaves of the latter are always pinnate, those of the former never. Our British representatives of the two genera are the common barberry, *B. vulgaris*, which is probably native in a few places in England, and the Oregon grape, *M. aquifolium*, the density of which as a naturalised plant is exactly correlated with the areas where pheasants, hapless creatures, need cover. Incidentally, why this particular species of Mr M'Mahon's genus should be neuter when all the rest are emphatically either feminine or else possessive, I cannot think. Anyhow, we inherited both these plants in the garden; the former in a very beautiful variety, which I cannot off-hand find in any catalogue but which is presumably var. *purpurea* of the *Dictionary*, with very deep reddish-purple leaves; the latter, in its most common or pheasant-cover form, growing contentedly where we have found nothing else except *Cyclamen hederifolium* and *Helleborus foetidus* to survive for long, in the dehydrated dust at the very foot of our chestnut tree. Apart from *B. vulgaris*, the *Dictionary* lists about eighty barberries, either species or hybrids and not including countless varieties, more or less warmly recommended for cultivation in British gardens. And incidentally it prefaces its discussion of them with the extremely interesting information, which is so simple that I find it hard to believe, that those with yellow flowers come from Asia, those with orange from South America. Of this unmanageable total I doubt whether we can claim even a nodding acquaintance with as many as twenty, and we grow, varieties this time included, only about half a dozen. Apart again from *B. vulgaris* var. Purpurea, which, still in its original position, blends to perfection with our own combination of the blood-red climbing rose Scarlet Fire and *Clematis × jackmannii* Superba, we find that the popular *B. darwinii*, whose bright orange flowers betray its origin, makes an exquisitely contrasting support for *Clematis alpina*; while its diminutive variety, which I bought from Joe Elliott under the name *corallina compacta*[1] and which, as he says, 'smothers itself in early summer with a mass of glowing orange flowers,' so well lives up to its last name that it does not look in the least out of proportion in by no means the largest of my sinks. One other barberry which we were lately given, with no name attached, is too young to have yet flowered, but already, with its long narrow spiny evergreen leaves, makes a handsome upright bush about a yard tall. Another of the popular favourites, *B. × stenophylla*, we have no great desire to grow, because we regard it as markedly inferior to *B. darwinii*, which is one of its parents. But our own favourites are *B. thunbergii*, which we grow in the semi-wild garden partly for its dark

[1 Now considered a form of the hybrid *B. × stenophylla*]

red shoots but chiefly for its colouring in the autumn, when leaves and berries alike are brilliant red, and its variety *atropurpurea* and the variety Nana of the variety. The former of these varieties has, as its name suggests, deep purple leaves, while the latter, which is a true dwarf of only about two feet and has, if anything, even darker leaves, is the best of all shrubs for near the front of a purple border.

After Berberis neither Mahonia nor Epimedium need long detain us. Apart, once again, from the aforementioned neuter species, we grow only one feminine, *M. lomariifolia*, and one possessive, *M. bealei.*[1] Both are beautiful, evergreen, winter-flowering shrubs, with long, broadly pinnate and very sharply and irregularly prickled leaves and lax clusters of flower-spikes like yellow lilies-of-the-valley. The former is looking too ill at present to show any signs of flowering, but the latter is to-day, 13th January, looking as if it would be in its full beauty by the end of the month. And as for the Epimediums, of which by sheer chance we happen to grow four out of the five that the *Dictionary* stars for garden merit, they all make excellent and virtually evergreen ground-cover for unpromising corners of the garden, but with one exception they all, including *E. alpinum*, the one which is very locally semi-naturalised in Britain, can hardly be distinguished from one another by the layman unless by the colour of their pretty but usually not very showy flowers. The exception is *E.* × *youngianum* Niveum (evidently a mathematically-minded plant since, to cite from the *Dictionary* a detail which I confess I have never noticed for myself, its leaflets per leaf are '2, 3, 6 or 9 on the same plant'), which is much smaller and more compact than the others and has leaves of a much fresher green. For the rest, I have the leaves of each before me as I write and can easily see, on such close inspection, that at this time of year those of one, which are very firmly toothed and apiculate, have red veins deeply impressed into a shiny green surface, those of the second, which are for the most part roughly cordate in outline and as edentulate as I am, have green veins even more deeply impressed on a predominantly crimson surface, while those of the third, which are undulating and, in the botanical sense of the word, crisp and have equally minute and sharp teeth as the first, are, veins and all, of a uniform green. But even with the *Dictionary* as well as the leaves before me, I have not the patience or energy to decide here and now, that is, until they flower, which is which. But when they bloom, and two of the four produce relatively large flowers of primrose and buttercup-yellow respectively, it will be a different matter.

The very next family in our flora is that of the *Nymphaeceae*, or

[1] And even *M. bealei* has recently abandoned mere possessiveness for femininity and become *M. japonica* instead.

water-lilies, of which we do, in fact, grow two, one large white one and one small red, in the tiny rectangular pool in our formal paved courtyard. At this point, therefore, I should by rights launch into a well-deserved eulogy of the numberless colour varieties of water-lily, which are most easily procurable from Perry's of Enfield. But since, in my judgment, the most beautiful of all hardy water-lilies is a native of northern Scotland, including the Hebrides and Shetland, and of Connemara in Ireland, I shall do no such thing. The taxonomic status of the plant in question is uncertain, but for the sake of simplicity let us accept the view of Clapham, Tutin and Warburg, which is, however, revised in the *Flora Europaea*, and regard it as a distinct species called *Nymphaea occidentalis*. Anyhow, it is in all respects a perfect miniature reproduction, immeasurably neater and more attractive, of the ordinary white water-lily. If you doubt my verdict on its superlative beauty, then I should advise you to take a drive, or better still a walk, along the very short stretch of road running due north from Salen in Ardnamurchan towards Acharacle and take a good look at the two little lily-lochans lying just below the road on your right. And with that I must pass on without more ado to the next family on my short list, that of the *Papaveraceae* or poppies, which comes, for horticultural purposes, in a wide variety of genera.

Just as, in an ordinary English garden, the place for the *Berberidaceae* is primarily, but not exclusively, in the shrubbery, so the place for the *Papaveraceae* is primarily, but again not exclusively, in the herbaceous border. Let us therefore start at the back of the border and, regardless of the amalgam of genera which you must take it from me belong to the same family, work gradually forwards.

The back row of all belongs, in this context, to the only two known species of plume poppy or Macleaya, formerly known and still listed in catalogues as Bocconia. Both are magnificent plants, attaining a height of at least six feet; both have large, cordate and somewhat glaucous leaves; and both bear flower-spikes suggestive rather of a Spiraea than a poppy. In fact the only noticeable difference between them is that, whereas the flowers of *M. cordata,* the one commonly in commerce, are buff, those of the slightly superior *M. microcarpa* are coppery-pink. But if your herbaceous border is restricted in size, be careful. We have ourselves twice moved or given away a large clump of *M. cordata*, and it is still growing where it was and spreading with undiminished aggression. Next, in the row in front, comes a genus which again embraces only two known species, both from south-west California and this time, for all practical purposes, virtually indistinguishable, the genus Romneya. Both are in this country generally treated, where they are entertained at all, as shrubs rather than as the herbaceous plants that they actually are; both have pinnatifid and very glaucous leaves; and both bear, throughout the summer and autumn, a non-stop sequence of enormous white flowers, at least four inches across, with a thick bunch of bright yellow stames in the middle. But again beware. They are both, though in our experience perfectly hardy, by no means easy to get established. The secret, which we learnt from some un-remembered quarter at, I think, our third attempt, is to plant the beautiful creature, in defiance of all the rules you ever heard about spreading out the roots and treading them well home, in the solid ball in which it arrives from the nursery. Then, in the next row forward, comes that exquisite genus Meconopsis which, with one notable exception of which more anon, we have sadly to assign to the damp peat of Ardtornish, and the true poppies of the genus Papaver, the most familiar of which, though by no means the only ones, are the numerous and usually beautiful colour varieties of the oriental poppy, *P. orientale*, and the detestable annual opium poppy, *P. somniferum*, which is detestable not so much for its various and dubious benefits to the human race as for the invariable and indubitable dinginess of the hues that its flowers, whether double or single, seem able to assume. And last but not least in the herbaceous border, we arrive, in the very front row, at the so-called Iceland poppy, *Papaver nudicaule*, which again can assume a great variety of colours but this time always pure and unalloyed.

And that still leaves no less than eight members of the family that I wish to mention, none of which seem to me to belong properly to the herbaceous border but the correct situation of all but one of which I leave each individual gardener to decide for himself. Once again, as in the herbaceous border, these eight species represent a disproportionate number of genera, in this case six genera to the eight species. We may as well deal first with the only one whose position in the garden is obvious, the relatively diminutive silver-leaved *Papaver alpinum*, which once again comes by nature in several pure colours and which is one of the finest adornments of the rockery or, as in our case, of sinks and troughs. Then follow five plants at least three of which must be familiar to any ordinary British gardener, even if he has never realised that they are all alike members of the poppy family. First, and most obviously one of the *Papaveraceae*, comes the little yellow Welsh poppy, *Meconopsis cambrica*, which is not only native, as its name suggests, in damp, shady, rocky places in Wales and elsewhere in the south west, but is so long-established and regular a feature of cottage gardens that it is thoroughly naturalised over much of the north as well. Despite its apparent daintiness it is an aggressive creature and, since its long tap-roots go too deep for the hoe, it can, and indeed has in our garden, become a minor menace. Scarcely less familiar, if far less palpably a poppy, is the yellow furmitory, *Corydalis lutea*, which again is completely established throughout much of Britain, though this time chiefly on old walls rather than hedgebanks. Like the Welsh poppy, it suddenly crops up in a new corner of the garden, and on the whole, though also somewhat invasive, it is more welcome than its tuberous pink congener, *C. bulbosa*, which we grow among the anemones in the semi-wild garden but which, owing to the mauvish tinge of its pink, we do not greatly admire. And last of these five, and superficially as unlike poppies as they could be, come two species of the genus Dicentra. The good old favourite from Japan, *D. spectabilis* or bleeding heart, with its much cut glaucous leaves and hanging pink and white flowers, is too well known to need any recommendation; but its counterpart from North America, *D. formosa*, seems in this country to be accorded less recognition than it deserves. It is a smaller and tidier plant, its leaves are even more glaucous and, a virtue indeed, it thrives and flowers for longer in at least half-shade.

So, finally, to two widely different members of the family which I hardly ever see in any garden except our own. The first of the two is *Eomecon chionantha* from China, sometimes called, presumably because of the shape of its leaves, the cyclamen poppy. These same leaves, which are borne singly on six-inch stems rising straight from the ground, are three or four inches wide, greyish-green, somewhat fleshy, and undulating at the edges, while the flower-stems, which come from the leaf-sheaths just above ground-level, are about twice the height and bear flowers that at first sight look just like miniature white Japanese Anemones. It is another mildly invasive plant, spreading this time by its rhizome rather than by seed; but give it a corner where it can run about as it pleases and you will be rewarded with a treasure as attractive as it is unusual. And the second of the two, positively the last poppy I shall mention and possibly the most beautiful plant in our whole garden, is our own native yellow horned-poppy, *Glaucium flavum*, of which I shall have a little more to say in a later chapter.

Next on the list come the *Cruciferae*, which I propose to treat very scurvily indeed. Simply because we have never found a suitable situation for them, that blessed trinity of A's, Alyssum, Arabis and Aubrieta is not for us; we prefer to admire, genuinely, the vivid colours of at least the first and last in other gardens in the village. Much the same is true too of wallflowers, the genus Cheiranthus, including those that are often wrongly distinguished as 'perennial wallflowers' such as Harpur Crewe, which we do actually grow because we were given it, or Moonlight, which is, in fact, probably not a Cheiranthus at all but an Erysimum. (I say 'wrongly distinguished' because, as is evident enough from many an old wall, the common or garden wallflower itself, given half a chance, proves to be a perennial.) And the same is true again, though less emphatically so, of both winter and summer stocks, the progeny of *Matthiola incana*, which seems to be native in southern Europe and which just touched our shores, or to be precise our sea-cliffs, at two or three places in the South. The best we do even for them is occasionally to buy a box of young plants and pop them in, not of course in straight lines, wherever we can find room. Indeed, the only one of the old cottage-garden favourites among the crucifers that makes anything of a show in our garden is the pale mauve *Hesperis matronalis*, sweet rocket or dame's violet, which I suppose we must have originally introduced into our herbaceous border and which we now happily leave to sow itself wherever it can find room there.

But the two genera of cruciferous plants which really interest me in our garden, of each of which, nevertheless, we grow only two representatives, are one a genus of giants, the other of pygmies. Seakale, or *Crambe maritima*, is a native of the shores of the Baltic, the Atlantic and the Black seas which again is to be seen on long stretches of our coast-line. It is most familiar, no doubt, as a perennial vegetable, the blanched young leaf-stems of which are among the most delicate culinary products of the garden. Few people seem to realise that, with its long, glaucous and exquisitely undulating leaves and its great bunches of relatively large white flowers, it earns as honoured a place in the herbaceous border as in the kitchen garden. And as for its enormous relative, *C. cordifolia*, that is, in its own kind, without a peer in any herbaceous border in the country. In this case the huge dark green basal leaves might even be thought rather coarse, but it throws up from them, when it is well established, three or four much-branched stems, in our case fully eight feet tall, starred all over with countless little white flowers. Its effect, in fact, is rather that of a giant Gypsophila, and it is enhanced by the fact that the flowers are so spaced that the whole inflorescence seems diaphanous as a gauze veil and you can see through to the colours of the flowers behind.

The two species of whitlow grass, or Draba, that I have in mind are, on the other hand, so diminutive as to find their proper niche not even in the rock garden but in a small sink. We have three British native whitlow grasses, all rather dreary little plants with white flowers, but one of them, the very rare Scottish *Draba norvegica*, distributionally interesting as one of the few exclusively arctic as opposed to arctic-alpine elements in our flora. And then there is a fourth, *D. aizoides*, a native of limestone in the Pyrenees, the Alps and the Balkans, which can easily enough be found, though its status there is doubtful, on rocks and walls around Pennard Castle in Glamorgan and which is a plant of a wholly different order of merit. I grow it in the smallest of all my sinks, where it sows itself like a welcome weed in the chinks of the Westmorland limestone, and so have the opportunity of observing it all the year round. It makes tight little green rosettes only an inch or so across, each very narrow leaf is tipped with a long white bristle and fringed with shorter bristles so that the whole plant has a hoary look, and when it flowers from March to May it is a solid mass of brilliant yellow. And in another sink grows an even smaller sample of the race, *D. rigida* var. *imbricata*, about the dwarfest of all cushion plants, which, at the approach of spring, turns brilliant emerald all over and a few weeks later bears little golden flowers on slender stems barely an inch high. Cruciferous or not, these two tiny yellow whitlow grasses, and doubtless others like them, are undeniably real gems for an old grey stone sink.

After mignonette, which I shall ignore, come four families in succession, the violets and the milkworts, *Violaceae* and *Polygalaceae*, the St John's worts and the rock-roses, *Hypericaceae* and *Cistaceae*, each of which deserves at least a paragraph and the last at least three.

Our native woodland violet, *Viola reichenbachiana*, has long been an uninvited guest in our garden and sows itself in masses in the beds and paths around the house. I tolerate it, Faith does not. And even I cannot deny that native in these islands we have immeasurably more beautiful members of the family, notably the mountain pansy, *V. lutea*, and the sand-dune subspecies *curtisii* of *V. tricolor*. Even the sweet violet, *V. odorata*, which we imported from a local hedge-bank, is, in other respects besides its fragrance, a better plant than its woodland cousin. But our two favourites among the violets proper, which we grow together at the front of the winter garden, are both foreigners. The use of the dark purple-leaved variety of *V. labradorica* is primarily as colourful ground-cover, while the huge, flat and very short-spurred flowers of the pure white form of *V. papilionacea*, from north-east America, put every other violet I can think of to shame. And similarly with what are commonly but unaccurately distinguished from violets as Violas. Though we do grow and treasure one which, to judge from its foliage and the size and shape of its flowers, is no more than a blackish-purple variety of our native *V. tricolor*, the one which we allow to sow itself wherever it will, except, as it often does, in my enormous trough and the adjacent sinks, is the beautiful pure mauve *V. cornuta* from the Pyrenees. As for garden pansies, the only one we take any trouble over is one we had from Valerie Finnis of Waterperry called Irish Molly, the flowers of which are basically black but strangely and metallically suffused with green and copper. And last comes our one and only alpine violet, the delicate little yellow *V. biflora*, which Margery Fish gave to the eldest of our children but I selfishly and perhaps rashly planted in the lime-free soil of my enormous trough. There, however, it produces its twin flowers freely enough and even seems to be spreading.

Of our odd half-dozen native milkworts, two of which, if they are really distinct, namely *Polygala amarella* and *P. austriaca*, are excessively local and rare, by far the most beautiful is the intense sapphire *P. calcarea* which, being almost confined to the chalk, is to be found only in the southern counties of England. On the other hand much the most variable, so polymorphic indeed that I have often unsuccessfully suggested to my botanical friends that it comprises three distinct species, is the widespread and common *P. vulgaris*. In its typical form it trails weakly through the grass, where it is often accompanied by the more compact and usually deeper blue *P. serpyllifolia*. But on limestone cliff-ledges in the mountains behind Sligo it suddenly appears, in what is sometimes called var. *ballii* or var. *grandiflora*, as almost a miniature tree, stiff and upright. And in a secret locality of my own near here, a little bank of absolutely bare, undiluted and undisturbed chalk, it reappears in quantity, yet again in quite a new form which momentarily baffled the pundits, completely prostrate and with countless short and leafy stems, each terminating in a compact head of brilliant blue flowers, radiating from the centre. This last form is the only one of our native milkworts that I have ever attempted to cultivate. I carefully transplanted a single plant into a corner of one of my most culcareous and sun-baked sinks, where I hoped it would trail contentedly and decoratively over the rough old grey stone. But it evidently so missed its monotonous diet of pure calcium that it speedily died of starvation. I shall try again with seed and watch with interest to see whether, with a change of soil, it comes true to form. And the only other member of the *Polygalaceae* that I have ever grown, this time with great success and again in a sink, which, however, I long ago had to leave behind in what used to be my father's garden in Cambridge, is the shrubby little *P. chamaebuxus*, whose large yellow and purple flowers, either solitary or in pairs, are finely offset by its dark evergreen leaves. We regularly see it in great profusion on limestone outcrops, and usually just coming into flower, when, as we occasionally do, we spend our Easter family holidays at Asolo, in the southernmost foothills of the Dolomites; but it has proved an exceedingly difficult plant successfully to uproot from the bed-rock in which it naturally grows there.

The next two families, unlike the last two, are predominantly represented in British gardens by woody shrubs and subshrubs. Apart from the very rare narrow-leaved St John's wort, *Hypericum linarifolium*, which is a beautiful feature of the steep banks of the River Teign in Devon, I am lucky in that my three favourites among our native St John's worts all grow wild in the garden at Ardtornish. They are widely different one from the other both in habit and in habitat. The little prostrate *H. humifusum* grows on the stony edges of the drive; the aptly named *H. pulchrum*, with its scarlet buds and anthers, abounds along the heathy river bank; and the shrubby tutsan, *H. androsaemum*, which bears large berries that turn from green to red to black, grows, for some reason always as isolated plants rather than in colonies, in several shady and rocky spots. It may have been from Ardtornish that we introduced a plant of this last into a qualid north-facing corner outside the scullery window at Shepreth. Anyhow, it and one or two uninvited but not unwelcome plants of the herbaceous *H. perforatum* are the only two of our natives to grace the garden here. And if it comes to that, we have only two foreign species either, though both grow cheek by jowl with their varieties. On our first joint visit to Greece, as a matter of fact, we collected on the rocky slopes of Mount Parnassus a solitary seedling of a third, which I judge from the *Flora Europaea* must have been *H. empetrifolium*. But with misguided generosity we gave it to the Cambridge Botanic Garden, whence, wrongly labelled *H. coris*, which goes no farther east in Europe than Italy, it figured in an exhibit of plants collected in the wild which won a gold medal at an R.H.S. show. Of those still with us, a number of the group formerly known as *H. patulum*, I think *H. pseudohenryi*, does very well at the south-east-facing front corner of the house, with the Hidcote variety close beside it apparently resenting the rigours of our winters; while immediately in front of them another Greek, the large-flowered little golden *H. olympicum*, along with its even superior very pale yellow variety *uniflorum* Citrinum, sows itself with careless abandon. Indeed it has gone so far, literally, as to insert a healthy young seedling into the very corner of one of my sinks, where, unlike *Viola cornuta,* I am suffering it to remain.

The rock-rose family deserves three paragraphs because, for garden purposes anyhow, it comes in three sizes, small, medium and large, representing, unlike the last three families, three different genera. I shall start with the smallest, the rock-roses proper, because they alone of the three are represented, and nobly represented, in Britain. If we ignore the pretty but very rare little annual spotted rock-rose, now called *Tuberaria guttata*, we are left with three native species of Helianthemum, the first two of which are among the numerous ancestors of the colourful garden hybrids. First, and so familiar that it needs no description, comes the common rock-rose, *H. nummularium*, which I associate primarily but by no means exclusively with chalk-down turf. The next two, on the other hand, are essentially plants of the limestone. It is perhaps surprising that the grey-leaved white-flowered *H. apenni-num*, whose specific name means what it says, should reach England at all; but it does in two places, both short rocky turf on cliff-tops, first at Berry head in South Devon, and second on Brean Down on the coast of Somerset. And third and last, slightly more widespread but still intensely local, comes the pretty little undershrub with small yellow flowers, *H. canum*. I shall say virtually nothing about the modern garden hybrids, several of them unaccountably named after Scottish mountains, because here again, as with hybrid Clematis earlier and hybrid tea roses later on, every man to his own taste in colour and form. We ourselves, as usual, abominate the double ones and rank as the three best singles, all grey-leaved, the pure white one called The Bride, the soft Wisley Primrose and, best of all, the shell-pink one which is listed by Alan Smith, as if it were a species, as 'Rhodanthe Carneum,' but which is in reality, I strongly suspect, the pink variety from the Balearic Isles and north-west Italy, sometimes known as *H. rhodanthum*, of our native *H. apenninum*. Instead I shall extol the merits of three genuinely wild species or subspecies, all of which I had from Joe Elliott; *H. lunulatum* from the Italian Maritime Alps; what he listed, fairly enough, as *H. alpestre serpyllifolium*, which would be more pedantically described as var. *serpyllifolium* of subsp. *alpestre* of *H. oelandicum*, from the mountains of central and southern Europe; and *H. oblongatum* from God knows where. All three have bright yellow flowers. The first is a tiny grey-leaved shrub which, when mixed with the blue *Lithospermum intermedium* [now *Moltkia intermedia*], makes a beautiful very miniature hedge. The second, the least interesting of the three, is, I found, too rampageous for a sink, but would probably drape itself elegantly and, for a long season, colourfully over a rock in the rock garden. And the third, whose slender reddish-brown stems are genuinely red when young, is so tiny and neat a creeper that it has proved itself, as Joe Elliott says it will, 'ideal spilling over the side of a trough.'

After Helianthemum the genus Halimium, the medium-sized version of the *Cistaceae*, need not keep us long. Although Notcutt's rank Halimiums as a separate section under Cistus and say of them that 'these differ from Cistus only in botanical detail,' I know of no Cistus with the yellow flowers that most true Halimiums in Europe have, including the two which Notcutt's list, *H. lasianthum* and *H. ocymoides*. These happen to be the two we grow or have grown at Shepreth. Both hail from Portugal, where they are not infrequent in the south; both are small shrubs some eighteen inches to two feet tall; both are greyish-white with down and silky hairs; and the bright yellow petals of both have a maroon or chocolate blotch at the base. Both, in fact, are very pretty little shrubs. But neither, in this part of the country at least, is at all reliably hardy. As I write, in mid-January, *H. ocymoides*, which is easily distinguished from the other by its smaller leaves, is still with us in our sheltered little courtyard. But how long, O Lord, how long?

The genus Cistus contains some of the most glorious of all flowering shrubs, several of which have proved decidedly hardier here than the Halimiums. At any rate three species, namely *C. ladanifer, C. salvifolius* and *C. albidus*, came virtually unscathed through the extreme and prolonged severity of January and February 1963. We saw plenty of the first of these on our first visit to Portugal, when our primary objective was miniature daffodils, growing in quantity as close to Lisbon as the fascinating promontory of Arrabida only just across the River Tagus. But as it was in full flower there was no seed available, and we did not chance upon any detachable seedling. A pity since, with its slender, shiny, resinous leaves, dark green above and palely glaucous below, and its huge white flowers with maroon blotches, it is one of our two favourites. The other two we did, however, import, in the form of young seedlings from the neighbourhood of the Riviera, and the latter especially, which had beautiful downy grey leaves but flowers of an ugly mauvish-pink, has actually multiplied. The second of our favourites, *C. palhinhae*, which is like a stunted *C. ladanifer* with unblotched flowers, we again saw in fair quantity on our second visit to Portugal, this time in the Algarve and notably as a prominent feature of the unique and fascinating flora on top of Cape St Vincent. Again, and for the same reason, we were unable to introduce it ourselves, but we have a young plant of it, raised from seed from elsewhere, on either side of the front door. Another which we did, however, import for ourselves is the neat narrow-leaved white-flowered *C. monspeliensis*, the seed of which I gathered in September 1967, along with that of *Clematis orientalis*, in a narrow natural thicket behind a sandy beach, on which Faith and our Greek host were risking a plague of wasps and bathing, on the west coast of the long narrow promontory of Kassandra in Khalkidike. Just over two years later we had about ten tidy upright bushes, already some two feet tall, of which I gave the majority away, one to the Botanic Garden, but transplanted three into small gaps in the border along the front of the house, one at the very foot of our huge old specimen, planted almost as soon as we came here and braving unprotected every winter since, of *C. ladanifer*. There they have all three already withstood twenty degrees of frost, and there, having never yet seen the plant in flower, I look forward to admiring, in five months' time, what must be a very elegant marriage between dark green linear leaves, again somewhat paler beneath, and pure white golden-centred flowers.

The following spring found us again in Greece, the happiest of all our hunting-grounds, this time mainly on Rhodes, where we collected, among other things that are still with us, the blood-red form of *Ranunculus asiaticus* and *Paeonia rhodia*, and the relatively tiny island of Cos, where I was completing my investigations of the plants mentioned in the Idylls of Theocritus. All round the town of Rhodes itself we encountered masses of *Cistus parviflorus*, the only really pure pale pink among the allegedly pink Cistuses, which was, of course, in full flower. Thwarted once again in exactly the same way as we were with *C. ladanifer* and *C. palhinhae*, we had recourse for the first time to cuttings, which are generally the easiest way to propagate the genus. When we got these cuttings, which we naturally took at the last possible moment, safely back home in a polythene bag, they incomprehensibly but resolutely refused to strike. And that leaves only two members of the genus which we grow or have attempted to grow. *C. laurifolius*, the dull leaves of which make it immeasurably the inferior of *C. ladanifer* but which is reputed to be the hardier of the two, perished during the unusually mild winter of 1968–9, which *C.* × *corbariensis* survived, in the same sheltered courtyard, wholly unscathed. This last, the result of crossing *C. populifolius* with the aforementioned *C. salvifolius*, both from south-western Europe, is one of the pick of the bunch. I have a sprig of it before me as I write, and it is now 18th January. It makes a low wide-spreading bush, eventually more than a yard across; its younger branches are red on the upper side and green on the under; its small, olive-green, cordate-lanceolate leaves are most delicately veined and their margins are elegantly waved and deckled; and its profusion of white flowers, which are flushed with yellow at the base, opens from buds of a pure rose-pink. And finally, the only reason why we have never grown the undeniably handsome *C.* × *purpureus*, the cross this time between *C. ladanifer* and the magenta *C. incanus*, is not so much that it is said to survive only the mildest winters as that, as may conceivably have become apparent, we prefer our Cistuses white.

Three families intervene in our flora, from which, for horticultural purposes, only the feathery tamarisks deserve as much as a mention, and they look to me all wrong away from the nourishing salt of the sea, before we are confronted with the formidable family of the *Caryophyllaceae*, which, since it contains at least twelve hundred species divided among some seventy-five genera, should by rights have a chapter to itself. However, of the twenty-five genera listed as relevant in the *Dictionary of Gardening*, I shall concern myself with only nine, and I shall divide the species involved, none too scientifically, into three categories: those that form tight mats or cushions suitable to the rock garden or even a sink; those that belong properly to the herbaceous border; and those of the genus Dianthus.

The genera falling essentially into the first category are Arenaria,

Minuartia and Sagina, between which, unlike Halimium and Cistus, the distinction really does rest only in subtle botanical detail. All three can boast, among many dreary and, in the last case, sometimes pestilential congeners, at least one British representative that could fairly be termed pretty. There is nothing much to choose between the three prettiest of our native Arenarias, the true *A. norvegica*, from five widely scattered localities in Scotland and one in County Clare, its subspecies *anglica*, whose only known station in the world is around Ingleborough in the West Riding of Yorkshire, and *A. ciliata* from the aforementioned limestone mountains behind Sligo. All make bright green mats or loose cushions, all bear numerous relatively large white flowers, and all, as I can certify for one of them, would embellish a sink. Their most familiar congener in British gardens, which has indeed naturalised itself thence in many parts of the country, is the tiny-leaved little creeper with solitary white flowers held on slender two-inch stems called, for obvious reasons, *A. balearica*; a first-rate plant for a dank and heavily shaded corner. Of Minuartia, on the other hand, and likewise of Sagina, we can claim only one pretty species apiece, namely *M. verna* and *S. nodosa*, but they are both as good plants for the rock garden as any of their kind. Indeed, I am so fond of the former that on our recent lightning tour of the Alps I collected seed of it from more than one mountain in the hope of growing it in a sink. Both these two, incidentally, can easily be distinguished from the best of our Arenarias by their much laxer habit and linear foliage, while the latter is best told from the former by the bundles of leafbuds in the axils of its mature leaves. I have yet to see another Sagina that I would wish to grow, unless for mere rarity's sake, but on this same Alpine tour I did collect seed, this time from well over nine thousand feet on the Gornergrat, of another and very different species of Minuartia, namely *Minuartia* (formerly *Cherleria*) *sedoides*, or mossy cyphel. Isolated plants of it were growing on a bare ridge among equally isolated plants of another member of the family, *Silene acaulis*, and though I had often seen it in the same company on Scottish mountains, its tiny dense cushions here made those on the Silene look so coarse and clumsy that I suddenly longed to grow it, as I already grow the other, in one of my sinks.

And that brings us to four other caryophyllaceous genera which, though by no means confined thereto, have a contribution to make to the rock garden, namely Cerastium, Lychnis, Silene and Saponaria. None of them need detain us very long. Our two mountain species of Cerastium, *C. alpinum* and *C. arcticum*, are both handsome plants, with much larger white flowers than the foregoing genera, but both, being used to a covering of snow, are said to resent winter damp; and the same will probably turn out to be true of *C. latifolium*, whose seeds I lately gathered at Arolla. Our native lowland *C. arvense*, the field mouse-ear, which is almost as handsome as its alpine and arctic cousins, would doubtless prove easier in cultivation, even though it seems to have a marked preference for sandy soils. But really the only excuse for mentioning the genus at all lies in the justly beloved *C. tomentosum*, dusty miller or snow-in-summer, the all-white effect of which is so regular a feature of cottage gardens that it has escaped all over the place. Our two mountain species of Lychnis, both of which were previously ranked under Viscaria, namely *L. alpina* and *L. viscaria*, are more refined plants for the rock garden, both as pink as their congener of the bogs, *L. flos-cuculi* or ragged robin, and once again I am hoping to introduce the former and smaller of the two into one of my sinks from seed lately back from the Alps. We have numerous native Silenes, to some of which, such as *S. conica* and *S. otites*, which are sometimes to be seen together on the Breck, I am, if only for sentimental reasons, deeply attached. Indeed, this past autumn I once again introduced, if this time only from just over the Suffolk county boundary, seeds of the latter and more curious of the two into our Shepreth garden. But our only native alpine species is the aforementioned *S. acaulis*, my single plant of which came actually, as a young seedling, from Morvern rather than the Alps for the two reasons that it is locally abundant there and appreciably less far from home. And that leaves only one species of Saponaria, not, alas, native in Britain, and for the time being we shall have done with the rock garden and our own substitute for it, the trough and sink. Unless you reckon Asolo, as you just might, as falling within the area of the Dolomites, the only time in our joint lives when we have spent long enough in any one place in the Alps to become really familiar with the local flora was when we stayed for a week in late June at Pralognan in Savoie. You can take a cable car from the village to the top of a high ridge immediately above, and on one side of the ridge you can follow a little path running along the top of the cliff that overhangs one of the two upper arms of the valley in which the village lies. One dazzling morning when we were up there, not only was this path ablaze wth the brilliant pink of the prostrate woody *S. ocymoides*, but the swallow-tail butterflies were continually settling on it with the same evident enjoyment as they settle on its relative, ragged robin, in the Norfolk Broads. It is only because, once mature, it would spread over too much of a sink that I have since refrained from introducing it into our garden.

While on the subject of the soapworts, the only other species, as opposed to a solitary hybrid of *S. ocymoides*, which is accorded a star for garden merit in the *Dictionary of Gardening* is the pale-pink herbaceous *S. officinalis*. But beware. Once in a border, it spreads fast and furiously and, since its method of doing so is much the same, it is almost as difficult to eradicate as ground elder. We ourselves took over a large colony of it in one of the borders in front of the house and, since it jarred with our proposed colour scheme of blue, yellow and white, which we have largely adopted so as to have no clash with the mellow red brick of our Queen Anne façade, we promptly determined to move it. I have lost count of the number of times we have done so over the past sixteen years but, like our *Macleaya cordata*, it is still there. No wonder people bung chunks of it out of their gardens so habitually and so ubiquitously that it is firmly established as an alien member of our flora, even though it may conceivably be native by streamsides in Devon, Cornwall and North Wales, in virtually every county south of the Scottish border.

Some people seem to fancy the double or various colour forms of our two common native campions, formerly *Melandrium album* and *M. rubrum*, now *Silene alba* and *S. dioica*, as herbaceous border plants. Although the most vulgar form of the white campion regularly sows itself from the wild garden, where we quite like it, into our herbaceous border just in front, we are not among them. So the next, and actually the last, of the herbaceous members of the family that call for a mention are three species of Lychnis. We once grew the popular favourite, *L. chalcedonica*, at the end of the herbaceous border reserved for red and pink flowers, but we found its proprietary brand of scarlet so strident that we speedily abolished it, and I still doubt whether it could ever blend with any other red in the garden. Its salmon-pink variety, eloquently called var. *salmonea*, sounds less anti-social. The normal pink form of *L. flos-jovis*, which the *Dictionary* calls 'purple or scarlet' and the *Flora Europaea* 'purplish or scarlet,' we have only admired and photographed at Pralognan. But we do grow *L. coronaria* from south-east Europe, which the *Dictionary* and the *Flora* are this time at one in calling 'purplish,' in three colour forms. (I shall have some more to say about the apparently almost universal reluctance to commit the word 'magenta' to print when we come, as we soon shall, to the Geraniums.) All three varieties share, of course, in the general characterisitic of the type, that the 'whole plant,' in the authoritative words of the *Flora*, is so 'densely villous with white hairs' as to look very pale grey. One of our three varieties, which sows itself all over the garden, is vivid magenta; another, which is more restrained and confines its philoprogenitiveness to the red end of the herbaceous border, is pure deep velvety red, a splendid plant; and the third, only just acquired from the Davenport Jones nurseries, of which again more anon when we come to the Geraniums, is reliably said to be equally pure white.

So to the genus Dianthus, which I have purposely left till last of the family for the simple reason that it has a generous contribution to make to every part of the garden. As before, we will start in the rock garden and work progressively thence towards the herbaceous border; and, as before, we shall have to be scandalously selective in our hasty progress. I shall, in fact, start from the larger of the two north-facing sinks which I reserve for alpine plants (in the strict sense of the word rather than by the common use or abuse of it for any old plant that is small enough for the rock garden) which we have ourselves, by one means or another, collected in the wild from various parts of the southern European Alps. There I grow a solitary plant of what I judge, from the horticulturally inadequate description in the *Flora*, can only be *D. pavonius*, and I have just been out to look at it. Anyhow, we came across a large quantity of it, in full flower, near the top of the Col du Lautaret. It was growing on a flat and rather bare moraine, and I dug up a young plant of it more in hope than in confident expectation. It now, with no cosseting whatever, makes a rather lax but agreeably glaucous cushion, about three inches across, and its flowers, when it vouchsafes to produce them, are large in comparison with their short stems, brilliant rose-pink above and beautifully burnished buff, if that is the colour of a biscuit, beneath. This particular plant in fact, if only because I am not quite sure of its name and therefore could not possibly purchase it, is a good example of the desirability of finding your plants for yourself. And with this somewhat uncertain species safely behind us, I feel on safer ground; for we come next to our native maiden pink, *D. deltoides*, which grows in abundance on top of two sandy hills not many miles from Shepreth. Only three or four years ago I decided off my own bat, and in the face of heavy opposition from the coherent members of the family, to plant, at the centre of the lawn in what passes for our rose and iris garden, a standard specimen of the wide-spreading *Catalpa bignonioides*. Once the fell deed was perpetrated we had, of course, to create a circular bed, only about a yard in diameter, around the tree's roots, and this bed we densely peopled, with an effect that seems to have silenced all concerned, with countless plants, raised from a purchased packet of seed, of an unusually dark and showy form of *D. deltoides*. And that brings us to at least five species, for I am, as usual, concerned with true wild species before we come to the beautiful modern garden hybrids, which fall in the intermediate zone between the rockery and the herbaceous border. These include, for instance, our own Cheddar pink, which in these days rejoices in the name of *D. gratianopolitanus*, and also the European ancestors of all our beloved Sweet Williams and garden pinks, *D. barbatus* and *D. plumarius* respectively. And they also include two strictly alpine species, *D. carthusianorum* and *D. furcatus*, the latter formerly known as *D. alpestris*, the seeds of both of which I lately brought back with the rest from our tour of the Alps, and which on that account prompt me to obstruct the already uneven flow of this chapter with an unashamed digression on sowing seeds. But before I launch into the digression let me first of all insert a word of advice to any aspiring collector of European species of Dianthus. Go East, young man, go East.

I have always instinctively believed that the right thing to do with a seed, as soon as nature has made it ready to drop to the ground, is to drop it there. When we got back, in the first week of October, from our tour of the Alps, I got Bob, nominally our gardener but actually our universal uncle and miracle-monger, to sift my seeds and sow them, well over a hundred packets of them, in a compound of about 90 per cent John Innes potting mixture to 10 per cent vermiculite. Although, in order not to interfere too badly with his other multifarious activities, I rationed him to about fifteen packets a day, he had finished the fiddling job in little over a working week. I had been gratuitously warned, of course, by all and sundry that 'they won't anyhow germinate until the spring, and even if they do they will damp off at once in our English winter.' But my mentors have been doubly confounded. Within a fortnight both the yellow sub-alpine foxgloves, *Digitalis grandiflora* and *D. lutea*, had germinated in scores, to be followed by a very short head by both these species of Dianthus. Next came sundry Veronicas, Campanulas and Phyteumas. And still they kept popping up until few but the gentians, the Potentillas and those berry-bearing plants, chiefly ericaceous and liliaceous, that we saw fit to sow in a surface of sphagnum have yet to appear. And what is more, not one single one of them, whether already individually potted up and put in the unheated greenhouse or left in their pans in the cold frame, has shown the slightest sign, by mid-January, of damping off. I am more than ever convinced that the reason why seeds bought from a seed-merchant often take an unconscionable time a-germinating is that the unhappy seed-merchant is usually in no position, or else in no mood, to obey the clear dictates of nature.

So we arrive, last of all the family, at what most people doubtless regard as its greatest glory, the countless hybrid pinks and hardy border carnations; and the last shall be first. There is no denying that, in this genus at least, modern methods of selection and hybridisation have produced some wonderful results, and for once I shall have to renounce my usual prejudice and admit that the double varieties in general outshine the single. I can still retain some prejudices and go on thinking, for instance, that good old Mrs Sinkins is still the best of the lot or that the modern hybrids of *D. alpinus* called *allwoodii alpinus* are hideous travesties. And I can still derive some quiet amusement from the fact that the exquisite pink called Fortuna, which is what I always call Faith's sister Fortune, should be described in Allwood's catalogue as 'a rose-cerise self.' I am afraid that our garden does not, nor do we intend that it should, move with the times. And so the best advice I can give anyone who is wisely thinking of investing in some of these glamorous plants is to write for the said catalogue to Allwood Bros. Ltd., Mill Nursery, Hassocks, West Sussex.

After this hectic scramble through the Caryophyllaceae, a brief breather is afforded by four families which have greater significance as noisome weeds than as welcome adornments to the flower garden, and we then embark upon the three last families before the Geraniums, namely the limes, Tiliaceae, the mallows, Malvaceae, and the flaxes, Linaceae. The limes are a taxonomically tricky family, better suited to a botanical garden or, better still, an arboretum than to our garden at Shepreth or, probably, yours. Admittedly we have three old trees of the common lime, *T.* × *europaea*, overhanging the high old red brick wall on our south-east boundary from the far side of the roadside path outside, and those three have to suffice. For I am bothered if I know where, in our garden of rather more than two acres, we could find room for another. As for the *Malvaceae*, they mean to me, for horticultural purposes, only some half-dozen plants, mainly of different genera and mainly plants of the herbaceous border. Of the mallows proper the best, in my view, is our own common native musk mallow, *Malva moschata,* whose stem leaves are elegantly cut into fine segments and whose flowers are normally pure pink but occasionally white. We imported the white form many years ago from a local hedgebank into a peculiarly dreary and discouraging corner of the garden, of which more when we come to the umbellifers, and for a while, until it was smothered by giant hogweed, it served its purpose admirably. We must introduce some more into the wild garden. And we grow another true mallow in the herbaceous border, the fastigiate variety of *M. alcea*. We were given two or three roots of it by Margery Fish, and its deep pink flowers perform the useful function of helping to prolong the colour of the border well into the autumn. Two other herbaceous members of the *Malvaceae*, the various pink Sidalceas and the many-hued hollyhocks, the offspring of *Alcea rosea*, are too familiar to call for more than a reminder of their existence. As for the tree mallow, *Lavatera arborea*, which used to grow at the back of our herbaceous border, we were so little enamoured of the colour of its mauvish-pink flowers that when, being a biennial, it naturally departed this life, we were in no hurry to replace it. And that leaves only two other members of the family that we grow, neither of them in the herbaceous border, namely the deciduous shrub *Hibiscus sinosyriacus* and the little-known trailing

Sphaeralcea munroana. I used to have a passion for the former, but I have outgrown it. Its flowers, which in these days can be single, semi-double or double and any colour from white, through sundry shades of pink and mauve, to deep purple, are undeniably showy and handsome, but they regularly appear and disappear while we are at Ardtornish for our summer holidays. And for the rest, its leaves are of no particular interest, and even without any pruning, at which, whatever the shrub, we are habitually far too lenient to satisfy any expert in horticulture, it makes a stiff and wholly graceless bush. But the Sphaeralcea, which we only quite lately acquired from Lady Aldenham's well-known garden at Briggins, is an altogether different proposition and makes an ideal edging to any border of any description. Although it can, according to the *Dictionary of Gardening*, attain a height of two feet, it rather tends in our experience, as I said, to trail. At first sight its three-lobed and blunt-toothed leaves might suggest a Pelargonium, but its long and liberal succession of flowers, which the *Dictionary* describes as 'scarlet or rose' but which are actually of an unusual and very attractive shade mid-way between those extremes, are of a typical mallow shape. If only I knew where you could get it, I should strongly advise you to give it a try.

And that leaves only the flaxes, of which we have never grown more than four. The crimson variety Rubrum of *Linum grandiflorum* is a beautiful and graceful little plant, but it suffers, in our eyes at least, from the fatal disadvantage of being an annual. *L. perenne*, on the other hand, whose subspecies *anglicum* shows in local abundance on the edge of the Gogmagog golf course, is, though about twice the height, an equally graceful plant, with flowers of an unalloyed pale blue, and is not only, as its name suggests, a perennial but one of those perennials which, in our light and chalky soil at least, sows itself with a cheerful abandon. Some years ago we were given, I forget by whom, a plant of the Mediterranean *L. narbonense*, the flowers of which are rather larger and brighter blue and come in more distinct panicles, and we planted it lovingly among its relatives in the front borders. But either I have developed a blind spot or else the plant is much more like *L. perenne* than its description in books might lead you to suppose, for I simply cannot find it any more. Or perhaps the sad truth is, as it well might be considering its origin, that it is not after all a hundred per cent hardy and has succumbed to the savagery of one of our Cambridgeshire winters. And last of all comes a flax of quite a different order, *L. arboreum*, the miniature tree flax, with rather glaucous, thick, spoon-shaped leaves and clusters of few but relatively very large bright yellow flowers. We did not see it two years ago when we were in Rhodes, which is apparently one of its stations, but I did see it in quantity in

1938, lighting up the cliffs and rocks in behind Sphakiá on the south coast of Crete, and was inspired by the sight to buy a plant of it on my return and grow it in the one and only sink that I then possessed. There, even though I disobeyed instructions and gave it no winter protection whatever, it flourished and flowered year after year. And I trust it is still doing the same in the same place. For when, soon after the war, my father had to move into a job to which there was no private garden attached, my one and only sink, which housed also the shrubby milkwort mentioned earlier in this chapter, was unable to move with him.

CHAPTER 4

Geraniaceae

NOW that we are embarking on the Geranium family, a relatively small undertaking in comparison with the foregoing chapters, I had better make myself clear at the outset. I shall do so, as often, on the authority of the *Dictionary of Gardening*, which any writer on botanical matters would be well advised to consult before putting pen to paper. The family embraces some five hundred species (as opposed, for instance, to the odd thirteen hundred of the *Ranunculaceae* or the two thousand of the *Rosaceae*), divided between only eleven genera. Of the seven genera treated in the *Dictionary* only three at most, namely Geranium itself, Pelargonium and possibly Erodium, would be of any concern to the average British gardener. Faith more than I has a lively interest in what, to the great majority of the population, the word Geranium suggests, the dubiously hardy bedding plants which come in such a dazzling range of colour, and we keep quite a number of the better varieties in the cool greenhouse or frames to plant out, along with Fuchsias, in the tubs of our paved courtyard. But, in the words of the *Dictionary*, 'the great range of Scarlet, Fancy, Scented and Show Geraniums belong, not to this genus, but to Pelargonium.' Since I am deliberately concentrating in this book on plants which are at least tolerably hardy even in the most inclement districts of these islands, and since I regard all greenhouse subjects as material for quite a different book, I shall be dealing in this chapter only with the true Geraniums of the rock garden or the herbaceous border. And furthermore, I shall confine my discussion almost exclusively to those of which I have first-hand knowledge and experience.

The Geranium family, like that of the spurges which I shall be talking about in a later chapter, is proportionately very well represented in the British Isles. There are, of course, no native Pelargoniums, but there are as many as a dozen native species of Geranium, as well as five aliens which are more or less thoroughly established, and four of Erodium. I shall not waste time and space on the latter because none of the four, and, if it comes to that, precious few of its foreign congeners, is worthy of a place in the garden. We ourselves grow only two of the alien species, both of them not only European but, by sheer coincidence, exclusively Greek in origin, and both, out of the total of about fifty species in the genus whose flowers are in the main of a nondescript and unattractive' colour somewhere between pink and mauve, thoroughly meritorious rock garden plants. *E. chrysanthum*, the better of the two, has silky, silvery and, like many of the genus, finely dissected leaves and pure sulphur-yellow flowers on relatively short stems. The other, which is, I think, the variety of *E. absinthoides* called, after the first thorough student of the flora of Greece, var. *sibthorpianum*, alias *E. olympicum*, is a prodigiously invasive plant with leaves of no particular distinction but with large flowers of, for the genus, an unusually pure pink. I originally planted it, in defiance of the instructions to give all Erodiums plenty of sun, in one of my north-facing sinks. But it so speedily took over the entire confined area that we have had to move it out not once but twice. The first time, though we took literally everything out of the sink and sieved the soil, we omitted either to scrub the lower sides of the chunks of Westmorland limestone which provide the mountains in the miniature landscape or, probably more important, to comb out the roots of the other mountain plants through which it was surreptitiously creeping. In no time at all it was back in full possession. The second time, which was only a few weeks ago, we took both these additional precautions, I hope with better success. And in the process we must have acquired rather more of it in another part of the garden than we really need.[1]

Our native geraniums are an altogether different cup of tea. For horticultural rather than scientific purposes they, like the ferns, may be divided into groups according to size. The small ones need hardly delay us. If your garden happens to contain an old flint wall or an outcrop of rock, preferably slightly acid, which naturally harbours the glossy-leaved *G. lucidum*, then you had much better leave it alone. But probably not even it, let alone any of the others which prefer light arable land, deserve deliberate introduction. The best of the medium-sized species is fortunately also much the commonest. Herb Robert, *G. robertianum*, needs no introduction either to you or to your garden. The mere facts that it, and even more its close relation on a smaller scale, *G. purpureum*,

---

[1] I am here guilty of a blunder which I detected too late to amend the text. Careful inspection during the summer of 1970 reminded me that, at about the same time as I acquired the Erodium, I also purchased, under the synonym of *Geranium farreri*, a young plant of *G. napuligerum*. Of two otherwise admirable plants it was the latter, not the former, that was the aggressor. The Erodium (and likewise its congener *E. reichardii*) has so far an irreproachable record.

bear masses of flowers of a pure unalloyed pink or red, and that its leaves tend to turn brilliant scarlet to crimson, immediately rank it far ahead of the others, such as *G. pyrenaicum*, which share with most of the Erodiums a certain lack of decisiveness in their colour. It is, in fact, only the large British geraniums, which include some of the most beautiful of our native flowers, that call for more extended treatment.

If you happen to have access to that magnificent monument to the collaboration between professional and amateur, the *Atlas of the British Flora*, which was published under the auspices of the Botanical Society of the British Isles, you will soon enough notice that certain plants, for one reason or another, have a remarkably restricted range. Some plants, such as *Gentiana verna* or the more interesting of our native orchids, grow where they do in these islands simply because they demand a certain type of soil and underlying rock. Others, which are really more interesting, reach the outermost fringe of their world distribution, North, South, East or West, within the narrow confines of our little islands. Perhaps the best of all examples, especially if you happen to be talking, as I am, without the *Atlas* readily available, is that of the white orchidaceous *Spiranthes romanzoffiana*, the natural range of which is almost exclusively confined to North America and Kamchatka but which has also six, or at most seven, outlying stations in Europe. All those six or seven stations fall, not only inside the British Isles but also on their most westerly extremities; two are in Ireland, two in the Hebrides, and two, one of which I discovered several years ago for myself but have not yet published, on the westernmost fringes of the Scottish mainland. I have yet to be convinced either that the record from Hampshire, where its near and equally rare relation, *S. autumnalis*, used to grow, is authentic, which question does not anyhow effect my argument in the least, or that, as has several times been suggested to me and as may well be the case with that major menace to our waterways, *Elodea canadensis*, it was originally introduced on the feet or through the digestive organs of migrant birds. The focal point in these islands lies in Counties Cork and Kerry, where plants of the Spanish peninsula, such as the two saxifrages, *S. spathularis*, or St Patrick's cabbage, and the kidney saxifrage, *S. hirsuta*, not to mention the glorified fly-eating butterwort, *Pinguicula grandiflora*, grow by nature in local abundance cheek by jowl with such North American elements in our flora as the inhabitant of peaty pools and bog-holes, pipewort or *Ericocaulon aquaticum*, and the blue Sisyrinchium, often and deservedly grown in rock gardens and for that reason locally naturalised elsewhere in Europe, *S. augustifolium*, alias, in defiance of grammar, *S. bermudiana*. Our larger native Geraniums, on both the edaphic and the longitudinal or

71

latitudinal scores, afford an admirable illustration of this natural limitation of range.

A good example of the kind of plant whose British distribution is determined entirely by the nature of the rock and the soil is *Geranium sanguineum*, the bloody cranesbill. Incidentally, why it should be called bloody defeats me. Admittedly different people's idea of colour can diverge very sharply, as Faith and I, for example, invariably disagree on where the dividing line should be drawn between blue and green. Clapham, Tutin and Warburg call the flowers of the bloody cranesbill 'bright purplish-crimson,' Keble Martin, though his painting of it is not unfaithful, simply 'Crimson,' which is palpably absurd, and the *Dictionary of Gardening* 'crimson to blood-red,' which is, if possible, even wider of the mark. To me it is the purest imaginable magenta. But whatever you decide its colour to be, it is essentially a plant either of the limestone or, in the procumbent form with broader lobes to its leaves known as var. *prostratum*, of fixed dunes. Though absent from south-east England and only very occasionally, as on the Devil's Dyke near Newmarket, straying not unnaturally from the limestone on to the chalk, it is widespread, if for obvious reasons local, throughout the British Isles from Caithness and the Outer Hebrides southwards. It lays on its most resplendent display in the Burren, that most fascinating district of deeply creviced limestone pavement on the north-western corner of County Clare, where, in places, with *Dryas octopetala*, the miniature yellow rockrose *Helianthemum canum* and *Gentiana verna* among its dominant associates, the vagaries of nature herself have furnished the most spectacular rock garden to be seen in Britain. Fortunately its prostrate, flesh-pink, purple-veined variety, once appropriately called *lancastriense*, now *striatum*, is so firmly established in commerce that there is not the slightest need to disturb it in its only known station in the world, the level sandy sward on the seaward side of Walney Island.

The other two of our native large-flowered Geraniums, *G. pratense* and *G. sylvaticum*, afford excellent illustrations, as a glance at the *Atlas* will show, of the second type of plant distribution. The former, which, from midsummer onwards, suffuses the roadsides in many a district in the southern half of England with a soft and, as even the rightly objective Clapham, Tutin and Warburg for once say, a 'beautiful violet-blue,' peters out gradually as you go northward to be progressively replaced by the latter. Moreover, it is to be found as a native in only one county in the whole of Ireland, County Antrim. *Geranium sylvaticum*, on the other hand, precisely complements the range of *G. pratense*. Although it has outlying stations, where, however, it is very local and scarce, in Gloucestershire, Monmouth and Glamorgan, its headquarters stretch in this island from Caithness in the north to

Yorkshire and Derbyshire in the south. Again, for reasons which must surely be more than merely coincidental but which are otherwise quite unknown to me, its only known localities in Ireland are in County Antrim. Incidentally, in case you are not already familiar with the differences between the two, *G. sylvaticum* can be immediately distinguished from *G. pratense* (the flowers of both of which, to underline their close kinship and to quote Clapham, Tutin and Warburg yet again, come 'in pairs on axillary penduncles') not only by its flowers which, to borrow a last phrase from the same indispensable source, are 'usually smaller and more reddish,' but also, a characteristic that I have not seen mentioned elsewhere, by its more narrowly upright and less diffuse habit. Both species appear, in Britain at least, to be indifferent both as to soil, in which respect they differ sharply from *G. sanguineum*, and as to altitude. *G. pratense* ascends to nearly two thousand feet, while *G. sylvaticum* is often to be seen in abundance, especially on the Lawers range in central Perthshire and frequently in the company of red campion, a lovely association, on cliff-edges well above the three thousand foot contour.

I have dilated at disproportionate length on these three native species for two reasons other than the valid one stated at the outset, both of which may strike you as more relevant. In the first place, all three of them are at least the equal of the great majority of their foreign congeners and on every score richly merit introduction, by seed of course, into any garden of whatever size. And in the second place, in addition to the pale Lancastrian variety of the bloody cranesbill, each of the other two has spontaneously produced an albino sport. Both of them are obtainable, or at any rate used to be, along with many other interesting and unusual species or varieties of hardy herbaceous geraniums, including the white form of *G. phaeum*, of which more very shortly, from the small nursery garden of the late Margery Fish at East Lambrook Manor, South Petherton, Somerset. By the same token, the pure white form of *G. sanguineum*, which I have not yet mentioned, is to be had from the gardens of the late Miss H. Davenport Jones at Washfield Nurseries, Hawkhurst, Kent. Both these good ladies died in the last year or two; both were, if in very different ways, enthusiastic amateur collectors; both started up small businesses which have luckily been carried on under their own names since their death; and the stencilled catlogues of both contain a more unusual and distinctively personal selection of plants than any we happen to possess.

In comparison with these three native species the five established aliens need not long detain us. They have anyhow only found their way into the British flora by dint of escaping from gardens, so that the proper place to discuss them comes, if anywhere, a little further on. But three out of the five can be dismissed without further ado here and now. Exactly as I shall maintain in a later chapter that almonds were intended by nature to be pink and cherries white, so, in my view, the geraniums of the herbaceous border or the rock garden ought to be blue, purple or magenta and never any nondescript shade of pink or mauve. That rules out the three in question straight away. *G. endressii*, a native of the Pyrenees, is the best of the three if only because its flowers are of a relatively pure and deep pink; and it has, of course, several hybrids, all of them, such as Rose Clair, A. T. Johnson or Wargrave Pink, named presumably after individual English gardeners or their individual English gardens, which seem to me to be disproportionately popular in this country. Next in the list come *G. versicolor*, which Linnaeus himself, who gave it this name, called also *G. striatum* and which sometimes hybridises, with results that reflect little credit on either parent, with *G. endressii*, and *G. nodosum*. For horticultural purposes there is nothing much to prefer one over the other, both having wishy-washy mauvish petals with veins of a somewhat deeper and purer mauve. The former is thoroughly naturalised, only a few hundred yards from a large colony of *G. phaeum*, on the verges of the road leading from Cambridge on to the Gogmagog Hills, and the comparison between the two, which can comfortably be made within five minutes, should leave you in no doubt as to which has the greater garden value. And that, apart from the said *G. phaeum*, to which I shall devote a paragraph on its own, leaves only *G. macrorrhizum*, a native primarily of the European countries bordering on the Mediterranean. I have only once consciously seen it in its native habitat, a rocky little olive-yard near the coast of Rhodes, where it was surrounded by anemones of every conceivable colour. Since it was only just coming into flower, with no seed available, and since I was deterred by its specific name, which means 'big-rooted,' from any attempt to dig it up, the only form of it that we grow is the white variety, once again procurable from the Margery Fish nursery, which we first saw and coveted in the National Trust's beautiful and highly individual little garden at Tintinhull in Somerset. I do not know Ingwersen's variety, which is the commonest in commerce and this time, among other sources, to be had from the Davenport Jones garden, nor do I know which variety it is that is admitted into our alien flora by Clapham, Tutin and Warburg. But since its range in Britain is evidently confined to village walls in a number of places in South Devon, it is of little consequence.

I have reserved *Geranium phaeum* till last for two reasons. First it is, in its typical form at least, of so dusky a purple as to be almost black; the only foreign species I know of with a colour said to vie with it is

G. delavayi, which we have only just succeeded in acquiring and are not yet qualified to judge. In its foster-home on the Gogmagogs, as a matter of fact, it displays a remarkable variation of colour, and the large colony, though clearly derived from the same source, may well include the variety called *lividum*, the flowers of which are said in the *Dictionary of Gardening* to be 'greyish-mauve.' We ourselves imported it early on into the most inhospitable of all the many corners of our garden, where it has sown itself with abandoned prodigality. And soon afterwards, to come to my second point, we were induced by a catalogue which this time I shall not specify to invest in another foreign species, which was said to resemble it closely but to have additional merit of leaves deeply spotted at the base, called *G. punctatum*. The undeniable spots, from which the plant derives its specific name, proved to disappear within a month of the leaves appearing, and the colour of the flowers turned out to be indescribably dingy. If ever you are offered this particular plant, decline the offer firmly in favour of *G. phaeum*.

So we come to the numerous foreign species which are commonly grown, or at any rate ought to be, in British gardens. And this time I propose to divide them, as unscientifically as ever, first by dimensions and then by colour. We may as well start with my habitual theme of size and consider first the relatively few hardy geraniums which belong primarily to the rockery.

The criterion by which I should admit a geranium to the rock garden is simple enough: in normal conditions it should not exceed a foot in height. When I write that there are relatively few such, I can actually, by this criterion, think of only four or five which we ourselves grow and a few others that we do not. First come two which I have already mentioned, namely *G. sanguineum* itself and its variety *striatum*, which is regularly listed in catalogues, simply but inaccurately, as *G. lancastriense*. If we had a rock garden, which as yet we do not, and if we grew the former at all, which again, for no obvious reason, we do not, I personally should put it in as isolated a position as possible there so that its flamboyant colour could not jar with ill-assorted neighbours. The latter, on the other hand, on grounds of colour alone, is much easier to accommodate. Actually, as well as the typical Walney Island variety, which I very briefly described higher up, there is another and in some people's eyes a better form available, the flowers of which are of a somewhat deeper and very much clearer pink. We have never succeeded in laying hands on it ourselves, but Faith's sister grows it in her garden in Westmorland and, with an honesty well becoming a Justice of the Peace, tells me on a postcard that it 'was a stolen root from a Yorkshire garden,' which does not help as much as it might. And while we are on the subject of pink geraniums suitable for the rock garden, there are two more, neither of which do I happen to know but both of which, if you like pink geraniums, sound well worth growing. *G. argenteum*, from north Italy, is listed among the fifty-one described in the *Dictionary of Gardening* and even given an asterisk for garden merit. It is evidently only about three inches high, its leaves, almost all radical, are 'hoary or silky on both surfaces,' its large flowers are 'pink, with darker veins.' The only trouble about it is that, short of going to collect it in its native country, I know of no means of procuring it. Unlike the next, it is certainly not to be found even in Ingwersen's catalogue. *G. dalmaticum* on the other hand, the belated inclusion of which in the Supplement to the *Dictionary* confirms an obvious but not invariably reliable conjecture as to its country of origin, attains a height of four to six inches, Ingwersen's description of it says of its flowers that they are rounded and clear pink, as opposed to Waterer's salmon-pink, while 'the glossy green leaves take rich red autumn tints.'

The precise line between pink and magenta, though I can draw it clearly enough for myself, is by no means easy to put across to other people. I can think of only two rock garden geraniums which I should call magenta, and one of these I have not only never consciously seen but I do not even know of what species it is a variety. It is listed by, among others, Notcutt's as Russell Pritchard. Notcutt's are the only firm I know which has the courage to use that apparently deterrent adjective 'magenta,' and the description of Russell Pritchard in their catalogue runs as follows: 'From June until autumn, lovely bright magenta pink flowers smother the grey-green leaves.' At the same time Reginald Kaye, the expert on ferns, describes its flowers, with the fashionable evasion, as 'bright crimson.' But the other of the two, which is invariably listed as *G. subcaulescens*, but which is actually only the Balkan variety of the Pyrenean *G. cinereum*, is one which I know intimately and is, in my opinion, the best of all the smaller geraniums. To all appearances it looks exactly like a true alpine plant. Having a memory like a sieve, I have just, on 2nd January, 1970, been out to inspect its leaves and have two of them before me, one of last year and one of this, as I write. Last year's, though still quite unwithered, is by now bright yellow, this year's, which is, of course, absolutely fresh, is slightly on the glaucous side of bright green. Last year's, which is naturally the larger of the two, indeed just about as large as it ever could be, measures only a very little over three-quarters of an inch across, while each has seven beautifully balanced lobes with three to five deeply incised and obtuse teeth apiece. You could not, in fact, ask for neater leaves or a neater habit. And as for its flowers, which are inevitably not on view at this season, they are larger than those of the typical *G. cinereum* and of a rather darker but no less pure magenta than those of *G. sanguineum*, with the added advantage of an almost black centre. Needless to add, they are described in the *Dictionary* as 'carmine, bright,' in Ingwersen's catalogue as 'glowing carmine-red,' by Hillier's as 'brilliant carmine,' and so on and so on. Heaven help all the readers of catalogues. As Christopher Lloyd writes in his book on Clematis, which is perhaps hardly relevant in the present context but is well worth noting by any writer or horticultural books, articles or catalogues, 'Descriptions in books might be thought to offer useful evidence, but here again one must be extremely wary. In most cases they are simply copied from one another, not from the plant itself, and the original description must often have been based on recollection, while the author sat writing (as I am)' and so am I 'by his winter's fireside. Recollection, even in tranquillity, of a flower's appearance is apt to be alarmingly inaccurate.' Hence my uncharacteristically precise description just above of the leaves of the plant usually called *Geranium subcaulescens*.

And that leaves, by my reckoning, only two of the smaller hardy geraniums, one blue and one white, that merit consideration. Unfortunately I know nothing whatever of the inhabitant of south Europe and Asia Minor, *G. asphodeloides*, beyond what the *Dictionary* tells me, which is to the effect that it is about six inches tall and that its few flowers are 'usually purplish-violet,' and so I am compelled by sheer ignorance to leave it out of account. But of those which I do know tolerably well, the blue one is the alpine variety of *G. himalayense*, which is appreciably dwarfer and has larger flowers than the type, itself a first-rate border plant. No known geranium, of course, not even *G. pratense*, is blue in the sense that either a forget-me-not or a gentian is blue, and I am for once reluctant to draw the line between blue, violet and purple. Suffice it that none of the three is the same as magenta. The flowers of *G. himalayense*, both the type from Sikkim and its alpine variety, are just about as blue as a geranium can ever be though they have red veins and a reddish-purple eye, and both are abundantly worth growing. And the same is true of the white *G. renardii* from the Caucasus. Given the right conditions, which we originally failed to observe, in full sun and with sharp drainage, it will soon form compact clumps, normally less than a foot high but more across, and, like most geraniums, bear a profusion of flowers which in this case are quite flat and on the grey side of pure white, with a purple centre and exquisitely delicate purple veins. Its leaves, moreover, which are velvety in texture and greyish-green in colour, are unique among the hardy geraniums in rivalling the sweet-scented Pelargoniums of the greenhouse in their fragrance. [*G. macrorrhizum* also has fragrant leaves.]

And after all that about the large-flowered geraniums which are either native or naturalised in the British Isles, and the smaller species and varieties, almost exclusively European in origin, which you might see fit to grow in your rock garden, there is precious little left to say about those bigger brothers of the latter which belong more properly to the herbaceous border. This time, in fact, there are only three that I feel called upon to mention, of all of which I have first-hand experience, plus one which I have very lately, contrary to my usual principles, ordered out of the blue from the description in my two favourite catalogues. Two of the three fall into my category of blue to purple and one is magenta. We ourselves grow the first two, *G. ibericum* from the Caucasus, and Buxton's variety of the Himalayan *G. wallichianum*, in our twin blue borders, which perhaps throws light on our interpretation of the word 'blue'; but the flowers of the former are described in the *Dictionary of Gardening* as 'blue to violet' and those of the latter as 'violet-blue.' Both would be a splendid adornment to any garden. But the third, the magenta one, which is still usually listed as *G. armenum*, which betrays its country of origin, but which in latter days is to be correctly known as *G. psilostemon*, is by as much the best of the big ones as the so-called *G. subcaulescens* is of the small. If your paradigm of magenta is, as it is mine, *G. sanguineum*, then, to exactly the same extent as *G. subcaulescens*, *G. psilostemon* falls on the dark side of it; and likewise, just as the former has a darker eye, so has the latter, which in this case is literally black. Since it can attain a height of about three feet, we grow it, in close proximity to other plants of *G. ibericum*, under the shadow of the chestnut tree at the back of the southern half of our herbaceous border. It is among the best of the well known herbaceous plants that we grow.

And that leaves only my dark horse, *G. malviflorum*, the flowers of which are alleged in the *Dictionary* to be 'pale purple with red veins,' in the Margery Fish catalogue to be 'mauve-blue,' and by the Davenport Jones nursery, from which I bought it, to be simply 'pale purple.' I have lately planted it, more in hope than in confidence, immediately beside the plant of *G. delavayi* which I acquired at the same time from the same source, in a gap in the blue border. May my faith be justly rewarded.

CHAPTER 5

Leguminosae

COMPARED even with the *Ranunculaceae* or the *Rosaceae* the family of the *Leguminosae* is an enormous one. It comprises about seven thousand species, divided among well over four hundred genera, of which no less than two hundred and seventeen are included in the *Dictionary of Gardening* as being, presumably, of relevance to British horticulture. Moreover, not only are these genera distributed between these sub-families called, respectively, *Caesalpinoideae, Mimosoideae* and *Papiliona-ceae*, but together they contain everything from a Laburnum or a Judas tree to a diminutive yellow clover which, if your grass seed was none too clean, you will find yourself mowing on your lawn. The *Caesalpinoideae*, so far as I know, contain only one plant worth growing out of doors in an average British Garden, though that one richly earns its place, namely the Judas tree itself, *Cercis siliquastrum*, from the Mediterranean region. The *Mimosoideae* are slightly more complicated because, in addition to the genus Mimosa, the chief pride of which consists in the two so-called sensitive plants from tropical America, they embrace the much more interesting genus of Acacia, which is nearly twice as large and includes what, in common English parlance and particularly in florists' shops, is invariably known as 'mimosa.' My main concern here is with the *Papilionaceae*, which I see to my dismay are now called in the *Flora Europaea* the *Lotoideae*. They are the only sub-family represented, and very splendidly represented too, in the British Isles, and they also comprise the two genera which, for horticultural purposes in this country, are of the most interest to me, namely Cytisus and Genista.

We have so many leguminous plants native in Britain that I shall confine my attention to the more glamorous of them, those which, if they found their way into my garden, I should welcome with tolerance if not with open arms. The largest and showiest of them all are, of course, gorse, *Ulex europaeus*, and broom, *Cytisus scoparius*, both so familiar that they call for no description and very little comment. Besides the ubiquitous species of *Ulex* there are, as a matter of fact, two others, much more local, in the British Isles, either of which, being only about half the size and much more compact in habit, would make appreciably better garden plants. *U. gallii*, the distribution of which in Europe is confined to the extreme west from Britain to north-west Spain, has, like the common gorse, golden-yellow flowers, while those of *U. minor*, whose headquarters in these islands lie in Hampshire, Surrey and Sussex, are very distinctly paler. And then there are the smaller brothers of gorse and broom, our three native species of Genista, none of which would disgrace even a small garden. In fact two of them, the very local and rare *G. pilosa* in the variety Procumbens and the double-flowered form of dyer's greenweed, *G. tinctoria*, are two of the only four species of Genista listed in Ingwersen's catalogue, while the third of them, *G. anglica*, which, as its specific name might suggest, is tolerably widespread on damp heaths in this island but absent from Ireland, would in my opinion, which you can check by looking at its picture in W. Keble Martin's *Concise British Flora in Colour*, prove at least the equal in the garden of the other two.

All the aforementioned have, of course, yellow flowers, while those of all three of our native species of Ononis, or restharrow, are pink; indeed, a clearer and purer pink than the illustrations on the same page of Keble Martin might suggest. The rarest of them, *O. reclinata*, which is so rare that outside the Channel Isles its only British stations, all in the short turf on top of sea-cliffs, are now one on the south coast of Devon, one in Scotland and two in south Wales, we can, in view of its extreme scarcity, fortunately afford to ignore. It is anyway an annual, only some two or three inches high, and with wishy-washy little flowers in proportion. But the other two are plants which, if only they were not so abundant in England, and not least around Shepreth, we should eagerly import into our gardens. In my opinion the erect *O. spinosa*, which actually only just reaches Scotland and is altogether absent from Ireland, would be of greater value in the garden than the much more widely distributed and procumbent *O. repens*, and it is only my habitual lack of initiative and memory that has prevented me from introducing it from one of the several large colonies only a quarter of a mile down the road into our wild garden.

Next among the British leguminous genera come the medicks and the melilots, Medicago and Melilotus. The latter, three of which are certainly only established aliens and the fourth very probably so, can be speedily dismissed. They look pretty enough, both the two tall yellow species, which are hard to distinguish from each other, and the single tall white one, on the waste places and derelict arable fields where they have very effectually established themselves. But, as they have demonstrated by the firm hold they have taken around London, they spread so rapidly by seed that only the most foolhardy would deliberately introduce any of them into his or her garden. The medicks, on the other hand, are an altogether different kettle of fish, for which I personally have a great fancy, and not only because one of the rarest of the British species, plus one hybrid, is restricted as a native to Norfolk, Suffolk and, though it only just crosses the county boundary, to Cambridgeshire itself. The two most familiar of our medicks are, I suppose, the purple-flowered lucerne, *M. sativa*, which may or may not be native in the Mediterranean region of Europe but was quite certainly introduced into Britain, and so became thoroughly naturalised, as a fodder crop, and black medick, *M. lupulina*, which is liable to become quite an invasive garden weed and which is all too often needlessly confounded, even by keen amateur botanists like myself, with the equally common hop trefoil, *Trifolium campestre*. My own special favourite among our medicks is the hybrid between lucerne and the very local East Anglian subspecies *M. falcata*, the flowers of which are pure buttercup-yellow and the pods, as again its specific name suggests, the shape of a sickle. This hybrid is, unlike the majority of hybrids, fertile, and it is so aggressive that on the Breckland it now immeasurably outnumbers both of its parents. It is aptly named *M. × varia*, for its flowers are, according to Clapham, Tutin and Warburg, 'yellow, purple, or yellow changing to purple through a series of dark greens and black.' How a flower, or for that matter anything else, can change from yellow to purple through a series of dark greens and black baffles me completely, but at any rate it is the green, not necessarily dark green, and the black varieties which fascinate me. This last autumn I have in fact, in triumph over what I said just now about my habitual lack of initiative and memory, introduced, along with those of the pale green wild liquorice, *Astragalus glycyphyllos*, which incidentally means 'sweet-leaved knuckle-bone,' a random selection of their seeds from Foxhole Heath on the Breckland into our garden at Shepreth. When I see what they produce I shall probably scrap all those which are neither green nor black, as may well be the case with most of them. As I remarked earlier in connection with hellebores, I have a weakness for green flowers, and the same is true of black ones; as witness my passion for *Hermodactylus tuberosus*, which is the only plant I can think of off-hand which combines the two colours.

We come next to the genus Trifolium, or in other words the clovers, which are for the most part either so familiar that they need no introduction to you and your lawns or else, as a rapid glance at the relevant maps in the *Atlas of the British Flora* will suffice to show, so relatively local and scarce, and incidentally also so undistinguished, that they need not detain us long. There are actually about twenty of them native in the British Isles, in addition to three or four more or less thoroughly established aliens. But of this large total only two, or at most three, are of any concern in the present context. The dubious case is that of the genuinely deep crimson *T. incarnatum* (and on the prevalent confusion between crimson and magenta please refer back to my comments in the last chapter on the colour of *Geranium sanguineum*) which, like lucerne but less frequently, was originally introduced into this country as a fodder crop and tends to persist beside roads and cart-tracks, and which has as a near relation, or even, according to the *Flora Europaea*, as a mere subspecies, the off-white *T. molinerii*, to be seen as a native in the British Isles, apart once more from the Channel Isles, only on the Lizard Head in southwesternmost Cornwall. The other two are *T. ochroleucon* and the hare's foot clover, *T. arvense*. Both happen to be locally abundant within easy range of Shepreth, but that again is not the reason for which I include them here. *T. ochroleucon*, the British range of which (like that of the true oxlip, *Primula elatior*, as opposed to the widespread but not very common hybrid between the primrose and the cowslip) is for no obvious reason confined to a small area near Shepreth, bears profuse rounded heads of distinctively pale yellow flowers, while *T. arvense*, a much more widespread inhabitant of sandy soil, including the Breckland, lives up to its English names by producing, after its insignificant white to pale pink flowers, exquisitely fluffy oblong heads midway between pink and grey. Both these native clovers, provided only that the soil happened to suit them, would embellish either the wild part, if there were one, or even, conceivably, the rockery in any British garden.

At this point I shall reserve till a little later, for reasons which will soon enough become apparent, no less than seven genera that are represented, if only monotypically, in our native flora, not to mention six others included in Dandy's *List of British Vascular Plants* which are more or less naturalised, and pass on to the two vast tribes of vetches and peas, Vicia and Lathyrus. There are eleven vetches native in Britain and eight peas, as diverse in colour as any two genera could reasonably be expected to be, but of this considerable total only one is worth deliberately importing into your garden. Admittedly one vetch, the blue tufted vetch, *Vicia cracca*, and one pea, the bright yellow *Lathyrus pratensis*, are among the most plentiful and colourful of the many adornments of our roadside banks and hedges. Admittedly also two peas, the blue *L. palustris* from the fens and the purple to magenta *L. japonicus* from the shingle beaches, would be abundantly worth cultivating if, as is extremely unlikely in the latter case at least, your garden happened to contain a suitable bit of ground. But the sad fact remains that, apart perhaps from the local native *L. sylvestris*, an inhabitant of woodlands and damp grassy sea-cliffs, the garden merits of which are reproduced on a larger and more colourful scale by the widely naturalised everlasting pea, *L. latifolius*, the solitary species from the two genera together which I would contemplate introducing on purpose into my garden is the wood vetch, *Vicia sylvatica*. Its map in the *Atlas* reveals it to be more or less evenly distributed, even if decidedly local, over this island and considerably more sparsely over Ireland. Personally I associate it primarily, along with the small teasel, *Dipsacus pilosus*, with the Cotswold woods, and I am relieved to see that the *Atlas* to a certain extent bears out my impression. But in the neighbourhood of Ardtornish we occasionally come across isolated plants or small colonies of it in rocky and usually bosky ravines, and it was there that my ever-increasing desire originated, with the usual negative results, to bring back two or three seed-pods to Shepreth. Whatever the Floras may say about its dimensions, a single plant of it is fully capable of scrambling through a hedge at least six-foot high and twice as wide and smothering it in the latter half of summer with its blue and white flowers. It would be a glorious acquisition for any garden in Britain.

That leaves, out of all the *Leguminosae* native in the British Isles, only the seven relatively small genera which I passed over just now for later consideration. Four out of the seven can, for horticultural purposes, be fairly summarily dispensed with. The genus of Lotus is one of those which (even though it contains, like the genera Vicia and Lathyrus, one or two species such as *L. corniculatus*, universally known in Britain either as bird's-foot trefoil or as bacon and eggs, and its bigger and less common brother in marshy fields and bogs, *L. uliginosus*, that are in their season a prominent feature of our countryside) every normal gardener would leave to introduce itself. The genus Ornithopus, however interesting one of its only two native species may be to a member of the Wild Flower Society, is horticulturally insignificant. And the genera Hippocrepis and Onobrychis contain only one British species apiece, both of them native only on calcareous soil, namely the prostrate and widely spreading yellow horse-shoe vetch, *H. comosa*, and the upstanding pink sainfoin, *O. viciifolia*, which, like lucerne, is commonly grown, or at any rate used to be, as a fodder crop. Once again neither of these last two, if they should happen to intrude into your garden, would bring discredit upon you or it.

If it comes to that, there is only one British species of Anthyllis either, namely *A. vulneraria*, kidney vetch or ladies' fingers; but that one, for garden purposes, is worth most of these last put together. It is widespread in Britain, with an apparent preference either for the chalk or limestone or (I know not why but the fact is evident from its distribution in Devon and Cornwall, Wales, Scotland and Ireland) for sea-cliffs. In its typical form, with yellow flowers and silky leaves, it is attractive enough, but in the local seaside variety called *coccinea* it is a great deal more than that. The best place I know to see it is once again the Lizard Head, a veritable paradise for leguminous plants, where it comes in every shade from the typical yellow to the pure crimson of the true var. *coccinea*. I should be proud to have any or every one of these colour varieties in my garden.

So we come, last of all our native genera in the pea family, to my two personal favourites, Astragalus and Oxytropis, which I suppose rank so high in my estimation primarily because each of them contains at least one genuinely alpine plant. The genus Astragalus contains only three British species, one of which, *A. glycyphyllos*, I have already mentioned in passing. I then said that its flowers were green, but I see that they are described by Clapham, Tutin and Warburg, and furthermore that the description is printed in italics as an important diagnostic characteristic, as 'creamy-white with a greenish-grey tinge,' and by Keble Martin simply as 'greenish-white.' But be that as it may, the plant is decidedly local in Britain, being centred mainly around Cambridge, Oxford and Hull, has a sprawling or scrambling habit and would probably be of little interest to any gardener who lacked my eccentric taste for green, or perhaps in the circumstances I should say green*ish*, flowers. On the other hand *Astragalus danicus*, the purple milk-vetch, is a plant which any gardener anywhere in the world ought to be glad to grow, if he could, in his rockery. Its map in the *Atlas* is one of the most eloquent of the whole lot, for it reveals at a glance that, apart from a very few isolated, widely separated and, to me at least, inexplicable localities on, for instance, the Irish Aran Islands, the Scottish Hebrides and the English Isle of Man, it is virtually restricted to the easternmost side of this island and especially the east coast. But wherever it grows it is much the same, seldom more than six inches high and with near pinnate leaves clothed with silky white hairs and many equally neat spikes of pure purple. We are again blessed in that its chief inland stronghold is roughly centred on Cambridge.

The third British Astrangalus is, like both our native species of Oxytropis, essentially a plant of the higher mountains of central Scotland. Indeed, if you are lucky enough to hit upon the right mountain you will find, at no great altitude and immediately beside the regular path to the summit, *Astragalus alpinus* and *Oxytropis halleri* growing side by side on a comparatively small outcrop of rock. The third of this alpine trio, *O. campestris*, which has only two known localities in the whole of Britain, calls in either case for a long trudge and, unless you happen to be as impassioned a field botanist as I am, is scarcely worth the fatigue. Compared with the other two it is a relatively coarse plant and its flowers, which are appealingly described by Clapham, Tutin and Warburg as 'yellow tinged with purple' and by Keble Martin as 'yellow, touched with mauve,' are in all honesty unutterably dreary. But the other two are altogether different. *Astragalus alpinus* is, in general habit and appearance, a slenderer version of *A. danicus*, but its flowers, instead of being pure purple, are of an equally pure pale mauve. *Oxytropis halleri* on the other hand, which I should without hesitation include in my list of Britain's ten most beautiful plants, is as compact and tidy in stature as any of the foregoing, the whole plant except the flowers is glistening silver with long silky hairs, and the flowers themselves, as usual defined in the Floras by the hopelessly vague adjectives mauve or purple, are of a vivid reddish-purple that is not far from magenta. It is true that I envisage the plant, from recollection of where I last saw it in flower, in the colours it dons on the north coast of Scotland; for unlike the other two alpines, it not infrequently descends from the mountains to near sea-level in our most northerly counties. But I do not think I am exaggerating and I would love to grow it in one of my sinks. As a matter of fact, among the loot that we brought back last October from our lightning tour of the Alps were the seeds of *Astragalus alpinus* and what I hoped, in the absence of flowers, might be *Oxytropis halleri*, both of them gathered just to the east of the top of the Little St Bernard Pass. Subsequent research in the *Flora Europaea* has more or less convinced me that the Oxytropis is more likely to be the pale yellow *O. pilosa* than *O. halleri*. But what does that matter? I can always try again next time I pay an autumnal visit to Sutherland or Caithness.

In addition to these numerous native genera of the family *Leguminosae*, there are also no less than ten listed by Dandy and at least seven included by Clapham, Tutin and Warburg as naturalised in this country. Of the former's ten, I wrote two or three sentences earlier about one, the genus Melilotus, of which one member, *M. altissima*, is apparently regarded by the latter as possibly native. Another, Tetragonolobus, need not detain us. It is native only just the other side of the Channel, and however it was introduced into southern England it was not, I fancy, from gardens. Its one British representative, *T. maritimus*, is, however, a pretty little plant, with solitary orange flowers about an inch long and curious winged pods. But since all the rest have unquestionably escaped from gardens, they afford an easy and natural transition from our native species to those which we grow from foreign lands. At least two of them, Laburnum and *Robinia pseudoacacia*, commonly known as the acacia tree, need no introduction or description. Nor does the yellow tree lupin, of which we used to grow the less common blue variety until it died, I think, merely of old age. But its herbaceous relation, *L. nootkatensis*, which makes great blue patches on the shingle banks of, for instance, the River Tay, is probably less well known. *Spartium junceum*, which looks rather like a large-flowered broom, is a familiar spectacle on the banks of the underground in west London, while to the east the senna-pod tree, *Colutea arborescens*, which is there more often brown than yellow, is established in equal abundance. Of our two naturalised Coronillas, I am ashamed to admit that I do not know *C. varia* or crown vetch, a native of central and southern Europe which has apparently succeeded in establishing itself in a considerable number of widely scattered localities in this island and which presumably owes its specific name to the fact that its flowers can be either white, purple or pink. But I am familiar enough with the other, *C. glauca*, with its rich yellow flowers and glaucous foliage, and since in an average garden it needs the protection of a warm wall, I am surprised that it should be sufficiently well naturalised to merit inclusion in Dandy's list. Goat's rue, on the other hand, *Galega officinalis*, I know to be well established, not least on railway banks between Shepreth and London, and as far as I am concerned it may as well stay there; its flowers, whether white, mauve or pink, are too pallid for my taste. Its less familiar congener, *G. × hartlandii*, which is known to me only from the descriptions in catalogues that liken its racemes of flowers to those of Wisteria, sounds an altogether better proposition. And that leaves, of these allegedly naturalised aliens, only *Dorycnium gracile* (really only a subspecies from the Mediterranean coasts of France and Spain of the widespread European *D. pentaphyllum*)[1], which again I do not know, but the close relative of which, another native of the Mediterranean region and of south Portugal, where we saw it among the unique flora on top of Cape St Vincent, namely *D. hirsutum*, is one of the plants we cosset, along with another leguminous plant called *Sophora tetraptera*, in the hottest corner of our sun-trap of a courtyard. Like *Coronilla glauca* it really requires, in Cambridgeshire at least, a warm situation and fortunately, in the not unlikely event of its capitulating to the rigours of winter, it can very easily be perpetuated in advance from cuttings. It is a small shrub, not more than two feet tall and a bit more across, which flowers very freely from June onwards and then produces a mass of distinctively chocolate-coloured pods. And for the rest I can do no better, to show that I am not unduly prejudiced in its favour, than to quote the brief description of it in Notcutt's catalogue: 'Attractive glaucous grey clover-like foliage portrays satin pink Broom-like flowers.'

---

[1] [Some botanists now include *Dorycnium* in the genus *Lotus*.]

I have already inadvertently strayed from the railway banks and waste places into the garden, and there we had better stay till the end of the chapter. I shall not linger there as long as I should, for although, as I said at the outset, we have a possibly disproportionate taste for the two shrubby genera of Genista and Cytisus, we have comparatively little use for their herbaceous brothers. In particular, though I sometimes admire them in other people's gardens, we have no desire to grow Russell lupins. Indeed the only lupin in the whole of our garden, apart from the late-lamented tree lupin, which was probably the variety known in commerce as Mauve Queen, is a solitary orange one in the herbaceous border, which I cannot remember our ever having planted but which seems mysteriously to advance every year a few inches towards the front row. All lupins in fact are supplanted in our affections by two of their relations which are comparatively seldom to be seen in British gardens but both of which could easily be mistaken at first sight for lupins. One is the bright yellow *Thermopsis montana*, the leaves of which are on the blue side of green, and the other is the equally bright blue *Baptisia australis*, a native of North America, which again has decidedly glaucous leaves. For some inexplicable reason neither of the two is to be found in any of the catalogues to which I regularly refer. We had the former from my mother-in-law's garden in Rutland, where, along with the gentian-blue calcicolous British native *Buglossoides purpurocaerulea*, it quite quickly increases in the long grass of the wild garden and, in the same association from the same source, it has happily adapted itself to our own counterpart at Shepreth. The other we have as yet only seen and coveted in another garden, but I have just discovered that it is procurable, or at any rate used to be, from Reginald Kaye of Silverdale and am taking the necessary steps forthwith.

To pass to the larger and woodier members of the family, we naturally inherited a perfectly ordinary Wisteria on the mellow red façade of the house, which, if only our predecessor had not absent-mindedly just sawed it down to ground level under the temporary impression that it was yet one more perfectly ordinary Virginia creeper, would no doubt by now be more gnarled and twisted than it is; and we have also introduced another, a white one, with a singular lack of success to date, on to the walls of our recently acquired courtyard. Of course there were at least three perfectly ordinary Laburnums already in firm possession of three distant corners of the garden. And of course there was the old Judas tree, a vastly welcome inheritance, to which I have already referred in an earlier chapter. All these are still exactly where they were when we first came and we are truly grateful for them all. We have never introduced either the intergeneric mixture between the Laburnum and *Cytisus purpureus*, which, with the flowers of both blooming simultaneously but separately on the same plant, is more of a curiosity than a beauty, or, more surprisngly, the lovely bright pink acacia, *Robinia kelseyi*, which, since it is reputedly very fragile, I long ago trained up the wall of one of the courts in my college, with the result I had hoped for but hardly dared to expect, that it was almost invariably mistaken for a unique pink variety of Wisteria.

And so, though I feel sure I must have forgotten several popular garden plants, to our favourite genera of Genista and Cytisus, or in common parlance, with very few exceptions such as Spanish gorse, quite simply broom.

Perhaps the most beautiful and among the most floriferous of all the Genistas is the tall, silky-grey, yellow-flowered *G. cinerea*, which for some unknown reason we do not grow. Instead we planted, as a specimen in the wild garden, a young shrub of *G. aetnensis*, the specific name of which betrays its origin. It is now some nine feet tall and rather more through, and when it smothers itself, every bit as profusely as does *G. cinerea*, with golden-yellow flowers it is a dazzling sight. The most popular of them all, the aforementioned Spanish gorse or *G. hispanica*, is too solid and graceless a hedgehog for our taste, and this time we deliberately planted in its stead the elegant little weeping native of eastern Europe, *G. lydia*, which, though allegedly less hardy than some, does very well among the white and yellow shrubs at the foot of the south-facing façade of the house. And finally, I hope it will shortly be joined there by another of the best of the smaller species, *G. sagittalis*, which has curiously winged and flattened evergreen stems and erect spikes of surprisingly large yellow flowers. At any rate we last autumn brought back several of its ripe seed-pods from the hills of the Jura, where it grows as a native in local abundance.

Our taste in Cytisus, as in one or two other genera, is, I fear, somewhat eccentric. In particular, with the solitary exception of the European purple broom, *C. purpureus*, which we grow underneath *Genista lydia* and which is frankly a dreary and dingy little plant, all the brooms we see fit to grow are either white or some shade of unadulterated yellow. That, of course, rules out straight away such popular favourites as the many particoloured varieties, such as Andreanus, Firefly or Lord Lambourne, of our common native broom, *C. scoparius*, and also, more sadly perhaps, the undeniably striking pink and crimson hybrid, raised at Kew in 1900 and named, presumably after its raiser, *C. × dallimorei*. Our own favourite is probably the small tree *C. battandieri*, which comes from north-west Africa but has what must be quite a close congener looking native enough on the artificial cliffs of the Corinth Canal. Its large silver trifoliate leaves are so beautiful and .its plump spikes of bright yellow flowers smell so deliciously of pineapple that we grow it in two separate parts of the garden one in the long grass close to *Genista aetnensis*, the other at the back of the winter garden whence it is chiefly to be seen from the courtyard behind. Next in our affections come two shrubs which tally more closely with most people's idea of a broom, *C. albus* from Spain and Portugal, which is a rather diffuse shrub of six or eight feet in height and bears a profusion of small pure white flowers, and the creamy-yellow hybrid between it and the golden-yellow *C. purgans* called either the Warminster broom, because that is where it was first raised, or *C.* × *praecox*. The former we again grow for no obvious reason in the winter garden, the latter above *Genista lydia* and *C. purpureus* in front of the house. The lovely procumbent *C.* × *kewensis*, which used also to be there, unaccountably died on us and is due to be replaced. And that leaves among our favourites only the dwarf golden-yellow *C. ardoinii* from the Alpes Maritimes, which we do not yet grow only because it is too big for a sink and we have not yet built a rock garden.

By all reasonable expectations that should be the end of the chapter. But I am prompted by circumstances to add, by way of postscript, three further paragraphs. The first at least can and will be brief.

A cousin of Faith's who has just been reading this chapter remonstrates with me that I have done scant justice to the rich and varied scents that are a major part of the point of leguminous plants: a vase of melilot, for instance, smells deliciously of hay and the pink alpine lady's fingers (presumably *Anthyllis montana*) of black-currant tart. I have never been quite sure whether, on balance, I lose or gain by an almost total lack of sense of smell, which even in a garden is hardly an unmixed blessing. One morning last summer, for example, some member of the household complained that there must be a very dead rat in the border towards the greenhouse, and I knew at once, though only by hearsay, of course, the nature of the very dead rat: that beuatifully sinister black Arum, the Cretan variety of *Dracunculus vulgaris*, had opened its flowers during the night. But it is painfully evident that I owe the *Leguminosae* at least an unreserved apology for my sensory deficiency.

My second afterthought is occasioned by looking again through Faith's plant photographs, from which I was parted throughout the writing of this chapter. There are naturally some plants we see on our travels which we admire and photograph but for one reason or another, and usually because they are large plants in full flower, never dream of collecting. There are no fewer than four such among the *Leguminosae*, one of which I had clean forgotten that we already grow and flower successfully. Its name, like those of distressingly many plants, has been changed more than once since I first made its acquaintance. I originally knew it and, unless I am much mistaken, bought it as *Orobus luteus*, since which not so distant days first its generic and then its specific name was changed (necessarily?) and it is now to be called (obligatorily!) *Lathyrus laevigatus*. And there is another species of Lathyrus, photographed this time on the Isle of Cos, which we should very much like to grow if only we could procure its seed, even though it is only an annual. It was growing on a bare, sun-baked, rocky slope, where we stopped to dig up a few blood-red anemones, only just above the north coast of the island, and at first I took it as *L. tingitanus*, which I know to be cultivable even in the coldest parts of Britain because I have lately scrounged some ripe seed of it off a gardening friend in Cumberland. Subsequent research in the *Flora Europaea* has, however, convinced me that I was wrong in my extempore determination, for the simple reason that this African species only touches Europe in the Iberian peninsula, Sardinia and the Azores, and that our plant must be *L. clymenum* instead. But I cannot see any reason why it should not be just as hardy as the other, and I should certainly like to grow it just as much.

The life of an amateur botanist is not an easy one, and I am in some slight trouble again over the last two leguminous plants I propose to mention. When I am in any doubt of a plant's identity I naturally refrain from labelling our slide of it until I can gain enlightenment from some authoritative source. In the two cases in point I was evidently in no doubt for I find the two slides labelled, and in my own hand too, *Astragalus alopecuroides* and *A. vicentinus* respectively; and I think I was probably right at the time about the former at least. After our stay at Pralognan in late June 1962, we just crossed the frontier and spent two or three nights at Cogne, the centre of the Italian National Park of Gran Paradiso. Taking one of the obvious walks from there on to higher ground, we soon enough lit upon a most beautiful plant. I see in the *Dictionary of Gardening* that *A. alopecuroides*, one of the only two members of that enormous genus starred for garden merit, is said to be native from Spain to Siberia. But I also deduce from the *Flora Europaea* that as lately as 1968 *A. centralpinus*, which is to be found only in the south-western Alps of France and Italy and in Bulgaria, was segregated from *A. alopecuroides*, which only creeps a little distance along the Mediterranean coast of France from its headquarters in Spain. So that is what our plant must be; and, which is the point, I can see no earthly reason why, if only seed were obtainable, it should not be one of the greater glories of an English garden. And the same would appear to be true, if less conclusively so, of our other Astragalus on Cape St Vincent, since our photograph of it shows it growing cheek by jowl with *Cistus palhinhae*, which has proved to be tolerably hardy in Britain. In fact the only thing to be added is that, as apparently no such plant exists, or ever has existed, as *Astragalis vicentinus*, we must henceforth remember to call it *A. massiliensis* instead.

And that is really enough about both British and foreign leguminous plants, for I cannot be bothered with peas and beans, and we must move on to the far more formidable undertaking of the rosaceous.

CHAPTER 6

Rosaceae

NEXT to the *Ranunculaceae*, but fortunately not in the same class as them, comes in the British flora, for sheer range of shapes and sizes, the family of *Rosaceae*. True, it contains nothing so superficially different as, say, an Anemone from a Delphinium or a Thalictrum, but the range from bird cherry, through dropwort, greater burnet, agrimony, the lady's mantles and marsh cinquefoil, to the brambles and roses proper is enough to give pause to any but the keen student of plant anatomy. And once again the family is very richly and variously represented in the British Isles. What native family could vie with one that contains, at the top end of the size scale, the wild cherry or *Rosa sherardii*, in the middle shrubby cinquefoil or meadowsweet and, at the bottom, wood or mountain avens or even silverweed?

Although the double form of dropwort, *Filipendula vulgaris*, is occasionally grown in gardens and is still in commerce under the misnomer of *F. hexapetala* Flore Pleno, I know of no garden except our own at Shepreth where the native plant is grown instead. And yet the single form is as usual, to my mind at least, far preferable to the double. Never attaining more than about eighteen inches in height, with its finely cut dark green leaves and its convex head of relatively large six-petalled white flowers, which are clear rose-pink while still in bud, it is not only the ideal plant for the front row of a chalky herbaceous border but it is equally at home in the crevices between paving stones where it happily sows itself. And for a different type of garden, damp and shady like Ardtornish rather than dry and chalky like Shepreth, *Geum rivale* deserves almost as much of a eulogy. The garden Geums tend to be rather too flamboyant for my taste, particularly the double scarlet Mrs Bradshaw. By way of contrast *G. rivale*, its orange-pink bell-shaped flowers drooping in hairy chocolate calyces, is almost too modest in its grace; but, as with anything graceful, the more carefully you look at it, the more keenly will you come to admire its virtues. Nor does it disclose all its merits to even a careful look. Although naturally at home on the edges either of a boggy clearing in a wood or a rocky mountain stream, it evidently has no objection to growing, flowering and spreading, admittedly under the shade of a barn, near the front of the same herbaceous border as, towards the other end, so happily accommodates the dropwort. And there is yet a third European member of the same family, *Alchemilla mollis*, which graces the front of the same border, the leaves of which, apart from the flowers which are much like those of any other bigger Alchemilla, are so densely and softly hairy that they retain the dew or the rain as little sparkling droplets on the concave upper surfaces. True, this is not a British species; it comes originally from the Carpathians. But though they are admittedly more prostrate in habit, there is no earthly reason why its place should not be taken at the front of a border, or again in paving stones as we grow them, by either of the native species, both embellished with gleaming silver undersides to their leaves, *A. alpina* or the very rare *A. conjuncta*.

But as well as the herbaceous border, both the rock garden and the shrubbery cry aloud for their rosaceous plants. Mountain avens and several of the Potentillas clamour for a place in the former, while no shrub border would be complete without its cherries, its crabs, its species roses and its shrubby Potentillas. Mountain avens, or *Dryas octopetala*, is all the year through perhaps the neatest of all British alpines, with its stiff, dark, little oak-like leaves with the white undersides, its relatively large white eight-petalled flowers with the bunch of golden stamens in the middle, and its wide fluffy seed-heads; but either Potentilla, *P. crantzii* or *P. tabernaemontani*, is a close runner-up. And if you want miniature trees in your rock garden as well, then the various shrubby Potentillas provide you with a wide choice of both size and colour. Indeed these same shrubby Potentillas are not far from being the best of all-purpose plants in a garden of any imaginable size. They have an exceptionally long flowering season; they do not exceed their limits; preferably when they have some lime in the soil, but not only so, they seem to tolerate almost any conditions; and they are an invaluable foil to any more flamboyant neighbour in almost any part of the garden from a formal paved courtyard to an informal shrubbery. The best of them by any standard is *P. Vilmoriniana*, with its silvery leaves and pale primrose flowers; but it seems to share, in these parts at least, with its relative *Rosa foetida* Bicolor, the Austrian Copper Briar, the habit of dying off a branch at a time and leaving an unshapely skeleton. Far more reliable among the upright section, though admittedly less lovely for the lack of the silver foliage, are the pale primrose Katherine Dykes and the buttercup Jackman's Variety; while *R. foetida* Austrian Yellow seems to lack the tiresome foibles of its congener. And among the decumbent species of shrubby Potentilla too there is a fair choice of both size and colour. *P. Manchu*, the smallest of them, being at most a yard across, has large white flowers among silvery foliage, *P. Tangerine*, which is more vigorous, provides a touch of orange, while the ordinary buttercup yellow is represented by *P. Longacre*.

Apart of course from the rose garden itself, the shrubbery is, however, the part of the garden where members of the rose family come most truly into their own. Here belong, besides the indispensable cherries, pears, peaches, plums, quinces, almonds and crab-apples, all the varieties of Cotoneaster, Pyracantha, Sorbus and Crataegus. The choice is here in fact so embarrassingly large that in all but the most extensive gardens drastic selection is unavoidable. By no means every garden, moreover, has a suitable site, nor every gardener a taste, for a shrubbery as such. In our Shepreth garden all that could strictly be called a shrub garden is a short deep border, backed by a south-facing wall and underplanted with snowdrops, aconites and violets, which we call the winter garden. At the back we grow, alongside the almond up which climbs *Clematis armandii*, large specimens of *Cornus mas* and *Prunus subhirtella* Autumnalis; the middle zone is occupied, on either side of the two specimens of *Viburnum farreri* which flank the exquisite *Prunus triloba* Multiplex in the centre, by *Corylopsis spicata*, *Forsythia suspensa atrocaulis* and *F. ovata*, and *Chimonanthus fragrans*; while in the front row, again alongside a pair of the purple-berried *Callicarpa bodinieri giraldii* which grow on each side of one of my old stone sinks, we have planted such relatively low-growing shrubs as *Corylopsis pauciflora*, *Daphne odora* Aureomarginata and *Mahonia japonica*. But for the rest we employ our selection of small trees and shrubs in virtually every part of the garden, and notably in the wild garden and at the back of the herbaceous border, as features providing variety of height, shape and colour.

The principles that guide us in our selection of these small trees are inevitably personal and arbitrary, but they are easily defined. Having decided that a particular part of the garden would be enhanced by the introduction of one or more trees or shrubs of a certain height and form, we simply choose our own favourites from the various candidates suitable for the situation in question. Although several of the Cotoneasters add an undeniable variety to the winter scene, we believe that in a garden of the size and nature of ours at Shepreth a more attractive alternative is almost always available; and the same is true, with the possible exception of the abundant native hawthorn, of the numerous species of the genus Crataegus. Of the Pyracanthas we have, after a good deal of hesitation, admitted only two, *P. rogersiana* and, I think, *P. atalantioides*, and I am still doubtful whether they merit the prominent position on a wall in the front garden that we have allocated to them.

Firmly convinced that the proper setting for the various species of Sorbus akin to the native mountain ash is neither the suburban garden where they are too often seen nor even such flat and naturally featureless gardens as our own at Shepreth, but rather the rocky slopes and glens of the north or west, we content ourselves with admiring two delicately graceful little trees, *Sorbus hupehensis* and *S. vilmorinii*, in the appropriate environment of Ardtornish and grow at Shepreth, at the back of the herbaceous border, a single specimen of one of the varieties of the native whitebeam, *S. aria* Lutescens, the function of which, along with the weeping standard *Pyrus salicifolia* planted close beside it, is to lighten with silver the darkness of a group of yews and the shaded bole of an enormous old elm behind.

So much for the large group of rosaceous genera whose genuinely indispensable value is, in our view, better appreciated in an urban park than in a relatively small garden in the country. And even now, before we come to the vast and varied tribes of Pyrus and Prunus and to the roses themselves, there are three other genera of the same family which deserve at least a passing mention, namely, first, the brambles, then the quinces, Chaenomeles and Cydonia, and finally the numerous species, mainly natives of north east America, of the genus Amelanchier. With two, or possibly three, honourable exceptions, the brambles are in our judgment best left where they belong, in hedgerows and thickets. The doubtful exception is *Rubus ulmifolius* Bellidiflorus, with double pink flowers, which we do not grow only because we much prefer various roses of the *filipes* and *wichuraiana* type. The two that we do gratefully grow are R. *thibetanus* and R. Tridel Benenden, the former for its waxy white stems and the white undersides of its leaves, the latter for its masses of large single white flowers. As for the quinces, our treatment of them is, I suppose, eccentric. We grow the quince proper, *Cydonia vulgaris* or, as it should now apparently be called, *C. oblonga*, in the dankest and shadiest corner of the whole garden, and we deliberately planted it there, where it surprisingly yields quite well, at least as much for the visual effect of its relatively large and pale foliage as for its over-rated fruit. Its infinitely more popular relative, on the other hand, *Chaenomeles japonica*, we use very sparingly. A shrub which, if it is to be induced to flower as flamboyantly as this one indisputably can, needs to be reduced by drastic pruning to the shape of a boot-brush or a hedgehog, fails to comply with our individual notions of garden design; and as the result, the two hybrids that we do grow, Knap Hill Scarlet and Rowallane, being allowed to develop to their natural size and shape, repay us with so sparse a flowering that they live under the constant and ever-increasing threat of replacement. I am indeed at present contemplating replacing one of the two, which grows on the other side of a narrow sunk path from the aforementioned quince, by a specimen of the only European representative of the genus Amelanchier, the comparatively low-growing and large-flowered species variously known as *A. ovalis, A. rotundifolia* and *A. vulgaris,* the young white leaves of which we have often admired, without ever attempting to uproot one of the numerous plants, on the lower slopes of the south-eastern outlier of the Dolomites, Monte Grappa. Such a substitution would not only introduce more light into the gloomiest corner of the garden; it would introduce also a relatively unfamiliar genus with which we have yet to make a first-hand acquaintance.

My taxonomy is, I believe, now out of date, but I still tend instinctively to think, as I always have thought in the past, of the recently segregated genus of Malus as a branch of that large and polymorphic genus Pyrus. But whether Pyrus and Malus are really one genus or two, they and the genus Prunus together provide between them many of the most invaluable of small flowering trees. The best of the pears I have already mentioned, the elegant weeping willow-leaved *Pyrus salicifolia,* which, when it attains a certain age, has a dark and gnarled trunk to offset the grace of its silver leaves. Though its white flowers are admittedly not very spectacular, I cannot understand why this exquisite tree is not more often seen. And as for the rest of the genus, since every pear tree is a thing of beauty, the obvious criterion for selection is the quality and quantity of the fruit.

The new-fangled genus Malus, which comprises the crab-apples, is more problematic for the simple reason that the number of species is very large and, since every one of them deserves a place in the garden, ruthless selection is once again enforced. Here, for once, we un-hesitatingly subscribe to the popular verdict and give pride of place to the relatively small semi-pendulous and wonderfully floriferous *Malus floribunda* and the hybrid × *atrosanguinea,* the latter of which, underplanted with Polyanthus and backed by a tall specimen of the bird cherry, overhangs the corner of one of our two rose-beds, while the former we have planted, to secure some continuity of colour and as a support for that loveliest of honeysuckles, the large-flowered bright yellow *Lonicera* × *tellmanniana,* beside the big almond at the back of the winter garden. Otherwise our choice was made for us. When we bought the house and garden at Shepreth we took over, as the back boundary of what was then the bare hen-run and is now the wild garden, a tall hedge of mixed crabs, with which the only fault we have to find is that it contains none of the varieties with yellow fruit. But if you are in a position to make your own selection, then there are three obvious criteria to guide you, namely height, which varies from about ten to well over twenty feet, colour of blossom, which embraces every shade from the deep wine red of *Malus* Eleyi to the white of John Downie, and, last but not least important, size and colour of fruit, which may be yellow, orange or almost any shade of red. And if you are in doubt as to the precise varieties which will best satisfy your requirements on these three scores, then you cannot do better than follow the guidance of the admirable selection offered in the illustrated and classified *Notcutt's Book of Plants*.

So we come, last before the roses, to the genus Prunus, which is, the roses apart, the most problematic of them all because it includes, besides the plums and the cherries, the almonds also and the peaches. As well as the justly beloved almond itself, *P. dulcis*, and the larger-flowered, deeper-coloured but, in our experience, much less floriferous *P.* × *amygdalopersica* Pollardii, there belong here also the beautiful double pink *P. triloba* Multiplex, the central feature of our winter garden, and the comparatively unfamiliar twiggy little shrub, usually only about three feet high, *P. tenella*, and its white and rosy-crimson varieties, *alba* and Fire Hill respectively. Fire Hill, which for no obvious reason we do not grow, is said to be the best of this trio of dwarf almonds, while we have never introduced the white form because we believe that almonds are by nature, like crabs, some shade of pink. But the type itself we do grow, on top of the low semi-circular flint wall, shrouded in miniature ivy, which surrounds a little artificial mound known to us as the Dog's Grave. This mound is topped by an ordinary Laburnum and backed by an ancient mulberry, and on its margin the dwarf almond performs its modest function to perfection.

The trouble about the peaches is, as every gardener knows, the unsightly affliction of leaf-curl, which, in this part of the country at least, is hard to overcome even by the most conscientious application of lime sulphur or Orthocide. But there is no denying that, if only this grave shortcoming can be mastered, then any of the peaches is, in the early flowering season, a glorious sight to see. After some experiments with free-standing trees of the variety Peregrine, which were totally frustrated by leaf-curl and so fairly promptly abandoned, the only peach that we now grow is the variety, whose name I have forgotten and which I cannot find even in Hillier's catalogue, with reddish-purple leaves. This we planted in front of an old red-brick wall, with *Berberis thunbergii* Atropurpurea Nana and the Rosemary Rose at its feet; these latter two we have in turn underplanted with the copper-leaved bugle and the late-flowering blood-red tulip, *T. sprengeri*, to repeat variations of the same theme at a lower level; and now, flanked as it is on either side by silver-leaved plants, this combination makes a spectacle which provokes a good deal of admiration. But the battle against leaf-curl continues with only moderate success.

As for the plums, they cause us little trouble because we happen to regard the foliage of the popular purple-leaved varieties, with the possible exception of the useful dwarf *Prunus* × *cistena*, as lifeless and lack-lustre, and though we tolerate the single specimen of *P. cerasifera* Pissardii which we planted in the same gloomy corner as our quince, the rest of our plums we grow, chiefly on the tallest of our old red-brick walls, for the sake of their fruit.

And so finally to the cherries, where again our views are eccentric. Just as the natural colour of crabs, almonds and peaches is in our view some shade of pink, so, we believe, cherries were intended by nature to be white. True, we took over, in the vicinity of the tall hedge of crabs, two mature specimens of one of the Japanese varieties with double flowers the colour of raspberry ice-cream, and these we have suffered to remain. True again that in a misguided moment, needing a tree the shape of a miniature Lombardy poplar to conceal a stretch of hideous corrugated asbestos roof, we deliberately planted a specimen of *P. erecta*, alias Amanogawa, and now that it is fulfilling its function we have not the heart to remove it. And true, finally, that in addition to the *P. subhirtella* Autumnalis in the winter garden, which as a matter of fact is scarcely flushed with pink, we grow *P.* Pandora which is indisputably pink, as a prominent feature in a little lawn across the road from our main garden. But nevertheless the positions of greatest honour are allotted, in addition to our two native species, the gean and the bird-cherry, to the two Japanese hybrids Okumiyako or Shimidsu-sakura, with its long-stalked, pendulous, double, pinkish-white flowers, and *P.* Tai-haku, the hanging clusters of whose huge single ivory flowers are so exquisitely offset by the copper-coloured young leaves. These two indeed should always be included in every list of the finest adornments of any garden of any size, and it is the greatest of pities that in the popular esteem they evidently do not begin to vie with the rather sickly pinks.

So at last to the roses themselves, which, though they call for and have indeed often enough been accorded a whole book to themselves, must here be treated with even more determined selectivity than the other genera of their family. We ourselves, though we grow well over a hundred different varieties, have scarcely touched the fringe of the subject; a catalogue such as Murrell's of Shrewsbury, from whom, regardless of the fact that far too few of their bushes are on their own roots, we nevertheless bought the majority of our roses, listed over six hundred and twenty. Here in fact, more than anywhere else in the whole garden, every man to his own taste, and here once again our own views are eccentric. Though we do, of course, grow a considerable number of hybrid tea and floribunda roses, partly in mixed borders to introduce variety of height and colour and partly in two relatively small triangular rose-beds with curving fronts which we do not hesitate to interplant with lilies and bulbous irisis, we once again, and this time without loss of flower, prune far too late and far too lightly to satisfy an aspiring exhibitor, and once again we show our usual preference for single over double flowers. Thus among the hybrid teas our favourites include White Wings, the coppery-orange Mrs Oakley Fisher, the very dark crimson Dusky Maiden and, above all, the pure pink Ellen Wilmott; and among the floribunda group the semi-double flame-coloured Anna Wheatcroft and the immensely strong and vigorous deep blood-red Frensham. The ubiquitous multi-coloured Masquerade, though we do grow it, along with Frensham, where little else will grow, in the impoverished soil beneath a large chestnut tree, we regard as a vulgar courtesan, and the same goes to a lesser extent for all the popular bi-colours, such as Tzigane, among the hybrid teas. As for the modern lilac-coloured roses, of which we were once beguiled by a catalogue into buying one or two, they are such unnatural monstrosities that after a year or two we unhesitatingly jettisoned them, the only roses apart from the old-fashioned curiosity, *Rosa* Viridiflora, to which we have ever meted out such heartless treatment. The moral is obvious: never buy a rose until you have actually seen it in flower. And as for the more popular double-flowered floribunda and hybrid tea roses, of which almost every gardener has his own favourites and of which from time to time lists are published of the best dozen, our own selection, based on first-hand experience and covering virtually the whole range of colour except mauve, would rank Iceberg, the Rosemary Rose and the lusty pink Queen Elizabeth Rose as the best of the former, and of the latter would name Spek's Yellow and Lydia as the best yellows, Mojave as the best orange, Shot Silk and Helen Traubel among the orangey-pinks and Monique among the true rose-pinks, Michèle Meilland and the irrepressible Peace among those whose precise shade is hard to classify, and finally Josephine Bruce among the reds.

The climbing roses present, if possible, even greater problems of selection than the bushes for the rose garden, for they range from the true species such as *Rosa filipes, R. helenae* and *R. brunonii*, through the various hybrids, chiefly offspring of *R. wichuraiana*, such as Albéric Barbier, the old favourite Albertine, Dr van Fleet and the enormously floriferous Wedding Day, to such climbing sports of the hybrid teas as Etoile de Hollande, Lady Hillingdon, Cupid, Guinée and Madame Grégoire Staechelin. Here, for once, we are liable to be untrue to our own principles in that we award the gold medal to two or three of the double-flowered hybrids. We do admittedly grow four of the climbers with large single flowers, three of them in the most prominent positions. The virtually evergreen Mermaid, with its handsome glossy foliage and huge single pale yellow flowers, has unfortunately proved not quite reliably hardy. We originally planted it, along with the vivid flame-coloured Réveil Dijonnais and the delicate white and purple variegated *Vitis henryana*, as the main feature of the low white-washed west-facing Elizabethan wing of the house, with the rampant scarlet Cape figwort, *Phygelius capensis*, attaining at least eight feet in front of it. No sooner, however, had it filled the space allotted to it and attained the full beauty of which it is capable than it succumbed, in common with several other evergreens, to the extreme rigours of the winter of early 1963; and its successor, which we planted with some hesitation after this experience, is taking its time to get away and after six years has barely attained so many feet. Meg on the other hand, which adorns the wall behind the larger of our rose-beds with abundant coral-pink flowers, is distressingly prone to mildew; while Silver Moon, which ramps healthily and strongly up the shady side of the leaning remnants of our ancient mulberry, condescends to flower so seldom and so sparingly that it survives only under the constant threat of replacement. In fact the only single-flowered climber with an irreproachable record in our garden is the blazing blood-red Scarlet Fire, one of the finest of the post-war introductions, which, along with the self-clinging *Hydrangea petiolaris* and the two varieties of Clematis, *C.* ×*jackmannii* Superba and *C. viticella* Royal Velours, smothers the tarred timber gable of one of our old barns with a veritable blaze of colour. Scarlet Fire alone among our selection of single-flowered climbers can in our estimation rival at least five double varieties.

We grow the majority of our more showy double climbing roses, all in various shades of pink, on the old brick wall at the back of the enclosed vegetable garden. Among those we already grow there are the climbing sport of Shot Silk, the familiar Albertine, Lady Waterlow and, the most vigorous and spectacular of them all, the wonderfully floriferous true rose-pink Madame Grégoire Staechelin. There they are about to be joined, indeed should have already been joined but for alarming delay in transit, by Climbing Caroline Testout and another of the single varieties, the huge-flowered shell-pink Cupid. But elsewhere in the garden we grow, three of them in splendid isolation, four others of the most resplendent of double climbers. Climbing Etoile de Hollande was already, when we arrived, vigorously established on the back wall of the house, which faces nearly due north, and we have never dreamt of disturbing it. Lady Waterlow climbs up the wall, eight feet or so tall, at the back of the winter garden, and her delicate flesh-pink flowers overhang the little paved courtyard with the lily pond, the only formal part of our whole garden, which lies directly behind. The early flowering Maigold, another of Kordes's most splendid post-war introductions, joins with *Clematis macropetala* Markham's Pink and *Lonicera periclymenum* Serotina in garlanding the lower of the two old brick walls that back our larger rose-bed. And last but by no means least, for in my opinion, despite a certain tendency to legginess, it is the finest of all climbing roses, the deliciously fragrant Guinée, the duskiest and most velvety of all red roses, clambers heartily at least twenty feet up the old tiled barn (itself, like the house, classified as an ancient monument) which forms one flank of the short gravel drive to the back door, and wreathes the flag-staff at the top.

The only other climbing roses that we grow on a wall, this time the high old red-brick wall along the other side of the short drive, are the semi-double canary-yellow Lawrence Johnston, which there at least suffers severely from black-spot, and the healthily floriferous and fragrant Wedding Day. These two share the same wall as our two Pyracanthas, a wall flanked at either end by the tall rose-pink hybrid *rugosa* Conrad F. Meyer and a rather stunted old fig tree; and it is Wedding Day in particular, with its abundant orange hips, which makes me doubt whether any Pyracantha merits so prominent a position. Most of the remainder of our climbing roses are asked to climb up sundry old trees and they respond with a will. Two of the best species, *Rosa filipes* and *R. multiflora cathayensis*, had already been planted in key positions by our predecessors, the former to climb up the tall and crumbling old brick wall that marks our front boundary into the branches of one of the three old limes that overhang the garden from beyond the path outside, the latter close beside it to smother the tall wrought-iron railings, dating from about 1720, which directly front the mellow Queen Anne façade of the house. And similarly Albéric Barbier, one of the best of the hybrid *wichuraiana* strain, was already when we came lightening the darkness of the sombre and rampant ivy that clothes our eastern boundary wall. Those that we ourselves have introduced are all in the remotest corner of the garden, which used to house the pig-sty and is on that account more fertile than the rest and which we have converted into the home of our old-fashioned roses and the best of our anemones, lilies and Alliums. Near the narrow entrance, flanked by box and yew, there is an old and barren plum tree, up which we climb the pale Madame Plantier, one of the new Noisette roses. In the tall lilac hedge which shuts off the wild garden we planted Dr van Fleet, which was sent to us in the days before we had learnt to say 'No substitutes, please' in place of the far superior New Dawn. Céline Forestier, which we intended to climb up another tall plum tree on the other side of a winding grass path from Madame Plantier, has unaccountably died and, since it is triumphantly survived by its companion *Clematis viticella* Alba Luxurians, has never been replaced.

And finally a small rooted cutting of an anonymous large-flowered crimson climber, which came to us from my mother-in-law's garden in Rutland and which we planted at the foot of a large and very productive apple tree, has shown such unforeseen vigour that for the past three years it has covered the broad crown of the tree with an ever-increasing mass of warm and vivid colour.

We are particularly attached to this remote and quiet corner of the garden because, having planned it from scratch and created it for ourselves, we were for once entirely free to follow our own fancies. The first thing we did, after we had reclaimed it from an impenetrable wilderness of nettles and demolished the brick and concrete pig-sty, was to erect, on the site of the said pig-sty and close to the old plum tree that supports Madame Plantier, an irregularly circular mound with a long narrow tapering spur running from it above the sunken path which I mentioned earlier in connection with our one and only quince. The mound itself we topped with *Rosa* Paulii, which delights to sprawl downwards from above and this particular specimen of which has produced first an enormous sucker of the ordinary dog rose, which is so safely protected by the densely intertwining tangle of savagely thorny branches that it is virtually impossible to eradicate, and then, by spontaneous layering, two robust offspring on their own roots; and at the far end of the spur we planted (in particularly successful association with the pink tree-paeony Moutan, the low, spreading and prodigiously floriferous white *Viburnum plicatum* Lanarth and, in the adjacent little lawn, a specimen shrub of the delicate weeping mauve *Buddleia alternifolia*) two tall bushes of what to my mind, with its exquisite rose-tinted glaucous foliage, is the best of all the many species roses, *R. glauca*. Between these two, on top of the tapering spur which is almost too densely carpeted with the beautifully variegated form of *Lamium galeobdolon*, Faith has planted a mixed hedge of her favourite old-fashioned roses. At the near end, cheek by jowl with *Rosa* Paulii, is the familiar *Rosa mundi*, the brightest and largest-flowered of the old striped roses; at the far end, blending to perfection with *Rosa glauca* and its carefully selected associates, is the rampageous dark purple-crimson Gipsy Boy, which, since it figures neither in Murrell's nor in the Sunningdale Nurseries' catalogue,[1] though I have since found it in Notcutt's, we were reduced to scrounging as a cutting from a friend in the north. And between these two, in a carefully premeditated order from the near end to the far, grow in succession, and all but the last of them of the *Rosa gallica* group, the pink Petite Orléannaise, the carmine

---

[1] I apologise: the Sunningdale Nurseries did list it after all, but, like Notcutt's, under its German name.

Surpasse Tout, the lilac-tinged Du Maitre d'Ecole, the huge-flowered plum-coloured Charles de Mills, the dusky purple Cardinal de Richelieu, the sumptuous deep purplish-crimson Tuscany Superb and, last before Gipsy Boy, alias Zigeunerknabe, and this time a Bourbon rose rather than one of the *gallica* group, the pale lilac, purple-striped Variegata di Bologna. And on the other side of the flat and winding grass path, from which, at the entrance to this secluded corner, the sunk path diverges to rejoin it again in the little hidden lawn at the far end, we grow, as individual specimens rather than as the constituents of a mixed hedge, four others of the showiest of the old-fashioned roses. First, against the background of a dense copper-leaved hazel and with the tall apricot *Lilium* × *testaceum* and the huge metallic mauve heads of *Allium christophii* in front, comes the grotesquely misnamed *Rosa gallica* Complicata, which, with its masses of large single flowers like those of a glorified dog rose, is the very quintessence of simplicity. And a little farther on, in front of a many-stemmed specimen of *Aesculus parviflora*, the miniature shrub chestnut with rich copper-coloured young leaves and long slender terminal spikes of white flowers, and just within touching distance one of another, grow the huge-flowered rich pink Bourbon, Madame Louise Laperrière, the purple moss rose William Lobb and the exquisite white damask with the green carpels in the middle, Madame Hardy. And that, with the exception of the dainty pink Cuisse de Nymphe or Small Maiden's Blush, which grows at the foot of Scarlet Fire, is all of the countless favourites of bygone days that we can find room for.

The hybrid musk roses, which form a small natural group of their own, fare even worse with us, for apart from the tall white Pax which, since the days before we came, has stood on either side of the front gate, and the pair of Buff Beauty which we have lately ordered to mark the end of our twin blue borders, they are confined to quite a small bed, roughly triangular in shape and underplanted with various hellebores and long-spurred columbines, which we have lately edged with York stone and of which the principal features have long been an old and gnarled Judas tree, a dark purple lilac and the ivory *Prunus* Tai-haku. The best of them, to our way of thinking, are the trinity consisting of the shell-pink Felicia, the creamy Penelope, its large semi-double flowers suffused with pale pink, and the lightly gold-tinged double white Prosperity; a small band admittedly, but with their characteristic clusters of flowers and their rich fragrance, one with a peculiar charm of its own.

Compared with this last group of delicate beauties, *Rosa rugosa* and its numerous hybrids are indisputably rather coarse. Accordingly, despite the fact that the leaves of some of them turn in autumn to a vivid yellow, we have until quite recently found room in the garden proper for two of them only. The tall rose-pink Conrad F. Meyer, which is not at all typical of the group, we found already in possession of the most prominent corner of the front garden and, though it does not accord with our chosen colour scheme, we have never had the heart to attempt to move so well established a bush. And otherwise the only one that we have ourselves introduced is the spreading semi-double pure white Schneezwerg, which we planted, along with the white varieties of several species of the herbaceous geraniums, in what is henceforth to be a white and green corner, a little artificial hollow below the mound topped by *Rosa* Paulii and near the base of Madame Plantier. But some three years ago self-interest impelled us, in the natural desire to protect our boundaries, to purchase the old thatched cottage and barns which have for years past made a truly rustic back-cloth to our vegetable garden and, in particular, to the twin blue borders on either side of the grass path down the middle; and with them came well over half an acre, rectangular in shape, of derelict orchard, a paradise for nettles and docks. When this area had been mechanically cleared, and then lavishly treated with various weed killers, we first of all turned the farther half into a playground for the children, a hard tennis court on one side and a lawn for cricket and football on the other, and moved into the near half, as well as our nursery garden, our taller fruit and vegetables. This latter half we divided by a straight grass path leading to the gate of the tennis court, and on one side of the path we planted, only about a year ago, a hedge of mixed *rugosa* roses. It is still too early to judge of its success, but with the relatively low-growing Frau Dagmar Hastrup, with its single flesh-pink flowers, the dominant theme, and other more vigorous varieties such as the wine-purple Roseraie de l'Hay interplanted, we are full of optimistic expectation.

Even after many centuries of skilful hybridisation the roses are still far from having exhausted their potentialities. With few exceptions the modern shrub roses, the most beautiful of all the products of complex cross-breeding, date at the earliest from the thirties, and more than twenty of them have been introduced since 1950. One of the few exceptions, whose origin is obscure but which anyhow dates from 1927, is Nevada, still in my judgment just about the best of them all. Once again we owe to our predecessors the superb specimen which grows against our front railings midway between Conrad F. Meyer in the corner and Pax beside the high wrought-iron gate; it is by now a very big rounded bush, nearly eight feet tall and rather wider than it is high, and at its first flowering in late May, when it is completely covered with almost single white flowers, at least four inches across and sometimes slightly flushed with pink at the margins, it puts almost every other rose in the garden to shame. With the possible exception of the hybrid musks, the only roses among those we grow at Shepreth that are nearly so floriferous are four others of this same group. One of them, Maigold, which we ourselves grow as a climber on a low wall, I have already, and perhaps inaccurately, mentioned among the climbing roses. The other three consist, first, of that wonderful pair of single hybrids of *Rosa spinosissima*, alias *R. pimpinellifolia*, Frühlingsgold and Frühlingsmorgen, and third, a hybrid of the sweet briar, the semi-double coral-pink Fritz Nobis. We grow Frühlingsmorgen, the flowers of which are pink at the edges and fade through pale yellow to white at the centre, in close proximity to the aforementioned *Sorbus aria* Lutescens at the back of the herbaceous border; and again, this time just within touching distance of its closest of kin, whose flowers shade from cream at the margin to gold at the centre, as a specimen bush in the little lawn the other side of the road. Fritz Nobis on the other hand, we long ago planted, as uniform and widely spaced hedges, on either side of the short mown grass path which leads down the centre of the wild garden to a shallow arc of tall bushes of the grey-leaved, orange-berried sea buckthorn, with a fine specimen, blazing scarlet in autumn, of the sadly neglected *Koelreuteria paniculata* in the middle. Two others of the group, Ballerina and Raubritter, which we have admired in other people's gardens, we have only this winter introduced and it is still too early to say how worthily they will adorn their carefully selected sites. The former we have planted, with sundry other pink rose bushes, at the foot of the long wall behind the kitchen garden, where, as I have already mentioned, we grow a variety of pink climbers, the latter, flanked on either side by *R. Paulii* Rosea, as the centre-piece of the Dog's Grave. And finally there are, I regret to say, three others of the group, all in shades of red, that we have either already discarded or are about to discard. Will Scarlet, which until this summer marked the end of our twin blue borders down the middle of the kitchen garden, was too strident for the purpose and has lately been replaced by the softer tones of Buff Beauty, while Bonn and Munster, which, between *Rosa moyesii* and Frühlingsmorgen, we planted at the back of the herbaceous border, so jar with our otherwise deliberately soft colour scheme that they are about to be replaced by a young but already vigorous rooted cutting of the tall and elegant white-flowered shrub, yet another of the rose family, *Sorbaria aitchisonii*.

The only other group of roses that calls for a mention, if only a very brief one, before we come finally to the species themselves is that of the miniatures. A suprising fact about them is that, contrary to all natural expectations, they do not blend at all happily with their bigger brethren. As there is no obvious place for them in the garden at Shepreth, we have never introduced more than three, one white, one crimson, and one, the most familiar of them all, the pink R. *roulettii*, out of the total of fifty-two listed in Murrell's catalogue. These three grow close together in one of the children's gardens, and they are as many, probably, as we shall ever bother to buy. But the relatively few climbers in the group, five in all in the same list, are a wholly different proposition. Though they too are best kept well apart from their relatives of a normal size, there is many a garden in Britain where an isolated stretch of comparatively low wall calls for colourful cover. So, at Shepreth, there is, at the north-west angle of the house, a small three-sided border, not more than five years old, where, between a wide projecting window and the actual corner, the old tiled roof drops to a height of little more than seven feet. Along the curving front of this tiny bed we first planted a miniature hedge, only inches high, consisting of two of the blue species of Lithospermum, almost the only two that positively like lime and now again re-named *Moltkia petraea* and M. *intermedia*, and the miniature yellow species of rock-rose, *Helianthemum lunulatum*. The flat border itself, which we underplanted with three of the best tulip species, was devoted to a mixture of prostrate thymes. And finally, the longer of the two walls behind, that which faces west, was given over to the pure rose-pink climbing Pompon de Paris, while that which faces north, only about half the length of the other, is the chosen home of the deeper Pink Cameo, with the true *Clematis alpina* trailing through it. Both have precisely filled the space allotted to them, and no two plants in the garden better fulfil their special function.

So we come, purposefully last of all of the groups of roses, to the species and their varieties; and here once again, for the first time for a long while, the British natives come splendidly into the picture. The hedgerows of Britain owe an overwhelming proportion of their unique beauty to the succession of rosaceous bushes that form their main ingredient. First comes the blackthorn, flowering profusely before it comes into leaf; next, the dominant feature of the early summer landscape, the hawthorn or may; and finally, of course, the wild roses themselves. In southern England the commonest of these native roses are the dog rose proper, *Rosa canina*, which is too commonly used as the stock on which to graft most of the garden roses, and, in some districts at least, the white R. *arvensis*, which is easily recognised, not only by the facts that its natural habit is lower and more sprawling and that its flowers come in clusters, but also by its prominently exserted styles. But the fragrant glandular sweet briar, R. *eglanteria*, is almost equally widespread. In the north and west, however, the dog rose is largely replaced by two more colourful species, the rich pink R. *mollis* and R. *sherardii*, which are most easily distinguished one from the other by the fact that the thorns of the latter, though relatively slender, are distinctly downward curving while those of the former are straight and narrow. The natural beauty of these two bushes is, moreover, greatly enhanced by their soft blue-grey foliage. But for all that, my own favourite among our native roses is normally an inhabitant not so much of the hedgerows, though in the farthest west it does tend to assume that rôle, as of heathy banks and commons and sandy pastures near the sea. Happily its correct name seems now once again to be *Rosa spinosissima*[1], but not so long ago that highly apt name had been infuriatingly replaced by the much less significant *R. pimpinellifolia*. But whatever its correct name may be, and both names, oddly enough, were given it by Linnaeus, the unique combination of its low-growing shrubby habit, its dense covering of straight and very sharp thorns, and its profusion of exquisite white flowers followed by almost black hips, is sufficient to distinguish it at a glance from any of its native relations.

Though all of these British natives, and many more besides, can be easily enough struck from cuttings, the best of them, with their numerous varieties, are to be had, at a price, from the Sunningdale Nurseries[2]. Besides, in most cases, the type from which the varieties have evolved, there are at least twenty varieties of *Rosa pimpinellifolia*, not to mention the hybrids which include Frühlingsgold and Frühlings-morgen, available from this one source; of the sweet briar group, apart from the type itself, *R. eglanteria*, there are only the various hybrids, fourteen in all but including the aforementioned Fritz Nobis and at least one highly characteristic copper-coloured Penzance hybrid; there are only one variety and two hybrids of the dog rose proper, *R. canina*; *Rosa mollis*, in the variety *pomifera*, is represented only by Wolley Dod's rose; and in the case of *R. sherardii* the type only is listed. Of this large number we have introduced deplorably few. We grow only four of the first group, but those four do at least include the two best that I have yet encountered, the tall and vigorously suckering variety *altaica*, the flowers of which are, like those of the type, single and very pale creamy yellow, and the relatively low-growing and large-flowered variety Lutea Maxima, whose flowers this time are as resplendently yellow as those of a buttercup. Of the second group we could until this winter boast only the type, which we grow primarily for its scent; but we have very lately invested also in the blush-white Double Marbled Sweet Briar and are on the waiting list for what is unquestionably the most striking of the Penzance strain, because it alone among roses vies with the deep and blazingly vivid orange tones of its other parent, *Rosa foetida* (or

[1] [The name *R. spinosissima* has since been again rejected for *R. pimpinellifolia*.]

[2] [This nursery regrettably is now closed.]

lutea) Austrian Copper, the hybrid Lady Penzance. Of the remainder, I admit to our shame, we possess not a single one.

And so, positively last of all, to the foreign species, which between them comprise so large a number and so wide a variety that no garden short of the very largest could accommodate more than a fraction of them. I have, as a matter of fact, already mentioned in passing over half of my own personal favourites: namely the two Austrian Briars; the vigorous climbers *Rosa filipes* and R. *multiflora cathayensis*; the best of them all, *Rosa glauca*, and the starry-flowered white R. Paulii and its slightly less rampant pink variety Rosea; and last but not least, the most familiar of the garden varieties and hybrids of our own British natives. But that still leaves, among the relatively few of which we have first-hand experience, at least half a dozen which are, in this brief and fragmentary survey, still awaiting recognition. We may as well start, because they are deliberately the predominant factor of this group in our garden at Shepreth, with those with flowers in various shades of yellow, which we grow either in front of the mellow red façade of the house or as specimen bushes in the wild garden. First and perhaps foremost among these, on account partly of the abundance of its pale yellow flowers and partly of its exceptionally delicate foliage, comes *Rosa hugonis*, which we grew originally in the form of four standards at either end of the two narrow borders flanking the cobbled path from the front door to the wrought-iron gate. The slender stem of one of the four snapped, however, before an unusually gusty south-west wind, which only at the front finds its way through the old railings into any part of the garden. Since we were unable to replace this one casualty, we moved the survivors into a more sheltered and less prominent corner of the garden and replaced the whole quartet by weeping standards of Albéric Barbier. Two others of the yellow species, the richly-coloured *Rosa ecae* and the pale primrose R. *primula*, we planted at each corner of the front façade, the former close to the Austrian Yellow, the latter behind *Potentilla fruticosa* Katherine Dykes. Unfortunately *Rosa ecae* soon produced an exceptionally vigorous sucker, which looked so promising that we allowed it to prevail, and when the sucker turned, apparently, into another R. *primula* we again permitted it, for the sake of symmetry, to have its own way. And the two last of the yellows which we grow, the rather deeper-coloured hybrid between *Rosa hugonis* and R. *sericea* known as R. Cantabrigiensis and the almost buttercup-coloured and marvellously floriferous *Rosa xanthina spontanea* Canary Bird, the habit of which is much lower and more spreading, we long ago planted, not far apart, as specimen bushes in the wild garden.

Of the pink-flowered species we have but three, *Rosa microphylla*, which is a low-spreading bush with leaves like an acacia's, the grey-leaved R. *soulieana*, and R. *webbiana*, which some fifteen years ago won an Award of Merit, somewhat surprisingly, for its hips. The former two, which have only just arrived and which we know, therefore, only in the gardens of friends, have their allotted stations among the miscellany of pink shrub roses at the foot of the wall behind the kitchen garden; the third, which was astonishingly sent us in error instead of the wholly different R. *nitida* that we had ordered, is nevertheless, though slow to put on growth, showing every sign of earning its place, for its single and very pure pink flowers rather than its hips, as another specimen bush in the wild garden. And of the true reds we have never attempted to grow more than one, *Rosa moyesii*, whose sumptuously rich blood-red flowers are followed by vivid scarlet hips the shape of a wine flagon. This particular rose is in fact such a favourite of ours that we found space for two specimens of it in different but adjacent parts of the garden. One of the two, as I said a while ago, is one of the shrubs and small trees which we have planted beneath the immemorial elm at the back of the herbaceous border; the other, along with two more species that I have not mentioned in this particular context, R. *glauca* and R. *pimpinellifolia altaica*, constitutes yet one more of the specimen bushes in the wild garden. But in both cases, I strongly suspect, we were sold a pup. Besides the true R. *moyesii* there are in commerce two others of the group, one a hybrid named R. High-downensis and the other a spontaneous variety called Geranium, the colour of both of which is immeasurably inferior to that of the type, and I remain convinced that in both instances we were inadvertently fobbed off with one or other of these. Fortunately the type, for which there is no adequate substitute, survives in fair quantity, with a variety of spontaneous hybrids, at Ardtornish.

That leaves us, at long last, with only one variety of rose yet to mention, but that one is something very special in the way of a curiosity. Inspired by an enormous bush of it at Ardtornish, which had been knowingly so planted as to enhance its particular merits, we decided some years back to introduce to Shepreth, as a feature of the little lawn across the road, a solitary specimen of *Rosa sericea pteracantha*, the last name of which means, for the benefit of those who have no Greek, 'with winged thorns.' This particular species is indeed probably unique among the roses in two quite different respects. In the first place its relatively insignificant white flowers have only four petals, and secondly it is to be grown, if at all, not so much for the sake of its flowers or even its hips as for that, as its name implies, of its thorns, which are not only enormously broad and winged at the base but pure blood-red in colour. The secret of its successful siting, which we learnt at Ardtornish, is simple enough: plant it, all on its own, in a position where the lowering sun can shine through and irradiate its ruby thorns.

So much by way of very partial introduction to the rose family, and all that remains to be said is that, of the numerous families that go to make up a tolerably well-stocked garden, the only one that can begin to compete with it in sheer variety of form and colour is that of the *Ranunculaceae*. In my own judgment, which is patently reflected in the great majority of English gardens, the *Rosaceae*, even if only marginally, get the better of the duel.

CHAPTER 7

A Second Miscellany

OF the twenty families that follow the *Rosaceae* in the British flora rather less than half, once again, would have much relevance to an average British gardener. As in my first miscellany, however, more than one of them, and the first two in particular, would be fully entitled, if only there were no limit to the length of this book, to a chapter on their own. From my point of view I confess that it is a relief to have to get over the most arduous part of the necessary task of selection early in the chapter, because then, unless I prove too sparing in my use of the axe, we should be able to relax a little.

Immediately after the *Rosaceae* come the *Crassulaceae*, of which by far the most important genera, in our climate at least, are Sempervivum and Sedum. I do actually grow in one of my sinks, simply because I was given it by a well-known gardener, a single member of another genus in the family, namely *Rosularia aizoon* from Asia Minor; but apart from scarcity value, it is nothing but an inferior blunt-leaved houseleek with a laxer and sparser inflorescence. The houseleeks themselves are, in my opinion, second only to the saxifrages, which come next in botanical order, as trough or sink plants. Since, like Sedums, they are virtually indestructible, we always collect a bit of any we see abroad, and I have also bought a number of species or varieties which we have never come across from Alan C. Smith, who is something of a specialist in the genus. The majority of the former are probably only subspecies or varieties of the widespread and polymorphic *Sempervivum tectorum*, which incidentally has become completely naturalised, I suspect for centuries, on the crumbling old brick wall at the back of our kitchen garden. But they also include two or three rather different forms of the best of them all, however common it may be in the Alps, the little cobwebby *S. arachnoideum*, and, I hope, though it has not yet had time to flower since I collected it last autumn on the Italian side of the Matterhorn, the big yellow-flowered *S. grandiflorum*, which we had photographed some years before in the Gran Paradiso. The best of those we have bought, on the other hand, which of course we bought for precisely this reason, are those with red or purple rosettes, notably the red form of *S. reginae-amaliae* from Kambeecho (though I never heard of such a place nor can transliterate into Greek) in the Epirus. The genus Sedum obtrudes itself into our garden in the form of the bright yellow *S. acre*, an abundant British native, which makes great patches all over the low-pitched pantile roof of the little barn on the north edge of our rose-garden, girdles the stone balls on top of the brick pillars on either side of our wrought-iron front gate, and from these two separate points of vantage peppers the vicinity with prodigiously fertile seed. It is a major menace in the sink almost vertically beneath the first of these stations, and it can become too much of a good thing on the cobbled paths in the front; but it is such a cheerful little invader that we let it be wherever we safely can. Why we have never introduced from Ardtornish its delicate pale pink counterpart, *S. anglicum*, which abounds on almost every seaside rock in the neighbourhood, I simply cannot think; nor can I think why this particular native of western Europe should have been called English when, as a rapid glance at the *Atlas* will show, it is far more widespread and abundant both in Wales and on the western coasts and islands of Scotland. We did, however, two or three years ago, bring down from one of the hills near Ardtornish, where it too is abundant, a single tiny seedling of *S. rosea*[1] or roseroot (whose English name explains its Latin except for the gender of the adjective), which is now waxing fat and fleshy in the border in front of the house. The place of *S. anglicum* is taken in our garden by the beautiful form of *S. album* aptly called Coral Carpet, which sows itself from the sink in which I grow it almost as freely, but not, owing presumably to its lower elevation, so far and wide, as *S. acre*. Then we have another fine Sedum for a sink in the Siberian *S. populifolium*, a miniature deciduous tree, less than a foot high, with deeply toothed fleshy leaves and white flowers faintly flushed with pink, which are alleged, by those with keener noses than my own, to smell strongly of hawthorn. And finally, my strictly alpine sinks can now boast two others collected, well past flowering, on our recent tour, which I fear will probably turn out to be only the yellow *S. reflexum* and the typical white form of *S. album*, much taller and more robust than Coral Carpet, both of which are thoroughly naturalised all over the place in England.

All the foregoing, like all the houseleeks, belong, if not to the trough or sink, at least to the rock garden. But there are, of course, others whose proper place is the herbaceous border. We have never grown

---

[1] [Re-named *Rhodiola rosea*.]

either subspecies of our own native orpine, *Sedum telephium*, which also grows, apparently quite wild, near Ardtornish, chiefly because we dislike its mauvish tint of pink. But we do grow, near the front of the herbaceous border, another with flowers that are even uglier, if only because they come in one large flat corymb rather than in several rounded cymes per stem, namely the typical form of *S. spectabile*, and every time it comes out I vow shall be the last. Quite close to it in the same border there are, however, two others which I thoroughly recommend, though again for their stems and leaves rather than their flowers. Both of them are varieties of the relatively tall *S. telephium maximum*, the leaves of which are, as usual, decidedly fleshy. In var Atropurpureum both stems and leaves are deep purple, while in var. Variegatum the glaucous leaves are variegated with silver and the stems are pink. I doubt whether I personally should ever have bought any of these last three, because I think there are many better herbaceous plants than any Sedum, but to the donor of at least the last two we are genuinely, and I hope lastingly, grateful.

The *Saxifragaceae* have become slightly less formidable than they used to be since they sloughed off into families of their own the *Hydrangeaceae*, including Philadelphus, Deutzia and, presumably, Carpenteria, the *Escalloniaceae* and the *Grossulariaceae*, or currants and gooseberries; but they are still quite formidable enough. Although the saxifrages themselves come first in their own family, I prefer to leave them till last and deal first, and very briefly, with several other and much smaller genera, namely Astilbe and Rodgersia, Heuchera, Tiarella and Tellima, Bergenia and Kirengeshoma, which still fall within the attenuated family. Unfortunately the pretty Astilbes and the even prettier Rodgersias, both of which bear so marked a resemblance to Spiraeas that it is a constant surprise to me that they do not belong to the *Rosaceae*, are not really for us; even the nurserymen who stock them and whose objective must therefore be to sell them to a credulous public agree that both need a moist and preferably peaty root-run, which is easy enough to provide at Ardtornish but impossible at Shepreth. Two years ago a friend did actually give us two Astilbes, the clear pink spiky Finale and the spraying white Professor van der Wielen, and by dint of planting them near the foot of a leaky rain-water pipe we have not only kept them alive but successfully flowered them. But how long they will survive I would not care to guess and I know that there is nowhere else in the garden where we could repeat the performance.

The genera Heuchera and Tiarella are a good deal easier to accommodate, if only because they seem to have no marked preference for peat. Every species of Heuchera and all but one of Tiarella come from North America and are absolutely hardy; they all have heart- or kidney-shaped leaves, attractively lobed and toothed, and those of some of the Tiarellas turn bronze or red-brown in the autumn; and all bear elegant sprays of flowers in the summer, those of Heuchera usually red or pink, those of Tiarella normally white. For some reason, probably because we are excessively liable to the prolonged spring droughts that they are known to resent, the Heucheras, which gaily sow themselves everywhere, and particularly between the paving-stones, in my mother-in-law's garden in Rutland, have never done at all well here. But the Tiarellas are a different matter. *T. cordifolia* spreads rapidly by stolons to make broad patches, while *T. wherryi*, which is not stoloniferous, makes compact and tidy clumps. And as for *Tellima grandiflora*, another North American with tall spikes of hanging bell-shaped flowers which turn from yellowish to reddish-green as they go over, it has so flourished in the narrow dusty bed at the foot of the wall near the mulberry tree that we have gratefully moved a whole lot of it to another almost equally inhospitable site.

Goodness knows why, but the insufferably coarse genus of Bergenia is apparently coming back into favour. If you grow Bergenias for their leaves you can have no appreciation of elegance and if for their flowers you must be colour-blind. I will say for the favourite of olden days, the Asiatic *B. crassifolia*, which was evidently so popular in western Europe that it is locally naturalised in France and Austria, that it is prepared to grow and flower where almost nothing else would; that, indeed, is the one reason why we have never disturbed the colony of it which on arrival we found growing in the arid bed at the foot of the high north-east-facing wall of the house. And I will also say for the hybrid, I know not of what species, called Ballawley, which, when we should have known better, we were beguiled by a catalogue into buying, that from the distance it puts on quite a good show of autumn and winter colouring. But for all that, I would gladly sacrifice all the beloved Bergenias in the world, and this time they all come from various parts of the Far East, for the sake of the sadly neglected *Kirengeshoma palmata*, the only species of its genus, which is as exclusively Japanese as its generic name suggests. If Bergenias neither need nor merit description, Kirengeshoma certainly merits it and may well need it. It is quite a tall herbaceous perennial, anything from two to four feet high, and, as it spreads quite rapidly, it can easily be multiplied by division. Its shallowly lobed and toothed cordate leaves, which extend up the purple stem in diminishing size and with progressively shorter stalks, are not only shapely but differ equally radically from those of any Bergenia in their delicate texture. Its five-petalled flowers, which come in threes to each peduncle, are campanulate in form, nearly two inches across, and of a characteristically soft shade of yellow. And as a final virtue, it seems perfectly easy in cultivation. At any rate it spreads happily and flowers freely in the narrow raised bed, admittedly well mixed with peat and leaf-mould so that we can grow Trilliums, on the shady side of our little courtyard. Since it is to be had from Hillier's and probably elsewhere, I cannot understand why the only garden where I have ever seen it apart from our own is Waterperry.

And now for the genus Saxifraga itself, starting with a single sentence of statistics. There are over three hundred species of saxifrage known in the world, not to mention countless hybrids, both natural and man-made, and one hundred and twenty-three of the three hundred are native in Europe, fifteen of them in Britain. Of these last, at least half a dozen are worthy of a place in the garden, though two of the best of them, the tufted and prodigiously floriferous yellow *S. aizoides* and the creeping purple *S. oppositifolia*, demand damper conditions than we could possibly provide at Shepreth without elaborate artifice. The two grow together in great profusion, along with an abundance of another of the best in the shape of the mossy saxifrage, *S. hypnoides*, on a mountain cliff near Ardtornish, the botanical riches of which (including another and rarer mountain saxifrage, *S. nivalis*, as well as the mountain avens, *Dryas octopetala*, and a large colony of the holly fern) I seem to have been the first to discover. But of the mountain's saxifrages, which actually number five because *S. stellaris* also grows here and there on damp stony patches, the only one I have ever transplanted into the garden, but that with remarkable success, is *S. hypnoides*. For three other mountain species you have to go to the west of Ireland. Another of the mossy group, *S. rosacea*, at least in the form in which I have seen it near Black Head in the Burren, makes a cushion, compact enough for a sink, which sometimes covers itself with pure white stalked flowers. But the other two, both Pyrenean and typical of the Lusitanian element in the flora of western Ireland, are plants of a very different appearance. St Patrick's cabbage, *S. spathularis*, is like a smaller and neater version of London Pride, of which it is actually one of the parents, while kidney saxifrage, *S. hirsuta*, is easily distinguished by the fact, suggested by the combination of its Latin and English names, that it has slender-petioled kidney-shaped leaves covered on both sides with long hairs. If you want an effortless inspection of these two, plus the vigorous and variable hybrid between them, I should advise you to go to the Ballaghbeama Gap in County Kerry, where, on the cliffs immediately beside the road, all three are abundant. I do actually grow a very small form of *S. hirsuta*, which however I collected in the Pyrenees rather than in Ireland, in one of my shadiest sinks, and I should be pleased to grow *S. spathularis*, the showier but less delicate of the two, beside it. And last of our native species, but perhaps the most beautiful of them all, comes the relatively widespread meadow saxifrage, which however, unlike the last three, is virtually absent from Ireland, *S. granulata*. Its fully double variety Flore Pleno, with white flowers almost an inch across, is occasionally to be seen in English gardens, but I have never yet seen the type in cultivation. It is locally abundant not far from Shepreth, and next time I see it, which you can hardly fail to do when it is in flower, I think I shall try propagating it from a few of the bulbils, its means of overwintering, which it produces in the axils of its basal leaves.

When we cross over to the Continent all but the specialist is bound to get lost in the welter of often critical species and varieties. As I regard saxifrages, as I said earlier, as the best of all sink plants, I have collected a good many in my day, chiefly but not exclusively in the Alps, and I am always guided by the simple principle of taking those which, even if I do not know their names at the time, strike me as the most distinct. I started as long ago as 1937, when I climbed to the summit of Mount Olympus and collected in the last few hundred feet, which consist of an almost vertical ravine, a young non-flowering plant of what subsequently proved to be either *S. grisebachii* or possibly *S. sempervivum*. Coming from nearly ten thousand feet it was naturally perfectly hardy and it settled down contentedly, grew in breadth and in due course flowered, in the sink, mentioned twice in Chapter 3, which I eventually had to leave behind in Cambridge. Its rosettes were silver hummocks, and the thick flower-stem, which rose some six inches from the middle of a rosette and at first nodded but gradually straightened up, bore on the lower half little reflexed leaves so densely covered in dark red glandular hairs that the whole effect was purplish-crimson and on the upper a series of solitary little pink flowers in large hanging hairy crimson calyces. Then there was a long interval during which I had no garden and gave what little I collected to the Cambridge Botanic Garden. But soon after our marriage in 1954, when we bought our present home at Shepreth, we started again in the Maritime Alps. It was in the rocky cliff-girt valley behind Ventimiglia that we collected, in early January, what has proved to be perhaps the best of all my sink plants, the saxifrage once given specific rank as *S. lantoscana* but now dismissed in the *Flora Europaea* as only a variety of *S. callosa*, alias *lingulata*. It seems, in common with all the rest of the saxifrages that we have collected in the Alps, to appreciate the north aspect that I have given it. At any rate if flowers lavishly, and when it is doing so it makes its more familiar and glamorous neighbour, *Ramonda myconi*, look almost coarse. On the other hand, since it was in full flower when we saw it, we contented ourselves with photographing it rather than collecting another of the same group, presumably, to judge from its distribution, *S. crustata*, which we saw on our first visit to Asolo. It was growing on roadside rocks less than a quarter of the way up Monte Grappa, whence I hope to add a young plant of it to our collection when we return to Asolo with the family this coming Easter. The next we actually imported, this time from the Col du Lautaret, is one which I imagine is more familiar to alpine gardeners, although I see it is not obtainable even from Ingwersen's, *S. bryoides*. It was doing nicely in another north-facing sink and beginning to form the tight mossy hummock from which it produces solitary cream-coloured flowers spotted with orange or red, when I carelessly allowed it to be suffocated by a rampant plant of alpine lady's mantle whose seed I must unwittingly have brought in with the gritty soil around its roots. We have now, however, removed the murderer to a chink in the paving where it can do no more harm and replaced its victim by another collected farther to the east on our recent tour. Indeed on that tour I ran amok among the saxifrages, collecting six very distinctive species in one lazy day up the Val Maggia behind Locarno. Two of the six, both of which grow on the rocky mossy banks of the little river near the top of the valley and may therefore be hard to accommodate in a sink, were at least easy enough to identify. One, *S. cuneifolia*, belongs to the same group as St Patrick's cabbage and looks, at least until it flowers, very like a diminutive version of it, while the other, *S. rotundifolia*, is a giant of a plant, with huge lax rosettes of rather hairy crenate leaves of the shape implied by its name. The remaining four are all plants of bare rocks or cliffs. Two of them which, where and when we saw them, invariably consisted of a single rosette up to four or five inches across, will prove when they flower, I fancy, to be *S. cotyledon* and *S. mutata*, both with large lax panicles of numerous white flowers. One, which has narrow lime-encrusted leaves, at present looks very like the aforementioned *S. crustata*, but in that case must be at or beyond the westernmost limit of its known range. And the last, which makes large compact cushions of inch-wide glaucous silver-margined rosettes, has me at present, unless it be *S. paniculata* alias *aizoon* itself, completely defeated. All I can say is that I have just been out to look at them and all six are still, towards the end of a damp winter, looking extremely pleased with the English way of life. I can only hope that, as and when they see fit to flower, I shall be able to name the last four with greater confidence.

Most of the saxifrages we have bought rather than collected for ourselves belong to a section I have not yet even mentioned, undoubtedly the best of all for sinks and troughs, the so-called Kabschias; but I will deal first with the only two that I can remember buying that do not belong to this section. They both came, like most if not all of my Kabschias, from Joe Elliott, and they belong to quite different sections. The first is much the smallest and neatest of the Euaizoonia or 'Silvers,' the group I have just been talking about, and forms little carpets of tiny silver rosettes with sprays of creamy-white flowers only about three inches high. Since it comes from Monte Baldo, it is listed by Mr Elliott as *S. aizoon baldensis*, but its correct name should, I think (and what's in a name anyhow?) be *S. paniculata* var. *baldensis*. And the second, a garden hybrid of the Pyrenean *S. umbrosa*, is listed as *S. primuloides* Elliott's Variety; in view of which Elliott's own description of it ought to be authoritative: 'Surely one of the ten best alpines. Like a small neat London Pride it grows with perfect ease in any soil or situation, making neat concise clumps of glossy, emerald foliage, and throwing out each spring a deep rosy veil of a myriad tiny blooms.' I think the first sentence goes a bit far, and I should be interested to hear what Mr Ingwersen, who sounds to have an even neater and brighter variety of his own, might have to say about it. But there is no denying that Elliott's Variety is a first-class sink plant.

And so to the best of all sink plants, the saxifrages of the Kabschia section, which are, I regret to say, the occasion for one of my rare lapses from my horticultural principles: I have always bought varieties or hybrids rather than true species and I have never regretted it. All make miraculously tidy, compact, rounded and slowly expanding cushions, composed of numberless sharp little leaves, nearly always silver-grey, and your choice of one in preference to another can depend on two factors only: the colour of the flowers and whether you like them one or several to each stem. My own selection, for what it is worth, has been, and would be again, first two varieties of *S. burseriana* (now called in the *Flora Europaea*, maddeningly but no doubt correctly, *S. burserana*), the snow-white Gloria and the clear sulphur-yellow Sulphurea; then, in logical order rather than order of preference, the bright yellow Faldonside, the shell-pink Jenkinsiae (which reads in other catalogues *jenkinsi* or *jenkinsii*) and the deep pink Cranbourne among the relatively straightforward hybrids; and finally two hybrids of a rather different type, the buff to apricot Iris Pritchard, which is somewhat laxer in habit than the foregoing and carries several flowers to a stem, and the dark purplish Riverslea, which makes flat rosettes and looks to me to have some of the *grisebachii* group's blood in its veins. And to complete this recital of their merits, I ought to add that most, if not all, of these have red or crimson stems and that several, notably Gloria, are already in the last week of January beginning to show their slowly unfurling petals.

A word about one last saxifrage which grows in our garden and I shall have finished with the family. Each year, on the rounded top of the low brick wall that separates the drive from our rosebeds, there reappears, wholly uninvited and unencouraged, quite a large and scattered colony of the annual native *S. tridactylites.* Owing, presumably, to under-nourishment, it is never more than two inches high, and for the same reason its little three-fingered leaves are bright red to offset its pretty but tiny white flowers. It is not a plant that I would ever have dreamt of deliberately introducing into our garden as I earlier today dreamt of introducing its very close relative *S. granulata.* But since it is there already, I find myself each year watching for its reappearance and each year I am quietly pleased to see it again.

After a brief excursion into a peaty marsh, which we possess only at Ardtornish, to admire the *Parnassiaceae,* including our own native grass of Parnassus, *Parnassia palustris,* surely one of the most delicately lovely of all our wild flowers, we move from my sinks into the shrubbery, which again we do not possess, to consider the *Hydrangaeceae.* I shall deal very summarily with the most popular of the Hydrangeas themselves, the so-called Hortensias (actually the all-sterile variety *hortensia* of the true species *H. macrophylla*), because, whether the nature of the soil turns them pink, blue or purple, they are further illustrations of the type of plant that we prefer to admire in gardens other than our own at Shepreth. As Aristotle wrote long ago in the last book of his *History of Animals,* where he was discussing the thorny question of the sexes of bees, 'Gaudy and showy bees, like gaudy and showy women, are good for nothing.' This particular brand of Hydrangea is emphatically a gaudy and showy bee, which steals the eye from the subtler charms of its less gaudy and showy neighbours. They look fine both at Ardtornish itself, where the vast vista of green and grey can well accommodate a few splashes of vivid colour, and in the tiny front gardens of the neighbouring crofts, where there is usually nothing much else, unless perhaps a hardy Fuchsia or two which can stand up to the competition, from which to distract attention. But we would rather be without them at Shepreth, which lies in any case far from the blue sea that is, in my own mind, their essential accompaniment. There we grow instead only two leggy, shrubby, lace-cap species in *H. sargentiana* and *H. aspera villosa,* both of them mauve, and one truly indispensable climber, already mentioned at least once in this book, in the lusty, self-clinging, white *H. petiolaris.* The only reasons why we do not grow the closely related *Schizophragma hydrangeoides,* which anyhow strikes me as very little if at all superior, are first that we have advisedly given up the only really suitable wall for it to the true Hydrangea, and second that I have good reason to believe, from my experience in my college garden, that it is by no means so easy a customer. And much the same goes for *Hydrangea quercifolia,* with its elegantly lobed and toothed leaves, which last summer we saw and coveted as a climber on the relatively low boundary wall of the National Trust's beautifully designed and imaginatively planted little garden at Tintinhull in Somerset. On the other hand, the most graceful and lovely of all the shrubby Hydrangeas, *H. paniculata*, we have perforce, and this time very reluctantly indeed, to leave to Ardtornish for the very simple reason that it would not for one moment tolerate our dry and chalky soil.

We naturally grow a good many species, hybrids and varieties of the genus Philadelphus, the mock oranges or so-called Syringas (and God knows when, how or why the correct botanical name for lilac first came to be attached to members of quite a different family), and it would be tedious to retail them all even if, as I cannot, I could remember them at this time of year. We inherited four or five mature bushes of the good old *Philadelphus coronarius*, which even I can smell, mainly strategically sited in unpromising positions in the hedges around what was then the pig-sty; but the rest we have had to introduce from sundry quarters for ourselves. My own favourite among the larger of them is one which we were given only as an unrooted cutting without a name attached, but evidently, like all the rest, it roots very obligingly from young wood. It bears a profusion of unusually substantial and regular pure white single flowers, and I can only think, from descriptions I have read of P. *inodorus* var. *grandiflorus*, that this is what it must be. Another large pure white one that we grow is the popular double Virginal, for which I used to have a passion on account again of the perfect button-hole regularity of its flowers but which, with my increasing preference for single over double forms, I am not now certain that I should buy again. More to my present taste are two varieties, both of which we grow in key positions in the garden, of the cross between the pure white P. x *lemoinei* and the magenta-spotted *"P. coulteri"* called P. *purpureo-maculatus*. Actually we grow the type of this last, a relatively low, lax and spreading bush, at the back of the herbaceous border, but it suffers in comparison with its varieties, in this garden at any rate where they all do equally well, by being much less floriferous. Of our two favourite varieties, each of which eventually attains a height of about eight feet and bears an abundance of white flowers smudged with purple at the centre, Beauclerk is slightly the tougher and stockier and Belle Etoile the more gracefully arching. But beautiful, fragrant and wonderfully easy as nearly all the larger varieties of Philadelphus may be, the one which perhaps suits our own peculiar horticultural taste best of the lot is the little P. *microphyllus*, a miniature version of the others, only about four feet tall when fully grown, with all its parts in perfect proportion to its diminished stature and with dainty pure white flowers giving off a fragrance out of all proportion to it. This alone is small enough to join the select band of yellow and white shrubs in the bed along the front of the house.

I am afraid I have nothing to say about Deutzias because we only grow one of them, a late-flowering white one, on the sunniest corner of the bed which houses our hybrid musk roses under the Judas tree, and we have both forgotten not only its name but even where we acquired it. Nor is there very much that anybody could say about Carpenteria, since it is a genus of only one species. That one species, however, *C. californica*, is as beautiful as any shrub in cultivation in this country outside a heated greenhouse. We first saw and fell for it, many years ago now, in an inland garden in cold Cumberland, where it was trained up the sunny wall of a courtyard and thus, unless my memory misleads me, comfortably exceeded what is usually said to be its maximum height of eight feet. But it was not until we quite lately acquired our own little sunny and sheltered courtyard, previously a corner of the farmyard adjoining the garden, and had cleared it of docks and nettles, paved it and built up with three courses of bricks the raised beds that now surround it that we ordered one for ourselves and planted it, free-standing, on the south-facing side. There, though it is still barely a yard high, it flowered prodigally last summer and justified the lavish praise I have just bestowed on it. Its evergreen leaves are narrowly lanceolate, tapering at each end and delicately veined, bright green above and glaucous beneath, and its flowers, which come in clusters of four or five, are more than two inches across and rather like those of a single white rose with a bunch of long and prominent golden stamens in the middle. I do not believe that it is really tender, indeed probably less so than the best Cistuses which superficially it somewhat resembles, but it does apparently demand, not unreasonably seeing where it comes from, a maximum of sunshine and a minimum of smog; and that at least we can and do give it.

I shall hurry over the *Escalloniaceae* as I hurried over the Deutzias, but this time not so much because I know very little about them, which I do, as because I have very little use for them and am not a whit grieved that without the protection of a warm wall, which we would accord to a host of plants in preference to Escallonias, they would probably capitulate to their first typical Shepreth winter. Even in the wide open spaces of Ardtornish, where there would appear long ago to have been a formal bed of them but where in these days they have every chance of concealing their modest charms in the jungle, they contrive to displease me every time I pass their way. And the same is to some extent true, if to a markedly lesser extent, of the great majority of the *Grossulariaceae*, which, as I suggested earlier, mean to me, whatever they mean to a professional botanist, nothing more nor less than the genus Ribes. Many years ago now, soon after we had demolished the pig-sty and poisoned the dense forest of nettles all around it, we went so far as to buy, even though neither of us had much liking for it, a young bush of the ever popular *Ribes sanguineum*, with the intention of planting it, such was our faith in its iron constitution, in the dreariest, darkest and least nutritious corner of the whole garden on the other side of the sunk path from *Rosa* Paulii. Our faith, of course, was justified, and what is more, there is no denying that its profuse racemes of deep pink flowers, even if they do smell of tom cats, go a long way in late spring and early summer towards lightening the local gloom. But for all its popularity and that of its various colour forms, it has one marked superior among the currants, while one of the gooseberries is in a different class. The currant is the much less familiar *Ribes odoratum*, a rather lower and laxer shrub, with much smaller and neater leaves, which colour splendidly in autumn, and hanging racemes of bright yellow and genuinely fragrant flowers. And the gooseberry is the so-called Fuchsia-flowered gooseberry, *Ribes speciosum*, which, solely because I have only seen it on the very warm and sheltered wall of the kitchen garden at Ardtornish, I had always assumed to be only half-hardy until I learnt from Notcutt's catalogue this morning, when for the first time I began to look into the matter seriously, that it is 'good on walls, especially in colder areas.' If the beautiful creature is really as unfamiliar as I suppose, it merits some description. It is a bristly evergreen which, on a wall, can attain a height, as it has at Ardtornish, of at least eight feet; its small, usually three-lobed leaves, almost round in outline and never much more than an inch wide, are of a rather dark and glossy green; and its bright red flowers, which hang in rows along the branches, really do look rather like tiny Fuchsias, with a long, thin, bell-shaped tube, four small petals, and four red stamens protruding nearly an inch from each tube. All in all a most engaging plant, for which I think we must now set about finding a space on a nice warm wall at Shepreth, definitely one of the 'colder areas.'

After three families that are of no use for horticultural purposes unless you have a bog in your garden (and, with the honourable exception of purple loosestrife, not a lot of use even then), we arrive at three families in a row which have a notable contribution to make to horticulture. First come the *Thymelaeaceae*, which probably mean to most gardeners, as they certainly mean to me, primarily if not exclusively the genus Daphne. There are two British representatives of the genus, both of which, if for different reasons, richly deserve a place in even a small country garden. The old and much loved friend of cottage gardeners, *Daphne mezereum*, which has been in cultivation in England for over four hundred years, is presumably too familiar to call for either description or praise. Incidentally, its status in most of its British localities is in these days open to grave doubt, and the reason for that is plain enough. Obviously, when our remote ancestors wanted to grow it in their cottage gardens, they simply walked off to the nearest native locality and dug one up, with the inevitable result that, as it became an ever commoner feature of country gardens, it became progressively scarcer in the wild. On the other hand birds have a great taste for its red berries, as they have, for instance, for currants, and birds neither stay put nor, so far as I know, suffer from constipation. And anyhow, according to Dioscorides (Book IV, Chapter 148), 'the fruit of it, as much as 11 grains being drank, do purge.' And so the plant began to reappear, and is still reappearing, in new places. It has actually done so in our garden. We evidently put our original plant of it in too dry a spot, for I can only think that that was the reason why, after three or four years, it suddenly died an untimely death. But by that time a considerate bird must have eaten and digested one of its ripe berries and excreted it from an old plum tree in the semi-wild garden into a damper and much more auspicious site. There it had already made a healthy little bush at least a foot high before we even noticed it, and there it should before long be showing pink. *Daphne mezereum*, of course, is deciduous and flowers before the leaves appear; but *D. laureola*, the status of which as a British native is not in dispute, is an evergreen, with long lanceolate leaves, broader above the middle, leathery and dark glossy green, and short racemes of yellowish-green, long-tubed flowers. It is surprisingly common in shady hedges around Shepreth and we have introduced three or four seedlings into the garden, where it has the great virtue of growing and flowering happily, where almost no other shrub except *Mahonia aquifolium* would even survive, at the very foot of trees or, as it does in nature, in perpetual and deep shade. And moreover it has the additional merit, as has *D. mezereum*, of coming into flower in the dead season of February.

The foreign Daphnes, most of them either European or from the Far East, are on the whole less accommodating in that they demand a fair amount of moisture as well as sharp drainage, not always an easy combination to provide. Long ago, even before my parents moved to Cambridge, my father successfully grew and flowered in his desiccated garden at Ely a little low-growing bush of the most beautiful and fragrant of them all, the pure pink *D. cneorum*; but I have long since forgotten, if indeed I ever knew, the secret of his success. Possibly the very similar *D. striata* from the Dolomites might prove easier in our soil. But for our own part we have hitherto ventured to introduce two only, which, however, no one could deny are doing uncommonly well. *D. odora* Aureomarginata, which comes into flower even earlier than our two natives, has survived many winters in the front row of the winter garden, where it is purposely sheltered, as the catalogues recommend, from the north and east; but then the variety is reputedly, if unaccountably (for this is certainly not the case with most variegated varieties), hardier than the type. And the spreading *D. blagayana*, whose cream-coloured flowers this time do not open until March, has actually exceeded its allotted space in the lime-free Norfolk soil in my enormous trough. It is a pity that, through sheer ignorance, I have not already pegged down one or two of its procumbent branches, which actually bend down to touch the soil and so invite such treatment, for this simple method of propagating the plant is apparently most effective when its branches are little more than a year old.

The family *Elaeagnaceae* comprises only three genera, Elaeagnus itself, Hippophae and Shepherdia. Of this last, which consists of silver-leaved shrubs to be distinguished from members of the other two genera by their opposite leaves, we have no first-hand experience whatever, nor can I find it in any of the obvious catalogues. Even Elaeagnus is a comparative newcomer to our garden, for only in the last two or three years have we come alive to its potentialities and by that time there were none but the most inhospitable sites left for it. We have, however, quite lately acquired, and planted, *faute de mieux*, in the border under the high east-facing wall of the house (the self-same border at the northern extremity of which, where it narrows to almost nothing, grows our aforementioned colony of Bergenia) a couple which, despite the rigours of their life there, are promising rather well. The first is the deciduous North American *E. commutata*, not only the oval and untoothed leaves of which are, as its name suggests, shining silver on both sides, but also, more surprisingly, the outside of the little clustered tubular flowers, the inside of which is yellow, and, most surprisingly of all, the egg-shaped fruit. The other is the evergreen *E. pungens* Variegata, a much more familiar plant, which is sometimes not unreasonably acclaimed as the best of all yellow-variegated evergreens. Its leaves are longer and narrower than the other's, again untoothed but rather elegantly undulating at the margins, dark glossy green above, like a bay tree's, but with a large and irregular bright yellow blotch, sometimes covering most of the surface, in the middle, and dully glistening silver beneath with an orangey-brown midrib. Though I have no great liking for yellow as opposed to white variegation, I have to admit that, especially in the colourless depths of winter, this is a very valuable acquisition. But for all that I remain unshaken in my long-standing conviction that the best of all the *Elaeagnaceae* is sea buckthorn, *Hippophae rhamnoides*, which is widespread on our coasts and almost certainly native from Kent to Northumberland. It is a small tree with a trunk rather than a shrub, usually not more than eight or ten feet tall, and with its shorter and leafless side branches often consisting only of a long sharp spine. Its very narrow and almost stemless leaves are reminiscent of some of the willows, grey-green above and silver beneath, its flowers are negligible, but its drupe-like fruit, which are its chief glory and are often in September thickly clustered around the leafless part at the base of its slender side-branches, are of a soft shade of orange which blends to perfection with the silver undersides of its leaves. As I mentioned in passing when I was writing about roses, we grow six little trees of it, three on each side of a taller tree of *Koelreuteria paniculata*, at the end of the mown path down the wild garden that we have hedged with Fritz Nobis, and it richly earns so prominent a position. But it is the occasion for another of my rare warnings. Since the tree is dioecious, since naturally only the female trees bear berries, and since even they will not oblige unless they are fertilised, you must grow at least two of them together, one of either sex, and if you see fit, as we did, to grow half a dozen, then you should specify in your order, which we absurdly omitted to do the first time, when I at least should have known better, that you want five females and one male. Thank Heaven for one thing: they have no more use for monogamy than the Turks.

The third of this trinity of successive families is somewhat more complex because, out of about three dozen genera, it contains as many as five which may be of concern to a normal gardener. I shall say nothing about Clarkias or Godetias, because they are not only all annuals but distressingly ugly annuals at that. But that still leaves the willow-herbs, or Epilobium, the evening primroses, or Oenothera, and the Fuchsias. Our own experience of willow-herbs is largely confined to common native garden weeds. We could easily be overrun at Shepreth, particularly in the beds in the semi-wild garden, by two of them, the broad-leaved willow-herb, *E. montanum*, and the stoloniferous short-fruited one, *E. obscurum*; but fortunately the very different roots of each come up *in toto* with a gentle pull at the base of the flower-stem. At Ardtornish on the other hand, where there are several others that I need not name, the verges of the drive are rapidly being taken over by the rather attractive little prostrate mat-forming alien from New Zealand, *E. brunnescens*, which has already proved itself the most rapid and effective colonist of the remotest mountain cliffs that has ever been introduced into these islands. If, in fact, you take the unsolicited advice that I proffered earlier in this chapter and go one summer day to the Ballaghbeama Gap in County Kerry, you will find it growing on the same cliffs, and in the same profusion, as the native Pyrenean saxifrages and will have difficulty in believing that it is not as genuine a native as they are. But the only willow-herb I have ever deliberately cultivated is another New Zealander, *E. glabellum*, which I bought on spec from

Joe Elliott and planted at the back of a sink. It did as it should and produced numerous stems clothed in oblong bronzy-green leaves and topped by a long succession of proportionately large creamy flowers. But though, as Mr Elliott says, it is not invasive, which is a great deal more than can be said of many of its race, it was at once too tall and too decumbent for a sink, and I moved it this past autumn to the front row of the newly designed white corner at the entrance to the semi-wild garden. One other true willow-herb and one very close relation I have so far done no more than ineffectually covet. The latter is the pale rose-pink form of the abundant rosebay or fireweed, once *Epilobium* but now *Chamaenerion augustifolium*[1], which I saw for the only time in my life on the same visit to our friend's garden in Cumberland as first introduced us to Carpenteria and of which, though the said friend is embarrassingly generous, I was firmly refused a small piece 'in your own interest.' Evidently, like its normal magenta form or like matrimony, it is so pervasive as not by any to be enterprised, nor taken in hand, unadvisedly, lightly or wantonly. And the other is the exquisite alpine *E. fleischeri*, which we saw late last September on the moraine below the glacier at the head of the valley just above Arolla in the Valais, where it was superabundant but in such full and spectacular flower that, alas, I could find no seed that was anywhere near ripe.

Of the evening primroses I have never ineffectually coveted any, but we do very effectually grow three, the first as one of the yellow punctuations in our blue borders, and the other two side by side in our second substitute for a rock garden, the broad flat sunbaked bed on the south-facing side of the larger and warmer of our two greenhouses. The first came to us, under the name of *Oenothera taraxifolia*, from my sister's garden in Kent, where it sows itself, as it does here, all over the place. But, as is so often the case with the less familiar garden plants, she had been given it and the name together by somebody else who had had them from somebody else, and so on. One thing is certain, that it cannot be *O. taraxifolia*; for that is a synonym of *O. acaulis*, which is, as its name suggests it should be, only about six inches high, whereas the plant in question is at least two feet. And of one other thing we have by now become tolerably confident, that the evening primrose in commerce that it most resembles is the one called Fireworks, which however is not such a pale primrose yellow, nor does it turn so pink when it begins to fade, as the plant which my sister was given by somebody else who had had it from somebody else, and so on. Happily we are in no such doubt about the identity of the other two, both of which are dwarf species, not more than nine inches high, and perhaps

---

[1] [At present it is back to *Epilobium*!]

better suited to the level bottom of a valley in a large rock garden than to the front of a herbaceous border. One is the relatively familiar *O. missouriensis*, which, from a rosette of long, entire and tapering glossy green leaves, produces trailing leafy stems nearly two-foot long and huge typically yellow flowers, fully three inches across, which, again typically, open towards evening. And the other, which we had from the Plantsmen only last summer under the name of *O. caespitosa macroglottis* and which may well be one of their own admirable introductions, is the grey-and-white counterpart of *O. missouriensis*, with irregularly toothed and equally tapering glaucous leaves with a broad white midrib and enormous white flowers, fading to pale rose-pink, held on short upright stems. We were so taken with this latter when we first saw it that we came away with two, one of which we planted out in the open ground near the greenhouse while the other, for fear that it might not be quite hardy, we have kept through the winter in a pot in the cold frame. Need I add that the former, having withstood twenty degrees of frost without protection, is already at the end of January throwing up a clump of tiny grey-green leaves while the latter looks to be at death's door?

As with Pelargoniums, so with Fuchsias, we grow some of the best of the modern hybrids, such as Ting-a-Ling, Flying Cloud and the tubular orange Thalia, in the cool greenhouse and plant them out, when the frosts seem to be over, in the tubs in our little formal courtyard. But once again these are not my concern in this book. We do, however, grow two out of doors which are, and though they are both cut right to the ground in all but the very mildest winters, they never fail to break through again and to grow so fast that by the end of the summer they have once more made sizeable and very floriferous bushes. One of them, which we have long grown at the red end of the herbaceous border, is the familiar variety Riccartonii of *Fuchsia magellanica*, the plant which makes the wonderfully colourful hedges in the west of Ireland. The other is unfortunately a mystery plant, with smaller and much more graceful flowers of a uniform and pure pale shell-pink. We first saw it, more than ten years ago now, in the front garden of a little croft near Sanna Bay, on the very tip of the Point of Ardnamurchan, and when we paused to admire it the old lady who lived there gave us a cutting. Like all Fuchsias it rooted without trouble, and our original plant of it, which now stands at the foot of the climbing rose Reveil Dijonnais in the sunny little border immediately beside the back door, has given rise by the same means to more identical children, most of them now in other people's gardens, than I could possibly count. Unfortunately I can find nothing that sounds remotely like it either in the *Dictionary of Gardening* or in any catalogue I can lay hands on. It is fair to add that, though most people are as captivated by its delicate charm as we were, a few with a passion for the flamboyant modern hybrids dismiss it as anaemic. But with that proviso, if anybody cares to come to Shepreth to collect a cutting, possibly even a rooted cutting, they are more than welcome.

After a wearisome wade through bogs and ditches in search of sundry dreary plants, of which only the gigantic Chilean and Brazilian Gunneras could be of the slightest interest to a gardener in his right mind, and next a scramble up a tree to pick a bit of misteltoe, we win through to the dogwood family, the *Cornaceae*. It is here that the gloomy Aucubas belong, commonly but erroneously known as laurels, and you are welcome to keep or destroy, according to your taste, any you are unfortunate enough to have inherited from your grandparents. And here belongeth also the striking *Davidia involucrata*, 'sometimes referred to,' according to Hillier's, 'as the "Dove Tree",' but known to me from youth up as the handkerchief tree. Since, without felling a mature tree to make way for it, we could not, regrettably, find room for it at Shepreth, we come at once to the genus Cornus. And here there are grounds for even greater regret. Forty years ago my father tried at Ely to grow a specimen of the lovely *Cornus kousa*, and twenty-five years later we experimented at Shepreth with the even lovelier *C. florida rubra*, but they were both dead in a trice, and we have reluctantly concluded that, if we are ever to succeed with any of this group, it can only be at Ardtornish, where, since we can never get there till the end of June, they will waste their sweetness, which is actually the one virtue they lack, on the desert air. But that is not quite the end of the matter. Apart from our own locally abundant native dogwood, *C. sanguinea*, which we found well established beside the french windows from the dining-room and have hesitatingly suffered to abide there for the sake of its dark red twigs in winter, the yard-high bush of *C. mas* that we planted fifteen years ago at the back of the winter garden is now fully five times that size and smothers itself in February and March with tight little clusters of bright yellow flowers, while *C. alba* Sibirica Variegata, alias *C. Elegantissima*, which, during our time here, we have planted in three separate parts of the garden, is a thing of beauty throughout the entire year. In the winter its shiny red bark warms the cockles of the heart, and when the pointed oval leaves appear they are of a soft grey-green with a broad margin and irregular markings of silvery white. It is so relatively small a shrub, not more than six feet either way, that room could be found for it in almost any garden of almost any dimensions, and for all-the-year-round effect there is no reliably hardy plant of comparable size to beat it.

And that, since the genus Hydrocotyle, which consists anyhow of horticulturally worthless bog and waterside plants, has again been subsumed under the *Umbelliferae*, leaves only the *Araliaceae* to be considered in the present chapter. And since I know nothing whatever of the genera Panax, Acanthopanax, Dendropanax, Echinopanax, Nothopanax, Oreopanax, Pentapanax or even Pseudopanax, let alone Tupidanthus, that means to me nothing more nor less than the genus Hedera or ivy. There is, as a matter of fact, one other member of the family, *Fatsia japonica*, which, since it has won an Award of Garden Merit for its enormous, glossy, evergreen, deeply-palmate leaves, I certainly ought to know and possibly ought to grow. But with my passion for botanical nomenclature, all that I can claim to know about the Japanese Fatsia, which apparently derives its name from the noises the natives make when they talk about it, is that it was happily married to the Irish ivy, *Hedera hibernica*, and gave birth to a child, a handsome tribute to intermarriage, with the seductive name of × *Fatshedera*. So I shall cling to ivy as ivy clings to the wall. And all I really know about even ivies is that they root as freely as they creep, and are on that account so easy to scrounge off neighbours and friends, that if only you have the patience you can acquire, without incurring the expense of as much as a postage stamp, as many varieties as you could possibly desire, though maybe not their names with them. We ourselves must grow at Shepreth, chiefly trailing over the low brick fronts of the built-up beds in the courtyard and on the Dog's Grave, at least a dozen different forms, of which we have certainly bought less than half. I have a leaf of all the more striking in front of me now and shall amuse myself more than you by trying as I write to identify them in Hillier's catalogue. But at least I can guarantee by way of recompense that any whose names I succeed in tracking down are plants which combine a distinguished character with an easy disposition.

The largest-leaved of those we grow, and also much the most vigorous, is *Hedera canariensis* Variegata, alias Gloire de Marengo. The leaf I have before me measures exactly four inches each way, is cordate in outline and entirely without lobes, and its matt dark green surface gives way in places to pale grey-green and then, especially around the margins, to creamy-white. The plant is too vigorous and on too large a scale for the courtyard but, particularly in winter, our carpet of it lightens the darkness of the Dog's Grave. A smaller and neater white-variegated form, which we do grow with great effect in the courtyard, is *H. helix* Tricolor, the leaves of which measure this time two and a half inches each way, are decidedly three-lobed with the central lobe much the longest, and change abruptly in colour, a hard irregular line dividing each colour from the next, from dark grey-green in the middle, first to very pale grey-green, then to white, and finally to a very narrow margin of rose-pink. This one makes a compact clump quite unlike the sprawling mat of the last and, since its leaf-stalks are also deep pink, it is on all scores one of the best. And we have another in the courtyard with exactly the same colouring, but it is only half the size, and instead of having three nearly equilateral lobes it has five long and very'narrow ones tapering to a point; though I cannot find it in any catalogue I possess, it looks like a *tricolor* variety, if such a thing exists, of *H. helix* Caenwoodiana. Then come three more, all in the courtyard and strikingly different one from the other, which are variegated with yellow rather than white, and this time there can be no doubt of the identity of any of the three. The most familiar is the variety of *H. helix* called Buttercup, Golden Cloud or Russell's Gold, the small and regularly five-lobed leaves of which are of a softer texture than the rest and are often yellow over almost the whole of the surface. *H. colchica* Dentata Variegata has rather larger leaves with markedly wavy margins, and their glossy upper surface is bright green liberally suffused, this time without any hard lines of demarcation, with primrose yellow. And last of this trio, but perhaps the most distinctive of the lot, is *H. helix* Discolor, or Minor Marmorata, whose short leaf-stems are again pink and whose small three-lobed leaves are basically very dark green overlaid with deep purple, but with a delicate tracery of light green veins and an irregular oblong patch of yellow in the middle which is here and there blotched round its edges with deep pink. And that leaves four last whose leaves, but for the lighter veining in every case, are uniform green, but which for all that could hardly be more distinctive. One defeats me; the five regular and unusually obtuse lobes of its two-inch leaves, its beech-green colouring and its pale yellow veins correspond with no description I can find. Another, whose scarcely lobed leaf-margins are wavy in both dimensions and whose rounded bases just overlap, may or may not be *H. helix* Deltoidea. The third, whose tiny very dark leaves are so crumpled and crimped that we call it the parsley ivy, sounds as if it could only be *H. helix* Conglomerata. And about the last of all there can be no shadow of doubt whatever; its three long, unequal, outstretched fingers and its two shorter ones deflexed like a Chinaman's moustache point unmistakably, as fingers should, to *H. helix* Digitata. I could go on to describe yet others, all varieties of *H. helix*, which are less interesting because less distinctive. But that, I hope, is enough to persuade any who think of ivy as nothing but a killer of trees and a crumbler of mortar to think again. And anyhow, though they are members of the same order of the *Umbellales* as the dogwoods and the ivies, it is high time we moved on to consider the *Umbelliferae* on their own.

CHAPTER 8

Umbelliferae

I HAVE only two excuses for devoting a whole chapter, albeit a short one, to the umbellifers, first that I am particularly fond of many of the British members of the family, and second because they include, among other good things for the garden, two superlative genera in the humble Astrantia and the proud Eryngium. At this point, in fact, I shall forsake objective statistics in favour of personal predilections.

The summer-long succession of umbelliferous flowers on the grassy roadsides is as characteristic and beautiful a feature of the English landscape as that of the rosaceous trees and bushes is of the hedgerows. The first of them to come out, which is also the most plentiful and on that account, among others, the most showy, is the familiar cow parsley or Queen Anne's lace, *Anthriscus sylvestris*. We have such a passion for it that we give it free rein in the wild garden and never scythe the grass until it and, a little later on, the ox-eye daisies are past their prime. Incidentally, I once had, at very short notice before a dinner party, to improvise a vase of flowers for the drawing-room. I went out into the garden and in less than half a minute picked, in the corner by the mulberry tree, three or four flowering branches of cow parsley and six or seven stems of the ordinary Solomon's seal. This impromptu combination, rapidly arranged in a black china bowl, proved so effective that I have since seen it plagiarised in the house of one of the evening's guests.

Next in the unbroken sequence come the pale pink hedge parsley, *Torilis japonica*, and, especially in damper places near rivers, the poisonous hemlock, *Conium maculatum*, which can be immediately recognised both by its taller stature and more upright habit and, the patent origin of its specific name, the lavish dark red spots on its stems. Then comes Angelica, *A. sylvestris*, which, though perhaps less plentiful than the others in any one place, is nonetheless the most widespread of the lot. And last of all, along with the coarse white hogweed, *Heracleum sphondylium*, and the equally coarse yellow wild parsnip, *Pastinaca sativa*, surely the most repugnant of our many inedible root vegetables, comes, in our part of the country at least, the delicate burnet saxifrage, *Pimpinella saxifraga.*

These seven species represent only a tiny fraction of Britain's umbelliferous plants, of which Dandy lists no fewer than forty-six genera. But they are the ones which any ordinary Englishman can hardly fail to notice, even though he may not have the faintest idea of their names, as he drives around the countryside on Sunday afternoons. In some quarters of the British Isles, or else in situations other than roadsides, there are, of course, many others which are equally prominent but of which, to avoid excessive tedium, I shall take only a random selection. To continue with the habitual inhabitants of roadsides, there are, for instance, near the Norfolk coast two other species, both yellow, which are locally more obtrusive than any of the rest, namely alexanders, *Smyrnium olusatrum*, which is alleged on the highest authority to have been first introduced into this country from southern Europe as a pot herb, and another which should never have been put to culinary purposes but may again have been misguidedly imported from the same area, namely fennel or *Foeniculum vulgare.* And likewise, in the northern half of this island, you can often see roadsides thickly colonised by sweet cicely, *Myrrhis odorata*, yet another alien pot herb, apparently most appreciated by the Scots, introduced from the mountainous areas of southern Europe or, much more locally, and in my experience particularly along the road from Selkirk towards Moffat, the yellow-leaved chervil, *Chaerophyllum aureum*, the original importation of which from the usual source I need no longer bother to explain. And finally, if you are very lucky, you might on a northern roadside, for instance in Westmorland or Glen Lyon, come across a colony of a plant to which I referred in a quite different context in the Introduction, to wit spignel, meu or baldmoney, *Meum athamanticum*, which is not only, for once, under not the slightest suspicion of being anything but native but also, with its exquisitely fluffy and finely divided leaves and its disproportionately broad white umbels, is considerably the most attractive of any of the members of the family that I have yet mentioned.

So much for the more characteristic of roadside species, and now for those that belong essentially to other types of habitat. The typical representative of those which opt for shady places is one that people often find it hard to believe to be a member of the family at all, sanicle or *Sanicula europaea.* Keble Martin's suggestion that it is confined to 'woods on basic soils' is conclusively refuted, if it needs refuting, by the fact, which I mentioned in Chapter 1, that it was one of the plants which we inadvertently brought into our fern border, along with the roots of either the beech or the oak fern which were the object of the exercise, from the very near neighbourhood, anything but basic, of Ardtornish. Some British native plants, but not very many, would seem to be totally undiscriminating in their demands. The first example that occurs to me, but not necessarily the best, is that of the little white purging flax, *Linum catharticum*, which, although by no means ubiquitous in these islands, is to all appearances as happily at home on the chalk downs around Shepreth as it is in the acid peat-bogs around Ardtornish. The corresponding species among our native umbellifers are, I suppose, either pignut, *Conopodium majus*, the raw roots of which, as I have lately been told by one of their number, are greatly appreciated, as part of their staple but unofficial diet, by schoolboys from Mill Hill and Highgate, or else wild carrot, *Daucus carota*, the origin of our least unpalatable root vegetable. In and around gardens the predominant species is ground elder, *Aegopodium podagraria*, which is commonly called, with scant respect for the customs of bygone clerics, either goutweed or bishop's weed, and which I would be thankful to be told, after several ineffectual experiments, how to eradicate. In salt-marshes, apart from the rare and beautiful sea hog's fennel, *Peucedanum officinale*, from either side of the Thames estuary, the typical representative of the family, itself by no means common and in Britain restricted to the coasts of southern and eastern England and of South Wales, but a member of a very distinctive genus of which more anon, is the slender yellow-flowered annual *Bupleurum tenuissimum*, alias, significantly, smallest hare's ear. And last, but certainly not least, come the three native inhabitants of our sea-cliffs and beaches, which deserve a paragraph or two on their own.

Samphire, *Crithmum maritimum*, is, as Shakespeare knew, essentially a plant of the cliffs.

> 'How fearful
> And dizzy 'tis to cast one's eyes so low!
> The crows and choughs that wing the midway air
> Show scarce so gross as beetles; half-way down
> Hangs one that gathers samphire, dreadful trade!
> Methinks he seems no bigger than his head . . .'

It is not, as a matter of fact, necessary to hang half-way down a cliff if, as seems improbable, your trade is gathering samphire. I do not actually know for what purpose it was gathered at all, nor can I find any book to enlighten me, but I could surmise that, since its leaves are exceptionally fat and fleshy and its fruit corky, it was in its day yet another of our umbelliferous pot herbs.[1] And in the case of the next on the list,

---

[1] I am wrong, but not too badly wrong, in this surmise. I have just learnt from the *Shorter Oxford English Dictionary*, of all unlikely sources of botanical or horticultural information, that its 'aromatic, saline, fleshy leaves are used in pickles.'

Scottish lovage or *Ligusticum scoticum*, there can be no shadow of doubt. It too prefers cliffs and cliff-top crevices to beaches, but its distribution in Britain is, as a rapid glance at the two maps in the *Atlas* will show, so radically different as almost precisely to complement that of samphire. Whereas the latter is tolerably frequent up the west side of this island and all along the south coast of Ireland but is virtually unknown in Scotland except on the cliffs of southern and western Galloway, Scottish lovage takes over, as both its Latin and its English names suggest, exactly where samphire gives out and is to be seen on almost the whole of the Scottish and Hebridean coasts, including, if very locally but not so locally as the *Atlas* might lead you to suppose, the peninsula of Morvern where Ardtornish lies.

I have left sea holly, *Eryngium maritimum*, till last of all not only because, along with the leguminous *Oxythopis halleri* which I tried to describe in Chapter 5, it would fill an honourable and unchallenged place in my personal list of Britain's ten most beautiful plants, but much more because it is one of the only two British representatives of a genus on which I shall be expatiating soon enough. The other, which is much rarer in this country and which I have only once seen here, on the almost vertical grassy bank immediately below the fort on Plymouth Hoe, is the white-flowered, widely-spreading and much less spectacular *E. campestre*, which we long ago introduced into our garden, with unqualified success, from Provence. Unlike samphire and lovage, sea holly itself inhabits the beaches rather than the cliffs and rocks, preferably but not necessarily sandy beaches, where it is sometimes associated, by one of nature's happiest combinations, with the pink sea bindweed, *Calystegia soldanella*. The British range of sea holly, incidentally, is much more like that of samphire than that of lovage, and it will be a sad waste of your time to look for it on any of the apparently suitable sandy beaches on most of the mainland of Scotland.

I said that these were the last of our native umbellifers that I was going to mention, but while writing the last few sentences I have, as I only too often do, changed my mind. There are two more that are not only characteristic of fens, which I have hitherto stupidly omitted, but also especially characteristic of our East Anglian fens. One of the two, whose only other native British congener I have already mentioned in passing, is milk parsley, *Peucedanum palustre*, which, as you could soon enough discover from any book about British butterflies, is the only food plant of the swallowtail, and the restricted range of which is alone responsible for the extremely limited distribution of the butterfly in England. And the other is *Selinum carvifolia*, which seems to have no common name, but which apparently has in these days only two British stations, both of which are very well known to me because both happen to be in Cambridgeshire. I will not dilate on these two plants at the present moment, beautiful as the delicately pinnate foliage of each may be, for two simple reasons. First because, if only we had a suitably damp patch in our garden, we should waste no time at all in importing the former, and second because, even if we do not grow, for the selfsame reason, *Selinum carvifolia* itself, we do grow, more for the sake of its elegant fern-like leaves than its flat and wide white umbels, its congener *S. tenuifolium*, seedlings of which we were originally given, with that name attached, by the head gardener of my college garden, and which seems to adapt itself more readily to the arid and alkaline conditions of south Cambridgeshire. The very existence of this latter was until lately stoutly denied by my old friend Professor Tutin, only alphabetically the second of the oft-quoted holy trinity, who used to maintain, at least until the publication under his aegis of Volume II of the *Flora Europaea*, that the genus Selinum was monotypic. He need only come to our garden, as he not infrequently does, to learn the error of his former ways.

And so, not before the time is perhaps long overdue, let us go out into the garden, where, apart from my two favourite genera of Astrantia and Eryngium, we grow, so far as I can remember without barging ahead of you, only about half a dozen species. I exclude, of course, all those unpalatable vegetables and pot herbs, such as carrots or parsley, which every normal English gardener feels himself under an obligation to his wife to try to grow, and shall mention, and very briefly at that, only those which we ourselves, for purely decorative purposes, see fit to cultivate. Three of them grow, more by chance than by design, in close proximity one to the other at the same end of the herbaceous border, namely the aforementioned *Selinum tenuifolium*, a really lovely and sadly neglected border plant, the taller, narrower and even more beautiful copper-leaved fennel, and the erect yellow-flowered hare's ear called *Bupleurum falcatum*. These last two sow themselves so freely that I am constantly giving away young plants of both, neither of which is often seen in gardens, to our gardening friends. The Bupleurum is or was possibly a British native, and our own seed of it came originally from what was already by then its only surviving station in these islands, a roadside near Ongar in Essex, where I am told it has lately been exterminated by road-widening operations. It is still, however, widespread and unquestionably native in southern, central and eastern Europe, whence its seed could be easily enough collected.

Talking of which, I hope this coming summer to have another European species of Bupleurum flowering in one of my stone sinks. It is certainly a Bupleurum and I judge from the *Flora Europaea* that it is probably the Pyrenean and Alpine subspecies *gramineum* of *B.*

ranunculoides. It is, however, only six inches high at the most, whereas the *Flora* suggests that the species in question can be as tall as sixty centimetres. But whatever it is, I gathered its seeds at the very end of September 1969, along with those of *Oxytropis pilosa, Astragalus alpinus* and many other lovely things, on the Italian, or north-eastern, side of the Little St Bernard, which is in my opinion the most interesting of all the passes through the western Alps. On the Italian side it appears to be pure limestone, the richest of all rocks for field botanists in Europe, whereas exactly at the frontier on the top you move on to an obviously acid rock which is dominated floristically by acres of ericaceous plants such as bearberry. In fact the only desirable plant I saw on the French side of the pass, and naturally added its seeds to my collection, was another native of the Pyrenees and Alps, the graceful little *Astrantia minor*.

The only other umbelliferous plants, apart from cow parsley, which we entertain for decorative rather than culinary purposes are the aptly named giant hogweed, *Heracleum mantegazzianum*, a native of south-west Asia which is by now widely naturalised throughout this whole continent, and the almost equally gigantic but much more delicate European species, *Angelica archangelica*, which is the plant used in confectionery and a liqueur. Both are prodigiously prolific and are often to be seen thoroughly established on, for example, waste places in and around London. We grow them both together, by design this time, on a primeval ash and rubbish tip at the foot of a tall elm near where the pig-sty used to be. Though both of them can be dangerously invasive, they are both so stately and architectural as to merit a place in all but the smallest of gardens.

Fond as I am of the genus Astrantia, there is not, as a matter of fact, a great deal to be said on the subject. The *Dictionary of Gardening* lists, apart from synonyms which obviously do not count, only seven species, one of which, *A. major*, as I should perhaps have mentioned earlier, is established in about twenty British counties, notably near Stokesay Castle in Shropshire, where it has been known for well over a hundred years. Furthermore, unless you happen to be a specialist, there can be little point in growing more than five out of those seven. *A. carinthiaca* is merely a more local subspecies of the widely distributed central European *A. major*, from which it can only be distinguished even by an expert by the length of its bracteoles, while *A. gracilis* is only a slightly larger version of *A. minor*. We ourselves have hitherto grown, all in the semi-wild garden, only three, namely *A. major* itself, *A. maxima*, and the variety *rubra* of *A. carniolica*. Our version of *A. major*, which came from I forget where, has pure white flowers and pure pale green bracts, but I am glad to say that the very day after I collected seeds of *A. minor* on the French side of the Little St Bernard I added, from hay-fields on top of the hills just north of Belley in Savoie, those of a form of *A. major* with pale pink flowers and bracts veined with pink. *A. maxima*, like the last, is anything from one or two feet high, but can easily be distinguished by the facts that its radical leaves have only three lobes instead of five and its flowers are of a distinctly deeper pink. And finally, *A. carniolica*, including the red variety that we grow, is usually much smaller and its flowers more clustered. Incidentally, two of these three[1] are natives of, among other places, the Alps, and I cannot wait to add a third in *A. minor* from the same source, for it is without doubt the most graceful of the lot.

The Eryngiums, according to the *Dictionary*, offer a very much wider choice, twenty-eight as opposed to a mere seven species, though how many of these are in commerce I am bothered if I know. The Plantsmen, who are a good source of several of the more interesting and beautiful, at present list thirteen, not all of them in the *Dictionary*. That is, I think, rather more than the number we grow, all but one of them in the blue borders. The exception is *E. campestre*, which, as I mentioned earlier, we imported from Provence and probably quite unnecessarily, for that reason alone, planted in the bed at the foot of the highest and warmest wall in the garden. We have never tried our much more beautiful native, *E. maritimum*, because until lately I had not realised that it is apparently content to grow in gardens far distant from the sea. Certainly we did know that the same was true of another and almost equally ravishing inhabitant of our shores, the silver-leaved yellow horned-poppy, *Glaucium flavum*, which, from seed from the shingle beach at Cley in Norfolk, has settled down most contentedly in our light and chalky soil and sows itself almost too freely in the adjacent asparagus bed. Not nearly so freely, however, to return to the subject in hand, as the biennial *Eryngium giganteum*, alias Miss Wilmott's Ghost, which, in common with another biennial in the form of the caper spurge, invades our gravel paths in such force that Faith has lately been reduced to repulsing it with weed-killer. It is a great pity that this particular Eryngium, the seed of which we originally had from our gardening friend in Cumberland, seems so hard to come by in this country; for with its blue flowers and its large involucral leaves that are so silver that they shine in the dark, whence presumably its familiar name, it is just about the loveliest of them all. Other tall ones with large conical or cylindrical blue heads, all first-rate garden plants and as hardy as rocks, are *E. alpinum* itself, a familiar feature of alpine meadows, the Pyrenean *E. bourgatii* and, perhaps best of all, the offspring of *E. giganteum* whose other parent

[1] [*A. maxima* is Caucasian.]

seems to be unknown called *E.* × *oliverianum*. Equally beautiful are the slenderer much-branched *E. planum* from central and south-eastern Europe, the round flower-heads of which, also blue, are much more numerous, and *E. variifolium*, which we had from the Plantsmen and which they rightly describe as possessing 'a striking rosette of cut, polished, green leaves, boldly veined with cream.' And last among those we grow or have grown come two that are quite different. *E. decaisneanum*, formerly *pandanifolium* from Montevideo succumbed to its first winter here before we had time to appreciate anything beyond its rosette of long, sharp-pointed, prickly and glaucous leaves. But the Mexican *E. agavifolium*, which we acquired at the same time and which is likewise said to be only half-hardy, is with us still. It, too, produces an evergreen basal rosette, this time very dense and composed of very narrow leaves with a regular margin of spines, and its tall upright stems, with similar but diminishing leaves up the lower part, bear, on short branches, many little round white flower-heads. All in all, though possibly more curious than beautiful, it makes a striking foil to the rest of a wonderful band.

I am afraid that once again, as in my chapter on the *Leguminosae*, I must just add a paragraph or two by way of postscript, and once again they are prompted by my return home after a few weeks away. But this time they will be even shorter than last.

To begin with, I was reminded, by going a round of my sinks to see how our recent imports from the Alps were standing up to the winter damp, that we grow another umbellifer which I had forgotten to mention. It is a curious little plant from Chile called *Azorella trifureata* (formerly *Bolax glebaria*). Its rather dark green leaves are three-fingered, jagged and leathery, and out of these it makes a compact evergreen cushion which differs in colour and constitution from that of any other cushion plant I know. Its umbels, which are composed of four little yellow flowers apiece and nestle snugly in the middle of the rosettes, are on that account, I admit, by no means conspicuous. But nevertheless it is an attractive and unusual little plant, as different as it could possibly be from that other miniature and uncharacteristic umbellifer, *Bupleurum ranunculoides*, which I look forward to associating with it in the same sink.

My second afterthought is occasioned once more by looking through our photographs, which have reminded me of a magnificent herbaceous plant, alleged to be perfectly hardy in this country and possibly even to be found in commerce, in the shape of the giant fennel, *Ferula communis*. We came upon it growing in quantity, along with an exceptionally fine form of *Artemisia arborescens* of which more anon, on the flat top of the mountain nearest the town of Rhodes, Mount

Filerimo. But whereas we successfully transplanted four or five very young seedlings of the Artemisia back to Shepreth, we could find none of the Ferula that were small enough to move. Would that some nurseryman might show the initiative to introduce this noble plant to the British horticultural market.

CHAPTER 9

Euphorbiaceae and Polygonaceae

AFTER the families so skimpily covered in the foregoing chapters the *Euphorbiaceae* come as a welcome relief. Leaving out of account, as the former at least fully deserves, both the perennial dog's mercury and the annual mercury, the spurges proper included in Dandy's *List of British Vascular Plants* number a mere seventeen, of which six are marked as aliens 'known or believed to have been introduced into the British Isles by the agency of man' and of which, the aliens apart, only four at most, those four including the Portland spurge which may be only biennial, are true perennials. The annuals on the whole are, so far as they allow, best ignored. In a south Cambridgeshire garden, unfortunately, it would be impossible for all but the purblind to ignore petty spurge, *Euphorbia peplus*, which, with the possible exceptions of ivy-leaved speedwell and groundsel, is the most prolific of all our annual weeds; while contrariwise every gardener, if there is any such, who numbers the Tintern spurge, *E. serrulata*, among his uninvited guests may consider himself fortunate indeed. Since I refuse to acknowledge the Channel Isles as botanically part of Great Britain, the purple spurge, *E. peplis* as opposed to *E. peplus*, falls virtually outside the scope of this paragraph and must anyhow be impossible to cultivate elsewhere than on a warm sandy beach. And for the rest these annual native spurges, though some of them such as the sun spurge, *E. helioscopia*, or the dwarf spurge, *E. exigua*, have to my eyes a certain charm, scarcely merit deliberate introduction into the garden.

The biennials, if *E. portlandica* really belongs to this class, fare much better; if it does not, then there is only the caper spurge, *E. lathyrus*, left. That the caper spurge should be classed, as it is, as a possible native of England and Wales is perhaps surprising; but be that as it may, there can be no doubt of its garden value. Apart from its traditional but scientifically unproven merit of repelling moles, it is, at all stages of its brief life, a striking and statuesque plant. True that, like at least two other outstanding biennials, *Onopordum nervosum* and *Eryngium giganteum*, it tends to sow itself anywhere and everywhere, particularly in gravel paths; but if only, unlike moles, you can endure its smell, there is not the smallest difficulty either in moving it to wherever you want it or, if you see fit, in eliminating it altogether with a hoe. And if only it were easier in cultivation, the same merits, though on a much smaller scale, could probably be claimed of *E. portlandica*. It and *E. paralias* occasionally grow by nature in Britain as the closest neighbours, the latter by preference in rocky clefts, the former in the sandy sward below. But whereas *E. paralias* sows itself happily in our dry inland garden at Shepreth, *E. portlandica* does no such thing. If only it did, it would bear an attractive if superficial resemblance to a miniature upright form of that fascinating spurge which we imported with the utmost success from the highest mountain in Corfu, *E. myrsinites*.

The prizes for garden merit should, however, go to the perennials, of which the gold medal rightly belongs to one of the three that are unquestionably British natives, *E. hyberna* or Irish spurge. Like *Osmunda* or *Dryopteris affinis* among the ferns, this beautiful spurge is one of the most prominent botanical features of the roadside walls and hedges of counties Cork and Kerry, and its prominence is enhanced when, with the advance of summer, it begins to turn bright scarlet. Although it is by nature an inhabitant of lime-free soils, it seems to be less particular than most of that class of plant and looks tolerably content in our Shepreth garden. Enough has already been said in the last paragraph about *E. paralias* as a garden plant, which leaves, among the genuinely native perennials, only the relatively widespread spurge of southern woodlands, *E. amygdaloides*. Its relative commonness should not, however, be allowed to detract from its charms. A single plant of it which we brought back to Shepreth some years ago from the Cotswolds and planted near some of its foreign congeners holds its own with unobtrusive dignity. And the aliens too are well worth growing. We are perhaps unduly favoured in that three of them, *E. cyparissias*, or cypress spurge, *E. esula* and *E. pseudovirgata*, all grow in local abundance on tracks or roadsides within a radius of, at most, some thirty miles of Shepreth. The cypress spurge is so invasive a plant that no great crime is involved in removing a single root from one of its larger colonies, while an appreciable proportion of the several separate stands of *E. pseudovirgata* is anyhow ploughed up every year. *E. esula*, being locally at least much the rarest of the three, we have left severely alone. The former two, however, make a splendid combination in the garden. Some friends and neighbours of ours, to whom we gave three or four roots of each, planted them in a small bed, *E. pseudovirgata* in the middle, *E. cyparissias* round the edge, and, with nothing else whatever, produced one of the most spectacular and unusual garden effects that I have ever seen. *E. cyparissias*, moreover, like *E. hyberna*, has the admirable habit, especially in an open situation in the poorest imaginable soil, of turning vivid orange-red in the autumn. Unfortunately it is, if possible, even more rampageous in the garden than it is in the wild, but that is a small price to pay for its many sterling merits.

Enough, for the time being at least, of the wild British spurges, both native and alien. As with the British ferns, the spurges have the great advantage of furnishing a garden with a wide variety of shades of green and, as again with ferns, a careful choice of the British species makes an admirable nucleus for a specialist collection. But with the spurges more than the ferns, a judicious mixture of foreigners, chiefly inhabitants of southern Europe, can greatly enhance the effect. Our own favourite is one or other of the two tall and stately species, *E. characias* and *E. wulfenii*, between which, despite the alleged presence of the black eye in the flowers of the former and their extreme proximity in the botanical garden at Oxford, I have always had such difficulty in distinguishing that I heard with considerable satisfaction lately that they had been merged together under the name of *E. veneta*[1]. Both species, if they really are distinct, grow to a height of about three feet, with the top quarter or so of their many miniature trunks covered in long narrow blue-green leaves and the flower-spikes, which hang down in bud like an elephant's trunk but eventually stand stout and erect, composed of numerous dark flowers each surrounded with pea-green bracts. There is indeed something faintly reminiscent of elephants about more than one of the spurge family, notably the trailing and very glaucous *E. myrsinites*. *E. rigida*, which we saw in quantity on the isle of Cos, is almost as glaucous as *E. myrsinites*, but shares the upright habit of *E. wulfenii*, while *E. polychroma* is, in spring, a veritable riot of beech-green and yellow. And if you want a touch of flame among your early spurges, then all you need do is grow *E. griffithii*, especially in the variety called Fire Glow. The only spurge that we deliberately grow which could conceivably be accused, when not in flower at least, of insipidity is *E. robbiae*, now regarded as a subspecies of *E. amygdaloides*, and that has the great advantage, to offset the dullness of its foliage, of providing an indestructibly hardy ground cover in the shadiest of borders. Indeed, with the solitary exception of *E. peplus*, which I have already dismissed as a pestilential weed, I have yet to encounter any single spurge that I would not welcome into my garden.

There are, of course, a great many spurges in cultivation that I have not mentioned and, since beginning to write this chapter, I have taken

---

[1] [The name 'veneta' has now been discarded, the two spurges being regarded as subspecies *characias* and subspecies *wulfenii* of *E. characias*.]

what steps I can to acquire those which we do not already grow. A good source for some of the better and more unusual of them, in case you do not already grow any spurges and should be thinking of investing in one or two, is the small nursery garden started by Margery Fish at East Lambrook Manor. Until her recent death we used, greatly to our advantage rather than hers, to exchange plants with her. The only two I was ever able to send her which she did not already possess were two which we had ourselves collected and which I have already mentioned in this book, namely the form of *Helleborus cyclophyllus* from Corfu and *Euphorbia pseudovirgata* from near home; in return for which we received a variety of good things, notably two rare and exceptionally decorative mints. Fortunately, as in the case of Miss Davenport Jones at Washfield Nurseries, Hawkhurst, Mrs Fish's nursery has, as I said in an earlier chapter, been carried on under her name since her death. Spurges and hellebores were among Mrs Fish's specialities, which is why I sent her the plants I did, and the current catalogue from East Lambrook Manor lists ten of the former. Six of these I have already discussed, but in addition to them there are *E. coralloides, E. dulcis, E.* Lambrook Gold and *E. pilosa major*. I know very little of *E. coralloides* or *E. dulcis*, neither of which, curiously enough, is mentioned in the *Dictionary of Gardening*, nor much of *E.* Lambrook Gold, apparently a spontaneous sport of *E. wulfenii*, except what its name suggests; and, since the plants received were, as usual from this source, very young, I may have to wait a while before my curiosity is satisfied. *E. pilosa major*, on the other hand, a golden-yellow variety of a species which may or may not be native in a wood and neighbouring hedgerows near Bath, is described in an article entitled 'The Showy Garden Euphorbias' by Christine Kelway, which we have preserved from the back number of *Country Life* dated 27th July, 1967, as follows: 'The difference between it' – that is, *E. epithymoides*, which, by the way, is synonymous with *E. polychroma* – 'and *E. pilosa major* is very slight in the early part of the year, though the latter gets longer in the stalk as it ages, and its colour is not quite so intensely bright; this increases during the autumn when it blooms again.' Incidentally, this same article, though it mentions no spurge that I have not already at least named, does contain also the following description of *E. dulcis*: 'The dainty, small-leaved *E. dulcis* is not the showiest of the family; rather is it a plant for the connoisseur, but it comes into its own with brilliant autumn tints.' That sounds to me distinctly encouraging.

Other species which I ordered last autumn from sundry sources, but all of which are awaiting spring delivery, are the aforementioned *E. rigida* from Hillier's, *E. palustris, E. sikkimensis* and *E. mellifera* from the Davenport Jones nurseries, and *E. nicaensis* from the Plantsmen. (I mention the names of the various nurseries to save any reader who sees fit to follow my example the considerable amount of time and trouble that it took me to track all these spurges down.) It is a truly astonishing fact that only one of the five, *E. rigida*, is to be found in the pages of the *Dictionary of Gardening*, which, though it lists and describes no fewer than seventy-eight species, lays an overwhelming and inexplicable stress on those from the Cape Province.[1] I am therefore reduced, in every case except that of *E. palustris*, which I already know in a friend's garden, to quoting or paraphrasing the descriptions in the catalogues in question. *E. palustris* is a taller and less compact plant than *E. polychroma* but resembles it in its showy greenish-yellow bracts in the spring (and bracts in spurges are again what you might be tempted wrongly to call petals), while in the autumn it has the advantage over its rival of delicate if not very spectacular colouring. *E. sikkimensis*, on the other hand, resembles *E. griffithii* in its red young shoots in the early spring and in its graceful red-veined upper leaves, and has the additional merit that its yellow flower-heads persist throughout the summer. *E. nicaensis* sounds like a hardier version of *E. acanthothamnos*, the rounded, spiny, yellow hedgehog which abounds not only in the Middle East but also, for instance, all along the coast of Attica from Athens to Cape Sunium, but which is yet again conspicuous by its absence from the *Dictionary of Gardening*. And finally, all that I can remember about *E. mellifera* from the Davenport Jones catalogue, which I have temporarily mislaid, is that it is appreciably taller, more bushy and less hardy than most of those I have tried to describe.

As usual, I cannot leave the spurges for the infinitely less attractive family of the *Polygonaceae* without a few isolated remarks by way of conclusion.

First, two or three summers ago we saw, in the justly celebrated island garden of Garinish in Bantry Bay, a species of spurge, exceptionally healthy and handsome, which, unless it be the midsummer form of *E. sikkimensis*, I have never been able to identify. One thing is certain, that although it was growing slap in the middle of the district famed, among other things, for the abundance of *E. hyberna*, it is emphatically not that species.

---

[1] It is scarcely worth tampering with the text but, since writing these paragraphs, I have lit upon the solution of this curious little enigma. The contribution on Euphorbia in the *Dictionary* is over the initials V.H. Belated reference to the Preface reveals that V.H. is Mrs Vera Higgins, an authority on Cacti and Succulents. That explains all. The precise figures, which I have just totted up, speak for themselves. Of the total of 78 listed, no fewer than 38, almost exactly half, come from the Cape Province alone (not to mention 20 which are native in other parts of Africa, especially Madagascar and the Canary Isles) as opposed to a mere 7 from Europe. This is of little use to any British gardener other than the specialist with a large heated greenhouse.

In the second place, it may be worth retailing the probably all too familiar fact that the correct name of the popular extravaganza universally known as Poinsettia is *Euphorbia pulcherrima*. This is, of course, even though it is a native of Mexico rather than of the Cape Province, one of the species described in the *Dictionary of Gardening*. Far as I am from sharing the evident predilection of the contributor to that work on the genus Euphorbia for plants which, on his or her own admission, can only be grown in our climate in a heated greenhouse, I am bound to admit, as I am not at all ashamed to do in view of my passion for spurges, that Poinsettia, especially its less vigorous white variety, is among the best of all house plants in cultivation.

And last of all, to ride one of my pet hobby-horses, a word about the name Euphorbia. It is said in the *Dictionary of Gardening* to be the 'name given by Dioscorides to this plant; said by Pliny to have been given in honour of Euphorbus, physician to King Juba of Mauritania.' This is, of course, rubbish. To begin with, it is absurd to suppose that Theophrastus, Dioscorides, or any other ancient Greek writer on matters botanical, sat down to coin a suitable name for a particular plant; they simply took over the popular names which, from time immemorial, the farmers, the shepherds and, above all, the ancient fraternities of *rhizotomoi*, or root cutters, and *pharmakopolai*, or vendors of drugs (all of whom were, of course, innocent of any but the most obvious botanical distinctions), had given to the more striking and distinctive members of the Greek flora. And to go on with, the Greek word *Euphorbia*, as Pliny, though a Roman, should have known better than I do, means, irrespective of the name of an obscure doctor, nothing more nor less than 'good fodder.' But be that as it may, here by way of illustration is what Dioscorides actually tells his readers about the plant, in the translation by John Goodyer first published in 1655 and religiously used by British physicians of the day:

'Euphorbium is a Ferula-resembling plant of Libya, growing on Tmolus, an hill by Mauritania; full of very sharp liquor, which ye men there being afraid of for ye extraordinariness of ye heat do gather thus; binding therefore about ye tree sheeps' mawes washed, and standing àfar off, they pierce ye stalk with long tools; and presently there flows out much liquor as out of some vessell into ye bellies, and being thus pierced, is also sprinkled on ye ground. But there are two kinds of ye liquor: One transparent as Sarcocolla, about ye bigness of ye Ervum, but ye other that is taken in ye bellies is of a glassy look and compact. But it is adulterated with Sarcocolla and glue mixed together. But choose that which is transparent and sharp, but that which is taken by ye tast is very hard to be tried, because ye tongue being once bitten, the burning doth remain for a long time, so that whatsoever is brought them seems to be Euphorbium. But ye first finding out of it is known to be when Juba was King of Libya. But ye juice hath a faculty of dissolving suffusions, being anointed on, but being drank it burns one through a whole day, whence it is mixed with Honey and Collyriums, according to ye proportion of ye sharpness. It is good also for griefs of ye hips, being mixed with an aromaticall potion, and so drank. It doth away scales from ye bones the self-same day, but it behoves them that use it to secure the flesh lying about the bones with linen cloths or Cerats. But some give out that no hurt doth follow upon them that are serpent-bitten, if one having cut ye skin of ye head even unto the bone, do pour in ye liquor beaten small, and sew up ye wound.'

Whatever Sarcocolla, Ervum or Collyriums may be, Dioscorides' Euphorbium is one of the tree spurges of Africa, the juice of which is indeed very potent. I choose to quote this particular paragraph of his Herbal in preference to many others which are perhaps more interesting only because it is for once free from the more horrifying obscenities.

So much for the spurges. And now, at lesser length, for the *Polygonaceae*, which I include in this chapter rather than in one of my so-called Miscellanies simply because, in the British flora at least, they follow immediately upon the *Euphorbiaceae*.

Under the heading of *Polygonaceae*, the *Dictionary of Gardening* first of all tells us that 'the family includes 30 genera of herbs, shrubs or trees', comprising in all 'about 750 species,' and then lists a dozen genera which its authors propose to include. Of these dozen, to betray once and for all my amateur standing as a botanist, I have previously heard only of our own native trio of Fagopyrum, or buckwheat, Polygonum itself, and Rumex, or dock, and of Rheum, or rhubarb. The remaining eight, in case any reader should wish to acuse me of scandalous omission, are Antigonon, Atraphaxis, Brunnichia, Calligonum, Coccoloba, Eriogonum, Muehlenbeckia and Podopterus. The only use I know for Fagopyrum in this country is as pheasant and chicken fodder. The less said about docks the better. Rhubarb, which is frequently established on roadsides, railway banks and waste places in Britain, and of which I have lately come across a single enormous plant, at least half a mile from the nearest croft, on the most isolated stretch of the western shore of the Isle of Mull, ought to be, but is not, on that account included in Dandy's *List of British Vascular Plants*. In cultivation it belongs, of course, along with sea-kale and the globe artichoke, to the kitchen garden. But it is undeniably a sculptural plant, and its red-leaved variety, known in commerce today as *Rheum palmatum* Bowles' Crimson, richly earns, again along with the other two just named, an honourable place in the herbaceous border. And that leaves, among the genera included in the *Dictionary of Gardening*, only Polygonum itself.

As a matter of fact the native British flora includes, besides the three genera already named, a fourth, called Oxyria, which is reasonably enough not included in the *Dictionary of Gardening*. Its solitary representative in these islands, *O. digyna*, is essentially a plant of damp rocky places among the hills, but it is often, as it is near Ardtornish, carried down by streams and rills to altitudes of well under a thousand feet. So, for the matter of that, are several other alpine plants, including the cruciferous *Cardaminopsis petraea*, which is locally abundant on the wide shingle banks of the Scottish Dee as low down as Braemar, the alpine lady's mantle, whose potential usefulness I discussed in Chapter 6, and at least three species of saxifrage all of which are worthy of a place in the garden. Since *O. digyna* is, with the possible exception of a few rushes, sedges and grasses, just about the dreariest of all our arctic-alpine plants, I mention it only to show that I have not forgotten it.

Of the Polygonums proper there are as many as eighteen species native in the British Isles, but of these eighteen only two at most deserve serious consideration as contestants for a place in the garden. Admittedly the alpine bistort, *P. viviparum*, the slender flower-spike of which consists in the upper half of pale pink or white flowers and in the lower half of reddish-purple bulbils, possesses, in its natural habitat of mountain pastures and grassland, a certain charm and curiosity value. But even if I owned the largest rock garden in the country rather than a few stone sinks, I would never dream of introducing it for decorative rather than strictly botanical purposes. If your garden happened to include a shallow muddy pond or a boggy patch of reasonable dimensions, it might just be worth your while to plant *P. amphibium*, whose specific name speaks for itself and whose tolerably showy spike of pure pink flowers is, compared with its congeners, relatively short and fat. And finally bistort itself, *P. bistorta*, which is distinctly local in Britain and rare, if indeed native, on chalky soils, and of which, I am fascinated to read in the somewhat academic Flora of Clapham, Tutin and Warburg, 'the young leaves are eaten as Easter-ledge pudding in the Lake District,' is the only one of our native species which appears to be in commerce in this country, under the varietal name of *superbum*. Notcutt's description of it as bearing 'magnificent light pink "pokers" ' seems to me to err on the side of exaggeration. Personally I would grow it in our garden only if, which heaven forbid, I could think of nothing better to plant in its stead.

Besides our own natives, however, there are, among the four alien species described by Clapham, Tutin and Warburg and the eight admitted by Dandy, at least two which merit a passing mention. As Hillier's catalogue all too justifiably says, '*P. cuspidatum* and *P. sachalinense*' – and where, or where, are the Sachalin Islands, which are apparently the one and only original home of the latter? – 'should be planted in confined areas in large wild or water gardens only. Both usually become pestilential weeds in good ordinary soil.' There is, however, a striking variety of the former, obtainable from the Margery Fish Nursery under the name *Tricolor*, of which we have lately been given an offset and on which Hillier's again justifiably comment: 'Handsome cream and pink variegated leaves on 6 ft stems, superb for waterside or wild garden, shaded from strong sun.' And according to the *Dictionary of Gardening* there is also a variety, var. *foliis pictis*, of another species of this same tall, leafy and dangerously invasive type, *P. chinense*, which is described as having 'some leaves green, others purple, all with V-mark margined on inner side deep purple or blackish-green.' If only you have the space, and if only, which I gravely doubt, you can find it on the market, this variety, unlike the type, sounds well worth trying.

And that leaves only three foreign species which seem to me to deserve a mention. If you insist on growing one of the tall and aggressive herbaceous species, then, next to the two variegated varieties just named, I would recommend *P. campanulatum*. It is less than half the height of *P. cuspidatum* or *P. sachalinense*, which may or may not, according to its chosen setting, be an advantage, and its pale pink or red flowers, which come, to cite yet once more the *Dictionary of Gardening*, in a 'drooping terminal branching inflorescence,' are far superior to the upright off-white spikes of the other two. Presumably because of the relatively mild climate and perpetually damp soil, all these three have firmly established themselves at or near Ardtornish, and for once I really do know what I am talking about. If, on the other hand, you want a genuinely valuable creeper to cover some dry, sunny and inhospitable corner of your rock garden, then try the completely hardy Himalayan *Polygonum vacciniifolium*, a woody mat-forming plant whose bright green leaves and equally bright pink elongated flower-spikes put it in a class on its own in the whole family. And if, finally, what you need is a climber to smother an architectural eyesore in record time, faster even and with even greater throughtness than *Clematis montana*, and in the process to unsettle most of the tiles or slates on its roof, or alternatively to climb up a tree and speedily suffocate everything in its neighbourhood, then waste no time in ordering *Polygonum baldsçhuanicum*[1]. The *Polygonaceae* have something to answer every question in the garden. But, as may possibly by now have become dimly apparent, I personally have not much use for them and it is high time we moved on.

[1] [NOTE. The Polygonums have undergone extensive revision. The herbaceous species mentioned here have been assigned to the genus *Persicaria*, becoming *Persicaria vivipara*, *P. amphibia*, *P. bistorta*, *P. campanulata* and *P. vaccinifolia*. The shrubby species were first separated into a series of genera (*Bilderdykia*, *Reynoutria*) but then reunited in one, *Fallopia*. Hence *Polygonum baldschuanicum* = *Fallopia baldschuanica*, *P. cuspidatum* = *Fallopia japonica* and *P. sachalinense* = *Fallopia sachalinensis*. *P. chinense* is merely another name for *P. cuspidatum* (*Fallopia japonica*) and "var. foliis pictis" is the variety Spectabilis. Though handsome, it is as dangerously invasive as the type.]

CHAPTER 10

Ericaceae, Primulaceae and Gentianaceae

IMMEDIATELY after the spurges and the Polygonums come the docks and the nettles, from which God protect us, and next the hop, which God preserve. Then we reach seven families in succession consisting of several large trees and a few shrubs. Here in our flora, for example, come the elms, the birches, alder, hornbeam and hazel, beech and oak, the poplars, the willows and the sallows. Few of these are my concern in this book; either you have them in your garden or you have not, and unless you plan for the distant future you are unlikely to plant very many. But before we come to the proper theme of this chapter, I must just say a few words about four of our native willows which fully deserve a place in all but the smallest of rock gardens. All except one of them are exceedingly local and rare inhabitants of rock-ledges, usually basic, in the Highlands of Scotland.

We may as well get the exception out of the way first. The ordinary form of the creeping willow, variety *repens* of *Salix repens*, is widespread on heathy ground, wet or dry, throughout most of the British Isles, especially Scotland, and is attractive enough, with its prostrate habit and neat little leaves, for us to have brought cuttings south from near Ardtornish, where it is locally abundant. But the variety *argentea*, which, apart from a few rocky heaths in north Scotland, confines its natural activities to colonising dune-slacks, is so entrancing a plant, with leaves silkily silver on both sides instead of only underneath and larger pussies that are shining pink and green before they expand, that it justly wins a place in Ingwersen's catalogue. And so, for the matter of that, do two more of my four, and again, in one case at least, very justly. Indeed the arctic and subarctic woolly willow, *S. lanata*, which reaches its southernmost limit in Europe in Perthshire and Angus, is bracketed in my esteem with the burnet rose, *Rosa pimpinellifolia*, as in its season the most beautiful of all our medium-sized shrubs. Its leaves and its catkins appear from fat woolly buds at the same time, which in its lofty native haunts is not before the middle of June but in a lowland garden may well be in April. Its young leaves, which are eventually broadly ovate, are silver and silky above and white-felted beneath, and its huge egg-shaped catkins, even before the yellow stamens or anthers appear, are already, to quote another of Clapham, Tutin and Warburg's infrequent aesthetic verdicts, 'beautifully golden-yellow' with the dense clothing of long silky hairs on the scales. On the other hand the third of my quartet, *S.* Boydii appeals to me as much for its curiosity value as for its beauty. William B. Boyd, of Faldonside, Melrose, achieved the remarkable feat of discovering in the Cairngorms, I think in the nineties, and of bringing into cultivation, two plants which nobody in the world had ever seen before nor, possibly because of their successful introduction into cultivation and commerce, has ever seen in the wild since. One was a hard hummock of a pearlwort, also known after him as *Sagina boydii* and also obtainable from Ingwersen's, and the other was this hybrid willow, which I have only very lately had in its infancy from Jack Drake and am therefore reduced to describing in Mr Ingwersen's words as a 'pygmy tree with tough, rounded, grey-green leaves and pretty rounded catkins.' And that leaves only the creeping *S. reticulata*, my passion for which is, I suppose, in small part due to the fact that I used always to be finding it on unexpected mountains in the Highlands but much more to my conviction that its little oval and exquisitely veined leaves, dark green above and glaucous beneath, are, at least when mature, the most beautiful of the whole vast tribe.

We shall have to spend much of the rest of this chapter, unlike its predecessors, wandering around the garden at Ardtornish, where, as I said in the Introduction, by far the greater part of the midsummer blaze of colour is contributed by ericaceous plants, notably Rhododendrons and Azaleas, and by Primulas. But before we leave the chalk for the peat, it might be helpful to say a little about the few members of the three families that are the nominal topic of this chapter which will tolerate a soil with as high a pH as that of Shepreth or, presumably, Cambridge. We, of course, cheat; as again I said in the Introduction, the lime-free Norfolk soil in our two vast troughs enables us to grow, and very successfully too, a considerable number of plants, medium-sized to small, that we could not conceivably grow in the open ground. Needless to say, others who garden on chalk could without undue trouble follow our example if they saw fit, and doubtless many already do. But in case there are any who feel that gardeners should make the best of the soil God gave them, I will deal very briefly with the plants which we can only grow by this simple artifice and hustle on to those which we do or could grow in our God-given alkaline soil.

Faith and I have one trough each, hers on the paving stones in the courtyard, mine on the gravel in the top corner of the drive, and we try to avoid growing the same plants in each. Faith's special treasures from these three families are first the two Kalmias, *K. augustifolia*, which flowered fit to bust last summer while still little over a foot tall, and *K. latifolia*, which has yet to flower and will probably grow too big before it does, and second two rare and beautiful Primulas, both grey-leaved, the soft mauve *P. bauhinii*[1], of which I know and can discover nothing save that she was given it by a friend who gardens on the heavy black soil of the Fens, and the huge-flowered ivory *P. reidii* from the north-west Himalaya. And she also grows a plant of our native cowberry, *Vaccinium vitis-idaea*, which we succeeded in rooting from a cutting off a plant near Dalwhinnie and which shall be joined in due course, if my seeds collected in the Alps eventually germinate, by four others of the same family, the first three again native in Britain, alpine bearberry or *Arctostaphylus alpinus*, lesser Wintergreen or *Pyrola minor*, wild Azalea or *Loiseleuria procumbens*, and the familiar Alpenrosen or *Rhododendron ferrugineum*. My own specialities, on the other hand, are dwarf rhododendrons and gentians. The best of the former that I know is *R. williamsianum*; but two others of which I am particularly fond, and which evidently reciprocate my affection, are the hybrid Blue Tit and the midget mauve *R. impeditum*. Of the gentians I now grow four, the fifth, the pure white *G. saxosa* from New Zealand, having apparently flowered itself to death in its first year. Actually three of them would probably survive in our local soil: certainly the cluster-headed *G. septemfida*, probably the Cambridge blue *G. farreri*, and possibly, though I know from experience that it would not flower as it does in my trough, the old favourite and quite unpredictable *G. acaulis*. But the best of them all, *G. sino-ornata*, would succumb to the first sniff of our chalk. And finally, the only reason why I do not add our own excessively local *G. verna* to this quartet is that, as its natural predilection for limestone might suggest, it is happier where it is in a stony mixture of our own garden soil in two of my sinks. And the same would go, I fancy, for the violet-coloured *G. pyrenaica*, which we saw in abundance some years ago high in its eponymous mountains, and for two others whose seed we lately brought back from the Alps, the exquisite annual *Gentianella cilata* from banks of bare limestone on the Jura hills and the stately herbaceous *Gentiana lutea* from Mont Salève above Geneva.

Many years ago, before I gladly handed over to a professional botanist, I was secretary of my college's garden committee and was given a more or less free hand to plant what I chose where I chose. When we suddenly wanted an impenetrable screen to shut off the view

---

[1] [True identity unknown. *P. bauhini* Beck is a robust form of the yellow-flowered *P. auricula*.]

of an adjacent new building from the Fellows' Garden, I planted a small grove of the strawberry tree, *Arbutus unedo*, the most northerly of whose native European stations is County Kerry. And when we decided to introduce perennial plants instead of Petunias into the little rectangular beds on the west side of our famous Gibbs' Building, I planted up the two beds on either side of the central arch with a mixture of the only two heathers that could be expected to tolerate the soil of Cambridge, the multitudinous colour varieties of the hummocky winter-flowering *Erica carnea* and its taller shrubby hybrid *E. × darleyensis*. All these proved their adaptability and performed their respective functions to perfection, and the only reasons why we have not repeated these successes at Shepreth are, in the case of the Arbutus, that we have not yet got around to it, though we shall any day now for exactly the same purpose as in King's, and in the case of the heathers, that our horticultural taste is so pure (or so perverse) that we do not really like even the brightest and best of winter-flowering heathers away from heather country. We do, however, grow in the courtyard two bushes of one of the only two Rhododendrons that would stand our soil, the bright rosy-purple February-flowering hybrid R. Praecox, and I have just, by way of experiment, ordered the other, R. *hirsutum*, which is the limestone counterpart of the Alpenrose, from Marchant's of Wimborne, along with that exquisite pseudo-Rhododendron from the eastern Dolomites, *Rhodothamnus chamaecistus*. And we do our best with Primulas too. Apart from cowslips, primroses and that speciality of our neighbourhood, the true oxlip or *Primula elatior*, we once bought a packet of seed, I thought from Thompson and Morgan of Ipswich but I can find no trace of the creature in their current catalogue, labelled Canadian Cowslip. We planted out the seedlings, as soon as they were ready, in the unmown grass of the wild garden, where they promptly proved to be exactly like ordinary cowslips in size and shape but to range in colour from orange through scarlet to crimson. If only I could remember where we bought them, I would strongly recommend them for any wild bit of garden, where they would reveal the additional virtue of spreading at a gratifying pace.[1] Then again, apart from the old favourite magenta primrose Wanda and some not very distinguished Polyanthus, which we grow under *Malus floribunda*, we have three colour varieties of the drumstick Primula, *P. denticulata*, none too happily housed at present in the dry border under the Judas tree, and, in the border under the greenhouse, several hybrid Auriculas of different colours, of which my

---

[1] I have just found 'Cowslip, Mixed Colours' in the current catalogue of Sutton's seeds, where the description leaves little doubt that this is the right plant. For once the common English name has helped.

favourite is the one which most resembles the true alpine *P. auricula* called Old Yellow Dusty Miller. I brought back young plants of two more alpine species, *P. integrifolia* and *P. hirsuta*, from our recent autumnal tour, and at present they are both looking tolerably happy in a north-facing sink; but I strongly suspect that they will prove as obdurate in their refusal to flower as did *P. minima* when we brought it back from near the Passo di Pordoi on our first visit to the Dolomites.[1] And of our meagre collection of Primulas at Shepreth that leaves only the tall yellow *P. florindae*, which we accepted from a friend with some hesitation since we were sure we were condemning it to a thirsty death and hopefully planted under the greenhouse where the overflow pipe from the rainwater tank inside trickles intermittently on to the border. There it has not only flowered each year since we had it but sowed itself so profusely that we now have flourishing colonies in three other of the few moist spots in the garden. But I fear that even in the dampest parts of our Shepreth desert its lowly and depauperated umbels will never hold a candle to the stately and colourful candelabras at Ardtornish.

A paragraph or two must be devoted, before we move up north, to six other genera of the Primula family, all but one of which consist of plants for the rock garden or even the trough or sink. Once again I will deal with the exception first, the genus Lysimachia, which is represented in Britain not only by the common riverside yellow loosestrife, *L. vulgaris*, but also by two bright little plants that are thoroughly useful in shady and preferably rather moist corners of the garden, yellow pimpernel or *L. nemorum*, which is abundant in the woods around Ardtornish, and creeping Jenny or *L. nummularia*, of which there is a thriving patch in a shady hedgerow only half a mile down the road from our house at Shepreth. But the member of the genus which we grow with the greatest pleasure is a neglected herbaceous species from south-west Europe called *L. ephemerum*. It bears long and slender spikes of little white flowers on yard-high stems that are fairly thickly clothed in narrow, opposite and very glaucous leaves. Since it is a tidily upright plant and, unlike most of the genus, immune to sun-baked drought, it makes an admirable constituent of our grey borders and is another of that large band of easy and elegant plants that deserve wider recognition than they get. And there is another genus too which, being not really suitable for a sink, we are still only too pleased to grow in the open ground, usually in inhospitable sites at or near the base of a tree, the hardy miniature cyclamens. If you make a

[1] My suspicion was unjustified; two plants of *P. hirsuta* flowered handsomely in their first year in England.

wise selection of these, you can have them, as you can species crocuses, flowering almost continuously throughout the winter. We have ourselves at various times brought four different species back from different parts of southern Europe, *C. graecum* from Olympia, *C. purpurascens* from the foothills of the Dolomites, *C. hederifolium*, which is conceivably native in Kent, from Corfu, and *C. persicum* from Rhodes. The first two keep flowering merrily away well into October and the third even into November, when in turn it is succeeded by the fourth. As a matter of fact we have not yet dared to entrust *C. persicum* to the mercies of our merciless winters, and we grow the odd dozen that we brought back in pots in the cool greenhouse, whence we had one in full flower indoors in the middle of January. It was immediately followed by *C. coum*, which, perhaps because its rounded and scarcely marbled leaves are smaller and less conspicuous than the rest, we have never found in the wild and were reduced to buying, but a large rich pink patch of which I can already see, on 2nd February, from the window where I am writing. And in a few weeks' time its place will be taken in turn by the last in the series, *C. repandum*, the leaves of which can be readily distinguished from the others by their numerous undulating lobes.

None of the four rock garden genera need detain us long, and one of the four, alas, can be dismissed without more ado. When, on one of our earliest visits to the Alps, we dug up an experimental root of the common *Soldanella alpina* and a few days later I lovingly planted in the dampest corner of my least dehydrated sink, it perished with such alacrity that even when we came across the much less common *S. pusilla* in the Dolomites we contented ourselves with photographing it. The same, I am sure, would happen with all the European Androsaces, with the possible exception of the densely hairy short-stemmed white *A. villosa*, but I have found that two pink Himalayan species, *A. sempervivoides* and the beautiful silver-leaved *A. lanuginosa*, provided you give them plenty of sun, are happy to spread and even to flower in a sink in the open. And exactly the same is true of the closely related and densely matted *Vitaliana primuliflora*, which we first saw in plenty near the Lac des Vaches above Pralognan and which now contentedly trails its yellow flowers over the front edge of the sink in the centre of the winter garden. But the last of this little band, *Dodecatheon meadia* from the woods of north-eastern America, demands quite different conditions and seems well satisfied with the sandy Norfolk soil under the shadow of the crimson-leaved Japanese maple at the back of my trough. No doubt all of these, and especially the Soldanellas, would do better in a proper rock garden, but I can vouch for the fact that, the Soldanellas excepted, they fare and flower well enough in a trough or a sink.

When we move north from Shepreth to Ardtornish, as I have actually just moved on the day before that on which I am now writing, it is difficult to know where to begin. The only one of the three families under discussion that can justifiably be dismissed in a single paragraph is that of the gentians. Since our beautiful native bogbean, *Menyanthes trifoliata*, which abounds in the shallow muddy pond at the bottom of the garden, has been separated off from the *Gentianaceae* and elevated into a new family named after it, there have only been two gentians that I can remember growing at Ardtornish, and alas, the better of the two, *G. sino-ornata*, which used to fill an oval bed near the drive gate, was crowded out of existence during a labour shortage even more acute than usual. The only survivor in these days, which however looks as contented here as in its native subalpine woodlands, is the tall and graceful willow gentian, *G. asclepiadea*, the seeds of which, gathered in plenty in the Val Maggia last autumn, are among the few which so far have resolutely refused to germinate at Shepreth. Since I very much doubt whether we could keep it alive there anyhow, and might well waste a lot of effort on the attempt to do so, perhaps its reluctance to co-operate from the outset should be interpreted as a token of its consideration rather than its obduracy. *G. purpurea*, whose seed, collected two days later at Cervinia, is already filling its pan to the rim, will probably prove in the end a perfidious flatterer.

The Primulas at Ardtornish present problems of an altogether different order. There is not the slightest fear of their being crowded out, since they spread like rampant weeds along the banks of any rill or ditch to which they extend their hold. But, as is liable to happen in any population explosion, they have in the process of territorial expansion indulged in the most promiscuous and bewildering inter-marriage. Our own three native yellow Primulas allow themselves quite sufficient licence in that respect, but as usual foreigners, and especially orientals, really do go too far. No doubt the original settlers at Ardtornish, coming from diverse parts of the East, were all of the purest strain, but the period of primal purity is irrevocably past. Along the ditch beside the track at the head of the main glen, the home of many of the best Rhododendrons, there is still a colony of unmixed *Primula japonica*, even if it is, as often, variable in its shade of crimson or magenta; and in swampy ground at the bottom of the glen *P. florindae*, apparently the least promiscuous of the tribe, stands stately and aloof among a many-coloured throng of hybrids that have seeded themselves down from above. But the floor of the glen between these two outposts is here and there carpeted by a motley collection in which the blood of *P. pulverulenta*, both the magenta type and its pink forms, and of the tall rich yellow *P. bulleyana* is most self-assertive, but in which a solitary specimen of the shorter *P. anisodora*, with its drooping bells of dark purplish-red, suggests at least one other more remote influence. Whatever its ultimate parentage, however, this random assemblage of Primulas, all of the candelabra type, ranges from yellow, through apricot, salmon- and rose-pink, to mauve, pure purple and vivid magenta; and while the eyes of most of them are bright golden yellow, those in which the *pulverulenta* strain seems uppermost sometimes have eyes of a brownish scarlet. Purists such as A. T. Johnson, author of *A Garden in Wales* and *A Woodland Garden*, evidently expend a lot of time and trouble in the attempt to keep their colonies of Primulas in splendid isolation; and there is certainly something to be said for knowing what the plants you grow in your garden are. But in the case of the candelabra Primulas, the random hybridisation which we anyhow have not at Ardtornish the time and energy to prevent produces a riot of flamboyant colour of which we should be sorry to be deprived.

But apart from a wide variety of unusual trees, large and small, evergreen and deciduous, the most prominent feature of the Ardtornish garden is its abundance of ericaceous plants. Nature herself made a good start: besides bell heather in the rockier parts and cross-leaved heath in the damper, the whole garden except the extensive lawns abounds in ling and bilberry. And by human agency long ago the Irish native, St Dabeoc's heath or *Daboecia cantabrica*, and Irish heath, *Erica erigena*, as well as *Gaultheria shallon* and *Pernettya mucronata*, have by now become thoroughly established. Indeed, on the level ground near the river there is an exceptionally fine and floriferous bush of *Kalmia latifolia*, beside the back drive to the farm there is an equally sumptuous specimen of *Pieris formosa*, and so on and so on. But to the casual visitor it would be the abundance and richness of colour of the Azaleas and Rhododendrons which caught the eye. As in most Rhododendron-growing areas, R. *ponticum* is a constant menace; it has to be uprooted by tractor and chains to prevent it choking its more refined relatives. But given only a modicum of breathing space and some protection from the south-westerly gales that all too often come blustering up the loch, both Rhododendrons and Azaleas flourish as the bay-tree in the acid peaty soil. Unfortunately the names of the many Azaleas, yellow, orange, flame-coloured and pink, are quite beyond me, and even those of the Rhododendrons, other than the species, are as difficult to remember as those of hybrid tea-roses or hybrid Clematis. Though I am confident that I could at a glance have distinguished in their human guise between, say, Admiral Lord Nelson, King George, Lady Chamberlain and Bud Flanagan, when they are all transmogrified into hybrid Rhododendrons the obvious distinctions become blurred. Now, however, I must struggle to overcome my chronic amnesia.

Even as he walks up the drive in springtime, any but the most myopic visitor will notice two species of Rhododendrons. R. *strigillosum*, which usually opens before March is out, bears trusses of bell-shaped flowers of a blazing colour somewhere between scarlet and crimson, and before it is over R. *oreodoxa*, whose wider bells have seven lobes rather than five, unfolds its clusters of pale pink. But though these two have the great merit of flowering freely every year, the colour of both is put in the shade by the hybrid between the former and R. *griersonianum*, aptly called Matador, which outshines even the most popular of greenhouse Pelargoniums in the brilliance of its scarlet. And while these three are blazing beside the steep and winding drive, elsewhere in the garden isolated patches of colour are provided by two other brilliant red Rhododendrons, R. *barbatum*, which has the added distinction of beautifully smooth pinkish-grey bark but which suffers somewhat from its over-compact trusses, and R. *thomsonii*, by the rose-pink R. *oreodoxa fargesii* and the larger-leaved and rather mauver R. *sutchuenense*, and by the blush-white R. *lindleyi*.

Before the last of this fine first flush has faded, it is succeeded by another brilliant batch spanning the months of May and June. Among the first of these to flower in our far nothern clime are three true species, R. *oreotrephes*, R. *concatenans* and R. *orbiculare*, and one hybrid aptly or ineptly named Letty Edwards. R. *oreotrephes*, the abundant flowers of which hover precariously between pink and mauve, is distinguished by its exceptionally glaucous oval leaves, R. *concatenans* by its almost circular leaves with grey undersides, and Letty Edwards, the hybrid between two phenomenally productive parents in the mauvy-pink R. *fortunei* and the soft yellow R. *campylocarpum*, by its yellow, crimson-throated flowers.

Expert Rhododendron growers, as that fabulous volume *The Rothschild Rhododendrons* shows eloquently enough, not only have their own taste but lay down the law of contemporary taste to the average British gardener. And what is more, this dictated taste is not only certified as authoritative by the annual publications on Rhododendrons of the Royal Horticultural Society but endorsed by the number of asterisks, ranging from nought to four, allotted to each Rhododendron, whether species or hybrid, listed in the *Rhododendron Handbook*. I am in no position to question this contemporary taste, but in my foolhardy fashion I do so nonetheless. My own three favourites among the Rhododendrons which flower in May to June are R. *cinnabarinum* and its varieties, R. *keysii*, and the hybrid between R. *williamsianum* and R. *griersonianum* which was first raised by Sir John Stirling Maxwell and christened after his son-in-law Jock. The first of this trinity, which is characterised by glaucous oval leaves and tubular flowers ranging, in its named varieties, from yellowish-orange through bright deep rose to purplish-crimson, is justly awarded the maximum four stars. The second, which belongs to the same series but has appreciably narrower leaves and flowers that gradually fade from scarlet at the base of the tube to the five pale yellow lobes, is deemed worthy of only two. And the last, a dwarf which smothers itself in a profusion of proportionately huge bright pink flowers with a faint touch of orange, is accorded a mere one. But be that as it may, all these flower prolifically at Ardtornish, chiefly on and around the top of a prominent rocky mound in the middle of the garden, where the typical orange R. *cinnabarinum* is flanked by its yellower variety Blandfordiaeflorum and the bright crimson variety Roylei. And a great deal more colour has been added to the area by a comparatively recent planting of several low-growing varieties; besides R. *williamsianum* itself, whose rose-red flowers usually open in April, there are three of its later-flowering hybrids in Bow Bells, soft pink with deeper shading outside, Temple Belle, clear pink inside and out (for its other parent is R. *orbiculare*), and the drooping crimson Hummingbird, and there is Jack Drake's richly coloured variety of the compactly carpeting R. *calostrotum* which he fairly enough calls Claret Form.

Meanwhile, if you walk two hundred yards farther along the top drive, you pass first, on the right, a clump of tall vivid red King George and a single small tree of the rich pink Lady Rosebery, and then, on the ledges of a low cliff on the left, six low and stunningly floriferous bushes of the aforementioned Jock. And that will bring you to the top of the glen, the floor and flanks of which, in late May and early June, are ablaze with Azaleas and dotted with Rhododendrons of many a shape, size and colour. R. *souliei*, Loder's White and Mrs Lindsay Smith provide the white element, R. *wardii* and R. *campylocarpum* the yellow, Fabia the orange, R. *insigne*, R. *smirnowii*, R. *albrechtii* and Dawn's Delight the various shades of pink, and Tally Ho, R. *sperabile*, R. *haematodes* and Cornish Cross a variety of reds ranging from vermilion to crimson. And if, finally, you care to climb the steep, narrow and slippery path up the right shoulder of the glen, you will come at the top, under the shelter of a tall Scots pine and a beech tree, upon a mauve and blue planting consisting, at the back, of a tall and branching specimen of R. *davidsonianum* with, in the foreground, clumps of R. *augustinii* and Blue Tit. And with that you will probably have had enough of Rhododendrons and, though there are many left to see in distant parts of the grounds, will be wanting a well-earned rest.

CHAPTER II

A Last Miscellany

I AM uncomfortably aware that owing to my instinct, born and bred at Ardtornish, to group the *Ericaceae*, the *Primulaceae* and the *Gentianaceae* together, I have been tempted to omit four whole families of our flora whose contribution to the garden deserves better treatment. I must now try to make them scanty but ungrudging amends, which may serve only to show that I have not completely forgotten them. First, and immediately before the Primula family, come the *Plumbaginaceae*, represented in Britain only by the sea lavenders and the sea pinks, both of which are colourful embellishments of our salt-marshes and seaside rocks but neither of which have I ever been under the slightest temptation to transplant from their native habitat into our garden. Apart from *Plumbago auriculata* itself, however, both the ordinary pale blue and the white varieties of which, planted in the soil in our cooler greenhouse, are a lavish source of autumnal flowers for our own and other people's houses, the genus *Ceratostigma* contains two thoroughly valuable and industructibly hardy plants. Both bear, at the end of nearly every branch, clusters of bright blue flowers in the late summer and autumn, and later on the unstalked and untoothed obovate leaves of both tend to turn flaming red. Whereas, however, *C. willmottianum* is a deciduous purplish-stemmed shrub two or three feet high and ideally suited to the front of a shrub border, the right place for the decumbent twiggy *C. plumbaginoides*, which only attains a height of about a foot but spreads at quite a pace horizontally, is the front of the herbaceous border.

Immediately in between the primulas and the gentians come, on the other hand, in an undivided trinity, the *Loganiaceae*, the *Oleaceae* and the *Apocynaceae*, and even if the names of these three families are as novel to some as they certainly would be, for instance, to the anti-botanical Faith (and they are; I have just checked), each contains at least one genus whose name and salient features must be as well known to every British gardener as his or her own. The pride of the *Loganiaceae*, which have nothing to do with loganberries except that they were so named in honour of a different gentleman of the same name, is the genus Buddleia; the most familiar of the *Oleaceae*, though not the only ones worth growing, are forsythia, lilac, privet and jasmine; the best known members of the *Apocynaceae* are the periwinkles, which, since there is not very much to say about them except that they are second only to the ivies as carpeters of unappetising sites, we may as well put behind us first. Whether or not either of them are actually native, both *Vinca major* and *V. minor*, the two most commonly seen in British gardens, are abundantly naturalised in England, especially in the southern counties. *V. major*, which has a form variegated with creamy-white, has the advantage, if advantage it be, of being larger in all its parts, but this is more than offset by the fact that its flowers, which only come in two colours, purplish-blue or white, are usually all over before midsummer, while *V. minor*, which has forms with leaves variegated either white or yellow and flowers of sundry colours from white through different shades of blue and purple to almost claret, often keeps going well on into September. I am sorry to confess that I do not know *V. difformis*, which comes from the western Mediterranean and is on that account less reliably hardy, but if Hillier's claim for it be true, that it 'produces its large, pale lilac-blue flowers in November and December,' it sounds quite a valuable acquisition.

Buddleia davidii is so popular and familiar a plant, indeed so popular as to have been, according to Clapham, Tutin and Warburg, 'common on bombed sites and the only garden plant recorded from them in London,' that I shall spend no more time on its numerous colour varieties than to remark that in my opinion the best of them are the long-spiked white one called Peace and the deep purple Black Knight. We have never had a sufficient fancy for the almost equally familiar orange ball tree from Chile, *B. globosa*, to induce us to grow it, though I for one would choose it every time in preference to the apparently beloved but, despite its Award of Garden merit, indisputably ugly double form of the orange-yellow rosaceous *Kerria japonica*. But its hybrid with *B. davidii* called *B.* × *weyeriana*, of which we were given an unrooted cutting that struck as obligingly as most of the Buddleias do, is an altogether different proposition. Seen from the distance it looks just like an orange variety, hitherto unknown, of *B. davidii*, but on closer inspection its spikes of flowers prove not only to be composed of lots of nearly contiguous balls but to be lightly suffused with mauve. The whitely downy *B. caryopteridifolia*, which is one of the shrubs we grow at the back of the herbaceous border and which produces relatively short and wishy-washy mauve spikes as early as May, has not been one of our more conspicuous successes, probably for the simple reason that it finds south Cambridgeshire too cold, whereas *B. fallowiana alba*, the young shoots and the undersides of the leaves of which are again densely felted in white while its flowers, in spikes at least twice the length, are milk-white with an orange eye, is one of the show pieces of our grey borders. But the most graceful and elegant as well as the hardiest of them all, to be distinguished from the rest by the characteristic its name suggests, is the Chinese *B. alternifolia* which, so I learn from Notcutt's catalogue, was aptly described by its first finder, Reginald Farrer, as 'like a gracious small-leaved weeping willow when it is not in flower, and a sheer waterfall of soft purples when it is.' Our own specimen of it in the semi-wild garden, to which I referred when writing about old-fashioned roses, makes a perfect curtain to shut off the most secluded little lawn in the whole garden.

When we first bought the house and garden at Shepreth we inevitably found two huge and probably ancient bushes of the most popular and floriferous of the Forsythias, the variety Spectabilis of *F. × intermedia*, already in undisputed possession; but since they had both been skilfully sited, one against the wall just inside the drive gate and the other on the edge of the wild garden, neither interfered in the least with our plans and both have been gladly adopted. But, almost equally inevitably, there was no other species in the garden, and so, having a preference for the more gracefully arching even if less densely flower-laden varieties, we wasted little time in introducing three others. *F. ovata*, which is the smallest of them all, usually no more than four feet high, and produces its first pale yellow flowers as early as February, and the taller and more spreading bright yellow *F. suspensa* have long been among the more showy shrubs in our winter garden, while the dark-purple-stemmed variety *atrocaulis* of the latter, which we originally kept in a large pot to bring into the house when it was in bud, eventually outgrew that purpose and was planted out as a colourful full stop at the far end of the belt of flowering trees and shrubs on the south side of the rose garden. Similarly, of course, we inherited quite a number of old-fashioned lilacs, mainly white or mauve but one bright purple one beneath the Judas tree, which again we welcomed and have left undisturbed in their carefully selected sites; and what is more, we have this time introduced no more to augment them. If we had, we should probably have chosen, in preference to the rather stiff and lumpy modern varieties of *Syringa vulgaris*, either the two miniature species, neither of them more than five feet tall, the rosy *S. microphylla* and the mauve *S. patula* or, if we had wanted something taller, one or other of the colour varieties of the more elegant and, in an aesthetic rather than a clinical sense, more delicate Canadian hybrid, which is named after its raiser *S. × prestoniae*. And yet again, two stretches of our many old walls were already occupied, to our unmitigated pleasure, by the two ubiquitous species of jasmine, the winter-flowering yellow *Jasminum nudiflorum* and the deliciously fragrant white *J. officinale*, and since the more aristocratic version of each, *J. mesneyi* and *J. polyanthum* respectively, can only be grown in these parts, as in fact we grow them to bring once more into the house, in a cool greenhouse, the only jasmine we have introduced into the open is the little shrubby yellow-flowered *J. parkeri*, which proved too small for the border in front of the house and now makes two tiny rounded bushes, not more than nine inches high, on the sunny side of the courtyard. As for privets, the genus Ligustrum, and especially the variegated and yellow-leaved forms, anybody who cares for them is as welcome to them, as far as I am concerned, as they are to the false laurels of the genus Aucuba. And that leaves only one member of the family that we have lately acquired from a cutting, *Osmanthus delavayi*, which looks rather like a small-flowered shrubby jasmine with leathery and sharply toothed oval leaves, and Hillier's description of which as 'one of China's gems' strikes me, but not Faith, as a dubious compliment to its motherland.

Even after the gentians there are still exactly twenty whole families of dicotyledonous plants left in the flora of Britain alone, more than half of which make contributions to British gardens of sufficient significance to entitle them to extended treatment. Since that is more than I can at this stage afford to give them, I shall take for granted at least a nodding acquaintance with the most familiar genera and species and concentrate attention on those relatively few which, though much less often seen in gardens, are just as deserving of a place there. The two families we encounter first, the *Polemoniaceae* and the *Boraginaceae*, illustrate the point at once, even if they do not raise it in its most acute form. To begin with, there are two species of the genus Polemonium itself which are not only very decorative in both leaf and flower but have also proved themselves here to be extremely easy-going and extremely prolific. Their rather fern-like radical leaves are virtually indistinguishable, but *P. coeruleum* or Jacob's ladder, a very local native which I have seen chiefly in the West Riding of Yorkshire, bears racemes of soft blue or occasionally white campanulate flowers and does best with us in almost full shade, while the Mexican *P. pauciflorum* had drooping tubular flowers, often solitary, of a brownish yellow and seems to thrive in full sun. Unfortunately the dwarf arctic species, *P. lanatum*, is difficult if not impossible to find in commerce, but those that are obtainable seem to present no problem of any sort, which is more than can be said of another constituent of the same family, the genus Phlox. The herbaceous Phloxes, mainly varieties of *P. paniculata*, which flourish so prodigally in cottage gardens in the wet north-west, regrettably fail to do themselves full justice, so light and dry is our soil, even in the damper and shadier parts of the semi-wild garden; and likewise we have no really suitable home, except perhaps the front of the raised beds on the sunny side of the courtyard where we do grow one or two, for their prostrate and sumptuously floriferous cousins, the numerous colour varieties of *P. douglasii* and *P. subulata*. But for all that, each of us contrives to grow one favourite. A tiny plant of the creeping rose-pink *P. adsurgens*, which Faith had at the same time and from the same source as her two precious Primulas, she planted with them, to satisfy its demand for lime-free soil, at the front of her trough, where it has not only, in under two years, made a solid mat more than two feet across but hangs very decoratively neatly half-way down the front. When it is in full flower, as it is for a long time, it makes a sheet of pure colour unsurpassed anywhere in the garden. By comparison with this aristocrat I admit that my own pet is a commoner, the variety of *P. douglasii* appropriately named Violet Queen, but it has the double advantage of being compact enough to trail unassumingly but brightly from the corner of one of my smaller sinks and of an apparent catholicity in its taste for soil. And that, even though there are seven other genera of the family listed in the *Dictionary of Gardening*, including the beautiful and miraculously rapid but, alas, half-hardy climber *Cobaea scandens*, will have to suffice for the *Polemoniaceae*.

The *Boraginaceae* present a graver problem if only because, even omitting borage itself, which you need only grow if you have a passion for Pimm's, they still confront us with as many as ten genera which call for at least a passing mention. Wherever possible I shall try to confine attention to the single species which we consider the best of the genus; we may as well first assimilate the simple fact that the flowers of the whole family are normally blue; and we had best take the genera concerned in an ascending order of complexity so as to harden our hearts for the ruthless elimination that will eventually be unavoidable. Blue-eyed Mary or *Omphalodes verna*, a root or two of which we brought back from the abundance in the woods around Asolo, is so much easier to accommodate in half-shade than either *O. cappadocica* or *O luciliae* that it must take precedence over them as a plant for the average British garden and gardener; and if it spreads too fast, as it has with us, there is no difficulty about finding grateful recipients of the surplus. Similarly nobody in his senses could fail to prefer the deep blue flowers of the narrow-leaved lungwort, *Pulmonaria longifolia*, which is indisputably native in the Isle of Wight and the New Forest but which we actually collected in the French foothills of the Pyrenees, to its mauvy-pink cousin *P. officinalis*, which is unaccountably much more often to be seen in gardens and has thence become more or less naturalised in many a shady place in England and Wales. Yet again, though the little yellowish-white comfrey, *Symphytum tuberosum*, which is an abundant native in several areas of Scotland, and for the matter of that two or three very similar foreign species, make very effective colonists of the least enticing and shadiest corners of the garden, there can be no doubt that much the most handsome member of the genus, and no less accommodating either, is the tall but graceful and genuinely blue *S. peregrinum*[1], the true form of which from the Caucasus is, I insist in the teeth of the Floras, palpably distinct from the indeterminately purple hybrid, increasingly common on roadsides, called *S.* × *uplandicum*. And last in this category, nobody should dream of growing any other of the hound's-tongues so long as the seed of the beautiful deep blue perennial *Cynoglossum nervosum* is still procurable from Thompson and Morgan.

The next category, which consists of the three genera Eritrichium, Mertensia and Brunnera, presents greater problems in that its representatives are either impossible to cultivate or impossible to acquire or both. The truly alpine *Eritrichium nanum*, which we have only once seen in a blizzard on cliffs high above the Col du Lautaret but which it is the ambition of every owner of an alpine house to induce to flower, falls squarely, along with its less known congeners from Asia, into the last of these three classes. I may have been unlucky, but the only species of Mertensia that I have ever seen looking at all happy anywhere in the British Isles is our own exquisite but sadly diminishing inhabitant of sand or shingle beaches in the north, *M. maritima* or the oyster plant. And as for the exquisite variegated form of *Brunnera macrophylla*, which until lately was called *Anchusa myosotidifolia*, it is at last available from the Bressingham Gardens at Diss, but only at a price which might well give pause to any but a fanatical admirer of variegation.

There seems to be a widespread but mistaken belief that none of the 'Lithospermums'[2] can stand a whiff of chalk or lime. That is probably true of *Lithodora diffusa*, the two bluest and best varieties of which, Heavenly Blue and Grace Ward, so prosper in the lime-free soil at either end of my trough, where I very effectually planted them to hang trailing down the sides, that their neighbours live under the constant threat of engulfment. But it is emphatically not true, as anybody would know who had ever seen our native *Buglossoides pupurocaerulea* flourishing on the limestone near Cheddar or who now saw it in the long grass of our chalky wild garden, of all the rest. As a reward for my previous irrelevances I need now only repeat that our experiment of growing

[1] [J.E.R.'s true *S. peregrinum* is probably *S. asperum*.]

[2] [The old genus *Lithospermum* has been redivided, the plants important to gardeners being ascribed to *Lithodora*, *Buglossoides* and *Moltkia*.]

Moltkia intermedia and *M. petraea*, together with *Helianthemum lunulatum*, in a dwarf hedge has been such an unqualified success as to dispel for ever any lingering doubts about their tolerance of lime. And of course the same is self-evidently true of the last two of my ten genera of the *Boraginaceae*, Anchusa and Myosotis. Indeed the more or less intensely blue varieties of *Anchusa azurea* were the original inspiration of our blue borders and now tend to crop up all over the kitchen garden, while all we have to do to ensure the perpetuity of the excellent form of forget-me-not that we inherited is to forbear to rake off its unsightly withered remnants until they have had time to drop sufficient seed for next year's blue haze. Their stunted but even brighter sky-blue cousin from the Alps, *Myosotis alpestris*, which is also to be seen as a native on Mickle Fell and Ben Lawers, I look forward to planting out shortly in two or three of my sunniest and least nutrient sinks; for its seeds which I brought back last October from the hills above Zermatt were not unexpectedly among the first to germinate.

The *Convolvulaceae* can boast one plant, the little silver-leaved shrubby *Convolvulus cneorum*, which ought to be in a sunny, sheltered and well-drained corner of every garden that is not liable to very heavy frosts; but for ourselves we have now lost it in so many winters, including the one which is not yet over, as almost to be deterred from trying again. The *Solanaceae*, on the other hand, are not for us for the simple reason that their greatest glories are either such annuals as the tobacco plants and Petunias or else, like the beautiful shrubby Daturas, subjects for a large greenhouse. And so we come quickly to the real crux of this chapter in the shape of the *Scrophulariaceae*, a family which, in the words of the *Dictionary of Gardening*, 'is an important one horticulturally for it contributes many beautiful plants to our gardens.' Out of the sixty-five of its odd two hundred genera that are listed in the *Dictionary* as playing a significant part in British gardens, it contains about ten which would demand a mention in even the most summary survey. Once again we had better deal first with those genera which need not detain us long, and the greatest of these is Antirrhinum, the ideal position for which is a roundabout. The closely related genus of Linaria, which no longer includes the jolly little ivy-leaved toadflax, now called *Cymbalaria muralis*, of many an old wall throughout most of Britain, is usually represented in British gardens, in preference to two much prettier natives in the abundant yellow *L. vulgaris* and the local and delicate mauve-and-white *L. repens*, by the insipid lilac or pink forms of *L. purpurea*; but it is redeemed by the existence, and indeed by the ease of cultivation in a sink, of the lovely grey-leaved trailing *L. alpina* with its mass of purple and orange flowers. And there is another colourful and prodigally floriferous member of the family, again ideally suited to a sink garden, the little ferny-leaved bright pink *Erinus alpinus*, which has not only a white variety but also a crimson one called, according to one of several current versions of the gentleman's name, Dr Hähnle. And before we leave the sink for the open ground, there are two species of Veronica and at least one of the closely related shrubby Hebe which, on grounds of size alone, find their proper place here. Although the two Veronicas, *V. fruticans* and *V. alpina*, are both natives, if very rare natives, of the central Highlands of Scotland, my seed of them was collected, as usual, on our recent tour of the Alps, and it is as yet too early to predict how either of them will stand up to the unaccustomed drought of even a north-facing sink. But the variety Minor of *Hebe buchananii* from New Zealand, a dwarf shrublet with close-packed tiny glaucous leaves and short spikes of small white flowers, fully deserves its place in Mr Ingwersen's useful list of 'plants specially suitable for troughs and sink gardens.'

We have no great liking for the majority of the Hebes, which tend to look too stiff and artificial for our taste. But we do grow two which on every score are entitled to a place in even a small garden. *H. pinguifolia*, alias *H. pageana*, a small and almost prostrate shrub with tidy, oval and very glaucous leaves and spikes of pale lavender flowers with blue anthers, is the smallest of the select band of shrubs in the border along the front of the house, where it is accompanied by its silver-grey-leaved cousin *Veronica spicata incana*. *H. hulkeana*, on the other hand, which is justly described in the *Dictionary* as the 'most beautiful in flower of all shrubby species,' is – or at any rate has been until this cruel winter – one of the most admired features of my trough. But we make more use in other parts of the garden of the showier and hardier herbaceous Veronicas. The most elegant of them is undoubtedly *V. gentianoides*, which, from rosettes of glossy lanceolate leaves, produces long spikes of relatively large pale blue flowers edged with deeper blue. But for some reason, probably, as usual, our habitual drought during the growing season, it does not at all enjoy life at Shepreth, and we have to make do instead with its gentian-blue relatives (and that accurate description makes me wonder why it should have been selected from them all for a name that means 'gentian-like'), which come in three sizes, all irrepressibly floriferous. The smallest, which belongs properly to the rock garden, is the mat-forming *V. prostrata*, which we grow, with other plants of the same habit, beside the paved path in front of the greenhouse. Second in size is *V. spicata*, a very local and rare British native, which can attain a height of nearly a foot but with us has yet to do more than throw up a mass of cotyledons from the plentiful supply of seed I brought back from Mont Salève. And the largest of them, even if you wish to specialise and grow such species as *V. spuria* or *V. longifolia*, which are normally intermediate in size, is *V. austriaca teucrium*, the variety of which called Royal Blue makes patches of intense colour on either side of the grass path between our twin blue borders. Of my four remaining genera one, that of the foxgloves, is exceptional in that all its members do better in at least dappled shade than in full sun. Although there is no denying Sutton's claim that their 'plant breeders have transformed this simple flower of the English woodlands' with their Excelsior strain, it is still legitimate to question whether the transformation is wholly for the better. We at any rate regard it as of the essence of a foxglove to hang its flowers down rather than to stick them straight out at you, and moreover to hang them on one side of the stem only rather than in serried ranks all round it, and we are therefore conservative enough to have so far remained loyal to the species. The white variety of our own abundant native is unsurpassed in the art of lightening the darkness of a deeply shaded corner, and it does it with a grace to which the Excelsior strain does not try to aspire. But maybe the two primrose-yellow species from the Alps, the large-flowered *Digitalis grandiflora* and the small-flowered *D. lutea*, the leaves of both of which are neater, narrower and darker green, have a more aristocratic air. Since both are perfectly simple, we have grown them for some years in various shady places; but though we could always, if we had taken the trouble, have greatly increased their numbers by seed ripened in our own garden, I derive a certain childish pleasure from the fact that they are shortly to be augmented instead by scores of seedlings from their native subalpine haunts. And they are to be joined too by *D. × mertonensis*, whose flowers are said in every available description to be the colour of crushed strawberries, and by the bronzy *D. davisiana*, the seed of both of which I have just ordered from Thompson and Morgan.

The genus Penstemon is nearly as versatile as the genus Veronica, since it too contains several species small enough for a sink. Of the three I have myself tried, *P. fruticosus* subsp. *scouleri*, with large lilac flowers, and the smaller deep pink *P. laetus* subsp. *roezlii* tend to suffer severely if the weather in August, when we are all up at Ardtornish, is too hot and dry, while the linear-leaved *P. pinifolius*, with narrow tubular flowers of a brilliant scarlet, remains unscathed. But I suspect that all Penstemons, much as they like the sun, like also a little more moisture round their roots than they can always get in a shallow sun-baked sink. Fortunately all the herbaceous varieties and hybrids, of which we grow too many to list but of which none, not even Garnet (alias Andenken an Friedrich Hahn), is quite dependably hardy, are just about the easiest of all plants to propagate from cuttings, preferably taken in late summer from the plentiful side shoots, and so there is really no excuse for losing them. And the perennial mulleins too, such as the yellow Gainsborough, the deep rose Pink Domino, both four feet tall, and the smaller and more graceful *Verbascum phoeniceum*, which is typically rich purple, are said to be almost equally easy to propagate from root cuttings. These three and many more besides, including particularly the unusual amber Cotswold Beauty and the terracotta Cotswold Queen, are admirable plants for the sunny herbaceous border, to be associated not, as the Supplement to the *Dictionary of Gardening* recommends, 'with lupins and delphiniums,' which merely repeat the same spire-like theme in different colours, but to be used rather, in the words of the *Dictionary* itself rather than its Supplement, 'for the contrast their frequently tall, erect, densely flowered inflorescences make with perennials of looser habit' such as Thalictrums, for instance, or Aquilegias. But, despite its ill-gotten star in the *Dictionary*, beware of *V. nigrum*, which not only has much smaller and dingier flowers than these others nor only sows itself with inconsiderate gusto but, since to leave only one thong of its great root in the ground is to stimulate it into further feverish activity, is the dickens of a job to eradicate. And beware too that you do not buy any of the biennial species, of which the most familiar in commerce is the stately densely-felted *V. bombyciferum*, usually listed as *V.* Broussa, under the mistaken impression that they are perennials. Several of them are noble plants as much as six feet tall, and I often collect seeds of them both on the Breck and abroad, but in our experience they do not reproduce themselves with the same uninhibited spontaneity as some other biennials such as caper spurge, giant hogweed or Miss Wilmott's ghost. Incidentally, much the most widespread and familiar of the British native biennials, *V. thapsus*, is the occasion for an unwonted extravaganza on the theme of popular English plant names in the *Dictionary*, where we are offered the following enticing choice: 'Aaron's Rod, Hag Taper, Torches, Adam's Flannel, Jacob's Staff, Shepherd's Club, Blanket Leaf.' After which the actual description opens soberly enough with the words 'Densely woolly.'

And that, since I cannot be bothered with Faith's pet variegated form of our own native figwort, *Scrophularia nodosa*, leaves only the so-called Cape figworts of the genus Phygelius. Seeing that both species in cultivation do in fact come from South Africa, it is remarkable how impervious they seem even to a temperature of zero Fahrenheit. Admittedly we grow both of them on warm walls, the scarlet *P. capensis* around the long, low, west-facing kitchen window and the indecisively pink *P. aequalis* in the hot south-west-facing corner of the courtyard. But *P. capensis* at least, which has been with us much longer and came unscathed through the rigours of early 1963, not only, as I said earlier in one of my recurrent fits of irrelevance, attains a height of at least eight feet on either side of the window but also throws out into the bed below a succession of vigorous suckers to stock many another garden besides our own. Maybe as the result it will one day become as familiar a feature of Cambridgeshire gardens as it deserves.

For all but the rabid specialist the next four families contain little of horticultural value. I regret to say that for me the leafless, parasitic and often brown-flowered broomrapes have a peculiar fascination, and if you have a willow or a poplar tree in your garden, it would be well worth your while, if you can obtain it, to sow some seed of the vivid purple *Lathraea clandestina* around its roots. Similarly, if your garden can boast a peat-bog or a muddy pond, try two glamorous members of the *Lentibulariaceae*, the giant butterwort, *Pinguicula grandiflora*, which is locally abundant in counties Cork and Kerry, in the bog, and the common bladderwort, *Utricularia vulgaris*, which you can see in plenty in some of the old brick pits at Wicken Fen, in the pond. Of the *Acanthaceae* the two species of the genus Acanthus itself, *A. mollis* and *A. spinosus*, are less exigent, and even without their spikes of curious mauvish-pinkish-greenish foxglove-like flowers, make splendidly sculptural features in a warm and sunny border. And to those with a taste for annuals even I am compelled to admit that the florists' Verbena, *V. × hybrida*, which is actually a perennial but habitually grown as a half-hardy annual, combines to an unrivalled degree a certain grace of growth with a variety and purity of brilliant colour. But I must not expatiate on the virtues or vices of any of these while the gigantic family of the *Labiatae* is only just around the corner.

The *Labiatae* are every bit as versatile in the garden as the *Scrophulariaceae*, furnishing plants for the sink or trough, the paved terrace or courtyard, the wild or semi-wild garden, the herbaceous border, the shrub or mixed border and, last but not least, the herb garden. The chief contributor to the sink, trough or rock garden is the genus Teucrium, of which we lately brought back two species from the limestone hills of Savoie, the seed of the pink-flowered cut-leaved germander, *T. botrys*, a rare native of chalk and limestone in southern England, and the seed and one young plant, which is so far doing very well, of the prostrate glaucous little sub-shrub with clusters of pale yellow flowers, *T. montanum*. Though the former is only an annual or biennial, I am hopeful of inducing it to sow itself in a sunny and chalky sink, while I am confident that the latter will prove as accommodating as two other species I grow in sinks, the variable but always densely hoary *T. polium* and another prostrate glaucous sub-shrub, this time with greyish-mauve flowers veined with purple, *T. aroanum*, which originally comes from Greece. The prostrate thymes, on the other hand, I long ago discovered to be too invasive for a sink and we now grow a tangled mixture of them in the little bed at the foot of our two miniature climbing roses, my own favourite among them being the true *Thymus pseudolanuginosus* (sometimes listed as *T. serpyllum lanuginosus*), which is so densely hairy that its fast-spreading mats are soft and grey. But we learnt a sad if salutary lesson from our tangled mixture. Before we planted the young thymes we had underplanted several species of miniature bulbs, notably the three tulips, *Tulipa linifolia, T. linifolia* Batalini and *T. orphanidea*, and we were soon taught that the only bulbs which did not so miss their customary baking in the summer sun, now denied them by the dense carpet of thyme, that they promptly died of deprivation were those of the tallest and toughest of them, *T. orphanidea*. Of course the ideal place for these mats of thyme is in the crevices between paving stones, where not only are they unable to stifle anything more delicate but you get the benefit of their fragrance whenever they are trodden as well as of their multitudinous purple, red, pink or white flower-heads. But our own paving stones in the courtyard were laid so close that it is impossible to grow anything between them except what sows itself there.

The genera which particularly suit the semi-wild garden are Ajuga, Lamium (and Galeobdolon), all containing at least one ground cover plant par excellence. We actually use the purple-leaved variety of bugle, *Ajuga reptans* Atropurpurea, as a burnished carpet, backed on each side of the sink in the middle by a fully grown bush of *Berberis thunbergii* Atropurpurea Nana, at the very front of the Copper Box, and first *Anemone pavonina* and then *Tulipa sprengeri*, both intense blood-red, are strong enough to thrust up through it. But for the rest we grow these carpeters in the shadier beds in the semi-wild garden. Two other varieties of our common native woodland. *A. reptans*, var. Multicolor which is variegated with bronze and red and var. Variegata in which the variegation is silver, spread apace (but not menacingly because you can always pull rooted pieces up around the edge to put elsewhere or give away) at either corner of the crescent-shaped mixed border at the far end. The compact but rather invasive *Lamium maculatum*, whose tidy green cordate leaves have a white stripe down the middle and whose clustered flowers are normally mauvy-pink but can be white, is a potential threat, against which we have to be constantly on our guard, to the best of our Anemone species under the old plum tree that supports *Clematis viticella* Alba Luxurians. And as for the variegated form of *Lamium galeobdolon*, sometimes still listed under its former name of *Galeobdolon luteum*, it is so aggressive a trespasser as to be often denied, as it is by Faith, its undeniable beauty. Even in early February, when I am now writing, its large but delicately crenate leaves, veined with deep purple and broadly splashed with silver midway between the midrib and the margins, give an unsurpassed effect of natural marbling to even the shadiest corner of the garden. But there is no concealing the other side of the picture either. When we first planted it, along with another ground-cover plant that I would have expected to withstand any invasion, *Euphorbia cyparissias*, on the long narrow ridge which Faith had topped with her mixed hedge of old-fashioned roses, it lost no time at all, while our eyes were averted, in using its lightning leapfrog tactics first to eliminate the spurge and then to entwine a young rose bush to the point of total suffocation.

The main contributor to the herbaceous border from among the labiate family is undoubtedly the genus Salvia. But before we lift our eyes as high as that, there are already three contestants, all very familiar, for places in the front row. First and lowliest come the various self-heals, of which the very local native inhabitant of chalk downs in southern England, *Prunella laciniata*, with its deeply pinnate leaves and heads of yellowish-white flowers, is among the prettiest. But I have yet to see it in a garden, where its place is taken sometimes by *P. vulgaris* form *incisa*, with similarly pinnatifid leaves but purple flowers, sometimes by *P. grandiflora*, the seed of which, in the normal purple form, I brought back last autumn from the Jura hills, but most often, probably, by *P. × webbiana*, which is to be distinguished by its shorter and blunter leaves and which has, besides the normal bright purple form, a lilac variety called Loveliness, a pink variety Pink Loveliness and a white variety White Loveliness. And then, of course, there are two universal favourites in the genera Stachys and Nepeta. Besides the familiar cottage garden plant called lamb's lugs, lamb's ears, lamb's tongue, or what you will, *Stachys byzantina*, whose glory lies not in its flowers but in the dense white wool in which, surely more like a lamb's ear than its tongue, the whole plant is clothed, there is another slightly less well-known member of the genus, *S. macrantha*, formerly often listed as *Betonica grandiflora*, whose broadly cordate wrinkled leaves and conspicuous whorls of large pink to purple hooded flowers fully earn it a place alongside its shaggier cousin. And similarly, besides the justly popular low-growing catmint *Nepeta × faassenii*, which is almost universally but erroneously listed under the name of one of its parents as *N. mussinii*, there is another twice the height and much more diffuse called Six Hills Giant which, though to my mind as to cats' much less attractive, is still worth considering for a place in the row behind. In that row too come not only the first and perhaps the finest of the Salvias, *S. × superba*, which is again almost universally but erroneously listed as *S. virgata nemorosa*, but also a curious plant, of better value perhaps for the entertainment it affords children than for beauty, called the obedient plant or *Physostegia virginiana*. The Salvia is tidier and more compact than most of its herbaceous relatives and produces a large number of upright branching stems, two foot or more tall, with each branch topped by a long spike of bright bluish-purple flowers arranged in close whorls and subtended by dull red bracts which outlive the flowers. For sheer mass of this particular colour there is no plant of comparable size to beat it, and the colour, even if somewhere between blue and purple, is both vivid and unalloyed. The typical form of the Physostegia on the other hand, which has however a white variety and another, called Vivid, which is said to be dwarfer, later-flowering and bright rose-pink, is of my least favourite shade somewhere between pink and mauve (or, as the catalogues prefer to call it, lilac), and its charm derives chiefly, as does its English name, from the fact that in whatever direction you choose to turn any or all of its relatively large and almost sessile flowers, which are arranged in straight lines both vertically and horizontally, there they will obligingly stay put.

At this point, two steps back from the front, we ourselves prefer to grow in our herbaceous border, rather than the taller herbaceous Salvias which tend, in our dry soil at least, to flop and straggle, the woody little evergreen shrub called Jerusalem sage or *Phlomis fruticosa*, which has thickly felted grey-green leaves, very pale and intricately netted with prominent white veins beneath, and one or two terminal whorls of many large yellow flowers. But we make amends to several of the Salvias by growing them in mixed borders in other parts of the garden. Perhaps the main point of *S. argentea*, which we grow for that reason in a prominent position in the relatively narrow bed in front of the greenhouse, lies rather in its wide flat rosette of silver woolly leaves than in its large branched panicle of distantly whorled white flowers; but at least, though it flowered heartily for us last year, it seems to be refuting the statement in the *Dictionary of Gardening* that it is a biennial by producing from the same root, as early as the second week in February, the unmistakable beginnings of a healthy new rosette. Nor do I understand the statement in the same authoritative work that *S. pratensis* Haematodes group is 'more or less biennial,' for unless by any chance I have confused it with *S. sclarea*, which is said to be neither 'more' nor 'less' but quite simply 'biennial,' it has unfailingly appeared and produced an abundance of pale blue flowers in precisely the same place for more years in succession than I can remember. The deeper blue *S. patens*, along with the shrubby rose-pink *S. involucrata*, is still no more than a healthily rooted young cutting in the greenhouse, whither for safety's sake the two will probably have to be returned after a summer in the open. And as for the rare native *S. pratensis*, the best blue of them all, it has as yet to produce anything more than cotyledons in the pan in the frame in which last October we sowed the seed I had just gathered in subalpine pastures. On the other hand we have long had another shrubby Salvia, the blood-red *S. grahamii*, which sometimes but by no means always survives our winters out of doors but can always, given the forethought, be easily replaced by a well-rooted cutting the following spring. And that leaves, among the more obvious labiates to grow in a herbaceous border, only the various colour forms of the two bergamots, *Monarda didyma* and *M. fistulosa*, of which the former at least, regardless of its having a variety called Cambridge Scarlet, took little time to discover that the soil of south Cambridgeshire was too dry for its constitution. Maybe, since *M. fistulosa* is said to thrive under drier conditions than *M. didyma*, we betrayed a lack of perseverance in not replacing the one with the other; but we found, perhaps unfairly, that we could live without either.

In dealing with Phlomis and the shrubby Salvias in the context of the herbaceous border, I seem to have left precious little for the shrub border. There are, of course, always the lavenders and the varieties of rosemary, but though they would all be welcome almost anywhere in our garden where they had a chance of survival, the one place where we should never put them would be anywhere in a collection of mixed shrubs. Indeed all the shrubby labiates that I know at all well look to me better, as does Phlomis, among plants of lower stature than among taller and more robust shrubs. *Teucrium fruticans*, for instance, which despite its reputation is hardy enough to have withstood unprotected our recent twenty degrees of frost, throws out its slender forked branches so nearly horizontally, rather like a young sucker from an olive tree, that if you want to appreciate its distinctive shape you must allow it room (and not much over a yard is required) to grow naturally and without impediment. The semi-woody *Perovskia atriplicifolia* on the other hand, the chief point of which is that the whole plant except the panicles of soft blue flowers is white with little starry hairs, naturally tends to grow, unless a strong wind thwarts its intentions, into a miniature silver reproduction, only a yard or so high, of a Lombardy poplar, and so is again best viewed rising above lower plants such as *Nepeta* × *faassenii*. In fact the only one of the three that can brook being overtopped or obstructed is the small shrubby relation of our common native horehound called *Ballota pseudo-dictamnus*; and why it should be called that when it bears not the remotest resemblance to a Dictamnus, God alone knows. Its flowers, apart from their broad grey-green calyces, are insignificant or worse, but the whole plant, which is less than two feet tall, is again so densely felted, this time in grey, that, being an ever-green, it has a modest decorative value throughout the winter months.

We cannot at this point move on as we should from the shrubbery to the herb garden for the simple reason that we do not possess either. Just as, however, we still contrive to grow a considerable number of flowering trees and shrubs, so there seem somehow to be quite a lot of herbs here and there, and mainly, for obvious reasons, round the edges of the kitchen garden. And moreover the most decorative among them, since we choose them almost as much for their looks as their flavour, seem to belong to the labiate family. We have never bothered with basil, hyssop or savory, which strike us as scarcely worth the space or the trouble, and even calamint and marjoram survive, the former by sowing itself in what is now the winter garden, from the days when there was far more bare earth in the garden than there was intentional vegetation. Though Faith is addicted to experiment in cookery, and not least with vegetables, we are in fact far from fanatical herbalists. But it so happens that three genera of the *Labiatae* that we do put to culinary purposes are, or at any rate can be, outstandingly ornamental as well. Apart from the common shrubby thyme, *T. vulgaris*, which, if given the chance, can make a grey-green bush eighteen inches high and more than a yard through and which, however small, smothers itself during the earlier half of summer in little pinkish flowers, the smaller lemon-scented thyme, *T. × citriodorus*, has a variety variegated with gold, Aureus, and another with silver called Silver Queen. Indeed, we grow a miniature thicket of the former and can testify that throughout the year, even now when the snow is falling remorselessly, it makes a welcome patch of colour. And there are at least four highly decorative varieties of the common shrubby sage as well, *Salvia officianalis*. There is a more compact version with golden-yellow leaves called Aurea; Icterina has the usual grey-green leaves liberally variegated with gold; Purpurascens, which is justifiably called 'a useful bedding plant' in the *Dictionary of Gardening*, is not only the most handsome, with stems as well as leaves rich reddish-purple, but also, which does not always follow, the easiest to procure; and Tricolor, which is the second best, has leaves which are variegated with pink as well as white, the pink predominating as the season advances. As a matter of fact, even before I was aware of the suggestion in the *Dictionary*, we had been using the purple sage very effectively to extend the influence of our Copper Box outwards from the centre in the form of colourful little islands in a predominantly silver sea. And the mints also, to come to the last of my selected labiates, have a number of elegantly variegated forms, notably var. Variegata of the hairy and woolly *Mentha suaveolens* (the leaves of which, in our version at least, are almost as much pure white, as opposed to the 'light yellow' of the *Dictionary*, as they are grey-green) and again var. Variegata of the lower red-stemmed *M. × gentilis*, the ginger mint (in which the leaves are this time richly variegated with gold). But in this case variegation smacks somewhat of gilding the lily. For there are at least two true species, *M. spicata* and *M. suaveolens*, the leaves of which are as different in shape, and in texture for the matter of that, as their former names (*M. longifolia* and *M. rotundifolia*) suggest, but alike in being soft grey-green above and whitely tomentose beneath; while what may or may not be the hybrid between the two (*M. × villosa*), the plant which Hull regarded as a distinct species and named *M. alopecurioides*, is a noble upstanding creature which, if only it were not so invasive, would be a heaven-sent addition to any grey border. Indeed, now I come to think of it, we grow a mint, originally given us by Margery Fish without a name and resembling *M. spicata* in every respect except that its leaves are silvery-grey on top as well as underneath, which, if only it could learn a little self-control, would strike a perfect balance with *Lysimachia ephemerum* in the farther Silver Box. And to complete this brief paean on mints I need only add that, if it too could sublimate its congenital tendency to trespass, the creeping *M. requienii*, which for all its diminutive stature is as aromatic as all the rest, would be an equally heaven-sent addition to a shady sink.

And at this point in our scramble through the flora we reach the *Plantaginaceae.* So let us leave my sinks, our herbaceous border, our non-existent shrubbery and herb garden, sit for a while on any of our lawns you choose and admire how luxuriantly the plantains grow.

CHAPTER 12

Campanulaceae to Compositae

OF the thirty-six orders of dicotyledonous plants in the British flora there are now only three left, the *Campanales*, the *Rubiales* and the *Asterales*; but each of these contains one family of paramount importance. The *Campanales* comprise, apart from the *Campanulaceae* themselves, only the *Lobeliaceae*, which, just as the *Paeoniaceae* have only lately been set up as a family on their own, were not long ago regarded as merely a genus within the large Campanula family. The *Rubiales* consist in these days of five families represented in Britain, two of which will call for a brief passing mention but one of which, the *Caprifoliaceae*, casts a shade, metaphorical as well as literal, over all the others. And the *Asterales* feature in these islands only in the guise, which in all conscience is enough in itself to keep many a British gardener happily occupied, of the polymorphic *Compositae*.

By as much as the family of the *Caprifoliaceae* dominates the order *Rubiaceae*, so does the genus Campanula dominate its own family; but this time there are several lesser lights in the same firmament to which we can spare an occasional glance while focusing on the Campanulas proper. The Campanulas proper, however, are again quite sufficient for the average gardener to be going on with; not only are there more than a hundred and thirty listed in the *Dictionary of Gardening*, not only indeed are more than thirty starred, but several of the best of them, especially where there are slugs about, are by no means easy in cultivation. Here again in fact, as with the alpine species of Ranunculus or the Soldanellas, a sink is no substitute for a proper rock garden complete with a proper moraine; for like these others, the alpine Campanulas demand, at least during the growing season, a constant degree of moisture in the soil such as is impossible to provide in anything as shallow and as flat as a sink. Consequently, though we have seen and photographed a fair number of alpine and sub-alpine Campanulas on our travels, we have as yet attempted to introduce only two into our own garden. *C. cochlearifolia*, which you can hardly fail to see on any excursion into the

177

Alps, is of course by any standards an exceptionally obliging as well as an exceptionally pretty little plant, and I had hardly planted it in one front corner of the largest of my sinks before it had spread by its slender underground runners to the other front corner as well. *C. barbata* on the other hand, which is perhaps too big for a sink, is the only one of the genus whose seeds I collected last autumn, and though it has again lived up to its reputation and germinated very freely, I can still think of no situation in a garden that lacks a rockery where its delicate colour and the long and characteristic hairs at the mouth of its bells can be best appreciated. We should have liked to try *C. alpestris*, whose disproportionately large hanging purple bells were mainly over when we saw it in the Gran Paradiso, but any reader of Reginald Farrer will think twice before attempting to uproot it; while as for the curious *C. thyrsoides*, which is abundant among other places in the hay-fields in the Val d'Isère, it loses much of its desirability in the eyes of a gardener as indolent as I am by being monocarpic. Whether the same is true of what appears to be its purple counterpart in the same district I am unable to say because I can find no trace of it in any book I can lay hands on.[1] But be that as it may, on our last visit to the Alps I paid more attention to the related genus of Phyteuma than to that of Campanula and collected seed of any species we found, including two dwarfs in *P. globulariifolium* and *P. hedraianthifolium*, wherever we came across them. All I can say as yet is that I already have a whole panful of healthy little seedlings of the latter, while the seeds of its bigger brother *P. scheuzeri* germinated and grew so fast that they had to be individually potted up within two months of sowing them. But how either of them, or any of the four or five others, will fare either in a sink or in the open ground, it would be premature to forecast. All I know is that I failed in a sink with the much more spectacular *Physoplexis comosa* from the Dolomites, which, since we have never even seen it, let alone collected it, in its native haunts, I was reduced to buying from Joe Elliott. But I can testify that another member of the same family which I had from the same source, *Wahlenbergia* (or *Edraianthus*) *pumilio*, is as obliging and floriferous in a sink as a plant could be.

The medium-sized Campanulas are as simple in cultivation as most of the small ones are tricky. Our own favourite among them is probably the white form of *C. carpatica*, which we honour with a place at the front of the sunniest of the narrow raised beds in the courtyard. Like all this type of Campanula it flowers prodigally, and it has the advantage, if such you deem it, of only coming into flower in the latter part of June, by which time the great mass of colour, in our garden at least,

---

[1] I have lately been told on the highest authority that it must be *C. spicata*.

is already beginning to fade. Even more colourful and even easier to satisfy are the two with impossible names, the starry purplish-blue *C. portenschlagiana*, which used more conveniently and suggestively to be called simply *C. muralis*, and the paler and even more rampageous *C. poscharskyana*. But if you follow the advice of some catalogues and treat them as plants for the rock garden, be sure to allow them plenty of room. In my own view the latter at least is best used to carpet an area less appetising and requiring less constant attention than the rock garden; for unlike many of its kindred, it is perfectly prepared not only to ramp but to cover itself in flower even in partial shade. Indeed, any of the refinements of the moraine would be wasted on any of this comparatively coarse group of Campanulas, in which should probably be included *C. garganica* as well.

At this point three other genera of the *Campanulaceae* raise their heads, though one of them not very far. The delicate, trailing, blue-flowered *Cyananthus microphyllus*, which is usually listed in catalogues as *C. integer*, and probably all the rest of its genus as well, not only require more moisture in the soil than they can get at Shepreth but equally palpably crave for peat or possibly leaf-mould and detest chalk. I suspect in fact that even then they need a good deal of care and attention, for they have done no good at Ardtornish either. The genus Codonopsis, on the other hand, with the apparent exception of the twining *C. convolvulacea*, which I have not consciously ever seen, suffers from the fact, freely admitted in the *Dictionary of Gardening*, that 'the outer colouring' of its petals is 'usually somewhat indeterminate,' and the hanging flowers have therefore to be either lifted or seen from below before they disclose the subtle beauty of their design. And last comes the genus Jasione, in which the rounded heads of powder-blue flowers are reminiscent of those of an elongated Globularia. Unfortauntely our own native *J. montana*, which blends so beautifully with the sea-pinks on, for instance, Holyhead or the Cliffs of Moher, is said on the highest authority to be 'usually biennial but probably sometimes perennial or annual,' so that even the most unscrupulous collector would have to select his victim with more than usual care and skill. But *J. laevis* from western Europe has presumably mastered this shortcoming, while another perennial from Hungary, *J. heldveichii*, is even procurable from Ingwersen's.

When we come to Campanulas for the herbaceous border, the native flora of Britain once again comes handsomely into its own. Apart from the four established aliens, rampion or *C. rapunculus*, the insufferably invasive *C. rapunculoides*, and the two most commonly seen in gardens, *C. persicifolia* and the Canterbury bell itself, *C. medium*, there are four other indisputably native species with so strong a claim to a place in the garden that two of them, *C. glomerata* and *C. latifolia*, or at least their varieties, have long been in commerce. Living where I do, I tend to think of *C. glomerata*, the clustered bell-flower, as essentially a plant of the dry chalk downs, and my mental picture of it therefore is always of a condensed little plant seldom attaining as much as a foot in height. I believe, however, that given a soil a bit damper and richer than it normally chooses for itself it can speedily double its stature. Even so its proper place in a border is well to the fore of the giant bell-flower, *C. latifolia*, which in normal conditions is at least a yard high. This time, as the result of the mere accident of having often driven from Cambridge to the west of Scotland, I tend to visualise the plant as suddenly becoming frequent in the hedgebanks as soon as you branch left off the Great North Road at or near Scotch Corner. But hardly less striking than these two are the nettle-leaved bell-flower, *C. trachelium*, which is widespread but by no means ubiquitous in southern England and would look very much at home in the wild garden, and the much more local *C. patula*, primarily associated for me with the by-roads of Hereford-shire, which holds its large, relatively shallow and vivid purple bells, presumably in reaction against the anti-disestablishmentarianism rife in the genus, not all together in strict spires but a few at a time on gracefully spreading branches. Although it gains no such recognition in the *Dictionary of Gardening* and none at all in commerce, it is, with the possible exception of the finest forms of harebell on certain roadsides in the west Highlands, the most beautiful as well as indisputably the most graceful of our native Campanulas, and the only reason why I did not last autumn bring back seed of it from the lowest stretches of the Val Maggia, as also of the lovely *C. rhomboidalis* which abounds in hayfields farther up, is that in neither case, even at the end of September, was the seed nearly ripe. There is indeed only one other of the larger Campanulas that I am as glad to grow in the garden, namely *C. Burghaltii*, and one, *C. lactiflora*, that I would equally gladly grow if I could. The former, which is yet one more of the countless plants that do not seem to have won the recognition they deserve, is another of the spire-bearing fraternity, but instead of lifting its many spires straight upwards, as *C. persicifolia* or *C. glomerata* do, it sprays them gracefully out in all directions so that it is appreciably wider than tall; and its large pendent flowers are of a unique and soft shade that is quite as much pale grey as blue. And *C. lactiflora* is a graceful plant too, despite its lofty stature of four or five feet, because it is another that has abandoned the spire habit in favour of large lax panicles of upright pale blue flowers. Inspired by its beauty and floriferousness on a very steep bank at the top of the drive at Ardtornish, where it is a deeper blue than usual and must presumably be the choicer variety *caerulea*, we early planted it, in close proximity to *Thalictrum flavum*, in the herbaceous border at Shepreth, and I can only reluctantly conclude from the fact that, whereas the Thalictrum, one of whose natural haunts is fens, is still in the rudest health, the Campanula never attains anything like its full stature, that it must be another and larger member of the genus which cannot wholly dispense with a modicum of moisture in the growing season.

One other member of the family, although not strictly a Campanula, looks so very like one and is so superlative a constituent of the herbaceous border that it cries aloud for a paragraph on its own. *Platycodon grandiflorus* is actually the only species in its genus, but it has several named varieties, of which var. *mariesii*, a lower-growing form with equally large flowers, is probably the best. As far as I remember, we bought three plants of the variety, which grow and flower happily towards the front of the herbaceous border; but the type we grew from a packet of seed with so little trouble and to such good effect that we now have two flourishing colonies of it, one on the sunny side of the courtyard, the other in the bed in front of the greenhouse. Its buds are of a characteristic shape, roughly that of a pear but with five regular corrugations radiating from the centre of the upper and broader end, and they open into wide and rather shallow five-lobed bells each measuring about two inches across. Both buds and flowers, which are normally two or three to a stem and on pedicels amply long enough to show them off separately, are of a purity and brightness of colour, distinctly on the mauve side of blue, as to put even most of the Campanulas proper in the shade; the best forms of the harebell and *Campanula rhomboidalis* are the only two I can think of off-hand that can vie with them, and in both these cases the flowers are, of course, very much smaller. Add to this that the narrowly ovate leaves, sharply pointed and finely toothed, seem always endowed with the bloom of health and you have yet another of the host of easy-going plants which richly earn a place in many more gardens than can at present boast them.

One last member of the *Campanulaceae*, aptly called *Ostrowskia magnifica*, is in truth so magnificent a plant that, although we have never attempted to grow it, I cannot forbear to mention it. And I know it can be grown too, even in Cambridge; for several years ago we were shown a superb specimen of it in full flower by a friend, admittedly a very skilful gardener, with a not very large garden there. From a tall stem with rather distant whorls of broadly ovate and toothed leaves it produces a spike of admittedly relatively few upright pale mauve bells each one of which measures nearly six inches across. Unfortunately it needs a deep and well-drained soil, preferably with a liberal admixture of leaf-mould, in an open sunny situation, as well as the protection in winter and early spring of a heap of leaves or ashes. But if you are prepared to give it that amount of mollycoddling it will put most of the Campanulas in your garden in the shade and all the Lobelias. For my own part, I cannot shed many tears that Lobelias not only, like *Campanula lactiflora*, hardly tolerate drought in the growing season but also, like Dahlias, have to be lifted and stored throughout the winter; for as it is, I can still see the small ones in other people's window-boxes and the large ones bedded out in municipal parks without thinking that we ought to try and grow them ourselves.

In defiance of the strict botanical order it will be best, while we are on the subject of herbaceous plants, to deal with the *Compositae* next and to leave the order of the *Caprifoliaceae* till last, the more so since I long ago foreshadowed our attitude to the *Compositae* as a whole in the Introduction and propose to deal with them almost as summarily as in an earlier chapter I dealt with the *Cruciferae*. There is, of course, no denying that the average British garden owes to the composites in general, and to Michaelmas daisies, Chrysanthemums and Dahlias in particular, the greater part of their autumn colour. It may be in part because we are regularly at Ardtornish from the last week of July onwards and do not see our garden at Shepreth again until the middle of September that we have progressively tended to aim in the south at a mass of colour in the earlier part of the year; but if that is a contributory factor in our injustice to these popular favourites, it is certainly not the main reason for it. The plain truth is that too many of the composites, and especially those which contribute most colour to an autumn garden, pay for the profusion and vivid colours of their flowers by the dreariness and inelegance of their foliage. Admittedly there are several notable exceptions. Most of the Achilleas, for instance, have attractively feathery foliage, and when it is hoary, as in the tiny high-alpine *A. nana* which is small enough for a sink, or silver, as in the herbaceous *A. aegyptiaca*, it would earn a place for that alone. And similarly the varieties of *Anthemis tinctoria*, notably Thora Perry, and of *Chrysanthemum coccineum*, better known as Pyrethrum, have finely dissected rather than the characteristically heavy leaves of so many of the family. Indeed in a very few genera, especially Santolina and Tanacetum, the foliage can be so delicate as to atone for the relative dreariness of the flowers that spring from it; and the same could almost be said of the shrubby relations of the groundsel, *Brachyglottis* (formerly *Senecio*) *greyi* and congener *laxifolia*, and the genuinely exquisite but, alas, even less reliably hardy *Senecio vira-vira*. So I could, and almost would, go on and on making exeptions until there was little room left in any ordinary garden for anything but composites. What, for instance, about those two species of Ligularia with purple-tinted leaves and stems, *L. dentata* in the variety Desdemona and the unpronounceable *L. przewalskii?* I have to admit that we grow them both in the herbaceous border, where the latter is liable to exceed its bounds. And at the other end of the size scale we even grow two species of Aster, *A. alpinus* itself and the bright blue *A. pappei*[1] from South Africa, which, until its numerous single-headed flower-stems begin to appear, looks rather like an infant larch tree. And finally I must admit that in the large selection of seed I brought back from our last tour of the Alps there were no less than seven species of composites included: two Alpine Erigerons, *E. alpinus* and *E. uniflorus*, the latter at least small enough for my smallest sink; an unknown Gnaphalium which may turn out to be only a stunted mountain form of our native (but attractive) *G. sylvaticum*; the variety *caulescens* of the carline thistle; and three giants in the shape of the yellow sub-alpine thistle, *Cirsium oleraceum*, another inhabitant of shady hedgebanks in sub-alpine regions, the tall mauve-flowered *Prenanthes purpurea* (which incidentally the *Dictionary of Gardening* dismisses, along with the other perennials of the genus, as 'hardy but of little garden value'), and last, but by no means least, that magnificent feature of high alpine meadows, so stately a plant that it once earned its place on Swiss postage stamps, the appropriately named *Cirsium spinosissimum*. And what is more, despite my undisguised prejudice, I hope they all germinate and flourish.

The full extent of our joint prejudice against the family of the *Compositae* goes in fact even deeper than I have yet suggested. Besides Aster, Chrysanthemum and Dahlia, several other popular genera fail to evoke in us the usual enthusiasm: Gaillardia, for instance, Helenium and Helianthus, Rudbeckia and, perhaps above all, Solidago. But for all our passionate prejudice there are, even apart from Artemisia, three genera that we would not at any price be without, the genera Hieracium, Cynara and Onopordum. The hawkweeds are all too often dismissed, as they are, for instance, by Mr Ingwersen, as 'a weedy race,' a generalisation which any gardener would immediately and uncondi-tionally withdraw who had ever seen the British *Hieracium holosericeum*, the most widely distributed of the alpine group of hawkweeds in these islands, on its native cliffs and rocky ridges. *H. holosericeum*, so far from being weedy, produces from a neat basal rosette a stem of about six inches, slightly nodding in the upper part, topped by a single large flower of pure soft golden-yellow and, which is the point, the whole plant except what you would call the petals, which are actually the ligules, is so densely clothed in very long silky white hairs that it looks from a little distance as if it were surrounded by a broad silver halo.

[1] [now *Felicia amoena*.]

Unfortunately *H. holosericeum* itself, possibly only because it is not uncommon on British mountains, seems not to be in commerce, but *H. bombycinum* from Spain, which is listed, as an exception from the general condemnation of the genus, by Mr Ingwersen, is a not unworthy substitute; and both *H. villosum* and *H. waldsteinii* reproduce, if somewhat less tidily, much the same effect on twice the scale. Nothing could be more different from this than the effect of the genus Cynara, the two most familiar of which are the cardoon, *C. cardunculus*, and the globe artichoke, *C. scolymus*. Faith and I can never agree as to the primary purpose of the latter, which incidentally is unknown in the wild anywhere in the world and appears long ago to have been derived from the former. Faith regards it, along perhaps with Asparagus, as the topmost delicacy of the kitchen garden; I regard it as one of the best of all plants for the back of the herbaceous border. But if you happen to share my view, you thwart your own purpose, of course, by decapitating the stately stems before the noble thistle flowers have a chance to open. Since fortunately the cardoon is, in Faith's view at any rate, less delicious to eat than the globe artichoke proper, we have only this past autumn arrived at a compromise that satisfies us both. A fine plant of *C. cardunculus*, with a main root about two foot long, has been moved to the back of the herbaceous border, where it joins the only other plant of equal architectural merit in *Acanthus mollis*, while the row of *C. scolymus* remains intact in the kitchen garden. I look forward to seeing how the long pinnatifid silver leaves of the Cynara and its huge globular heads, beside which those of the popular *Echinops ritro* are both puny and pallid, complement the dark glossy leaves and stiff flower-spikes of the Acanthus; and Faith can still glut herself on her favourite delicacy. Happily there is no room for difference of opinion on the last of our short list of assorted composites, *Onopordum nervosum*, because nobody has ever suggested that any part of it is edible; its function in the garden, which it performs as well as any plant of any family, is purely decorative. For the benefit of those who do not know it, a fully grown plant of it, even in our far from nourishing soil, is fully eight-foot tall, and it is so glistening silver from top to toe that, like the involucral leaves of *Eryngium giganteum*, it reflects the last rays of daylight in such a way that the whole of it seems to shine in the dark. Unfortunately it suffers from the same drawback as the Eryngium, that it is a biennial, and in our experience it is not nearly so spontaneously prolific either. But we have found that if you simply lay the whole plant flat on a bare bit of ground in the kitchen garden when it has finished flowering, you will by the following midsummer have a large brood of seedlings which you can with the utmost ease, as soon as the ground is damp, move to their ultimate destinations.

So we come to our beloved Artemisias, which are not only so decorative but also for the most part so easily satisfied that they put two other potentially valuable genera of the family to shame; the genus Anaphalis because it is coarse by comparison, the genus Helichrysum because it is much less tolerant of winter damp. The great glory of all the best of the Artemisias, though not quite all that are worth growing, is the incomparably delicate silver filigree of their foliage; the only one that is commonly grown for the sake of its flowers, and is on that account starred in the *Dictionary of Gardening* as 'a fine plant grown in a mass in a semi-wild garden,' is *A. lactiflora*, which personally I regard, and only after fair trial, as very little superior to our own common wormwood, *A. absinthium*, a dowdy dweller on derelict dumps. Fortunately there is no need to grow it either, for those with finely cut silver leaves vary in size from three inches to at least as many feet. The two smallest are *A. norvegica*, which was first found as a native of the north-westernmost Highlands of Scotland as lately as 1952, and *A. glacialis*, which is not uncommon on damp stony slopes at high altitudes in the Alps. Though they both make mats or cushions of finely pinnate silver leaves, the two plants could not be confused in flower because, whereas the former usually bears only a single flower on each stem, a nodding yellow button half an inch across, the latter produces little spikes, bending coyly over at the tip, of tiny closely packed flowers. Regrettably neither seems to be in commerce, and while the former could only be acquired, even if you knew where to go, by an act of the grossest vandalism, the latter appears, from our own experience at least, to be as impossible to satisfy in a sink as an alpine Ranunculus or Soldanella. The case is, however, gratifyingly different with the next in the size scale, *A. nitida*, which, though another inhabitant of the high mountains, is not only perfectly at home here both in a sink and in the open ground, but is exceptionally easy, like the biggest of its brothers, *A. arborescens*, to propagate from green cuttings taken in the summer. Then comes another pair of which one again, *A. maritima*, is not only another British native but this time, especially around the Thames estuary and on the north coast of Norfolk, a locally abundant one. If, for instance, you went to Burnham Overy Staithe, between Brancaster and Blakeney, and walked along the top of the dyke with the creek on your left, you would see, particularly as you approached the sand dunes, a broad zone of silver just above the high tide mark consisting entirely of the sea wormwood. And what is more, although it is by nature confined to sea-walls and salt-marshes, it is another of those plants which adapt themselves happily to gardens far inland, where it will spread apace and, apart from the fact that it grows a little taller, will produce the same effect of silver filigree as it does on the coast. And much the same general effect is produced by the other of the pair too, *A. alba* from the Mediterranean, though a closer inspection reveals that the individual leaves are sharper and dissected on a more regular and rectangular pattern. Then come two which do not really fall into the series at all, because their upper leaves at least, which are long and narrow, so far from being finely divided, are normally not divided at all. I confess that I am in a difficulty here over nomenclature, for were it not that the *Dictionary of Gardening* lists and describes them as distinct species, I would have sworn that the plants in commerce under the names of *A. palmeri* and *A. ludoviciana* were one and the same; and if they really are distinct, I am at a loss to know which of the two it is we have long grown in the herbaceous border. Whichever it may be, it is a rather invasive but quite easily controlled plant, about two feet tall, and, in the company of most other plants, emphatically silver. But in the company of the other of our pair, of the origin of which I can discover little but which is readily procurable under the name of Silver Queen, it would perhaps be more accurately described as silvery-grey. Yet two others of the genus, southernwood or *A. abrotanum* from southern Europe and *A. stelleriana* from North America, are often recommended as herbaceous border plants, but they both merit a position where the beauty of their individual leaves, grey and dissected in the former instance, pinnately lobed and silvery-white in the latter, can be fully appreciated. And the same goes even more for what is perhaps the finest of the whole genus, the feathery silver sub-shrub *A. arborescens*, a particularly splendid form of which, not only appreciably more silver but, as this winter has conclusively proved, incomparably hardier as well than the one in commerce, we successfully introduced two years ago, in the form of three or four diminutive seedlings, from the summit of Mount Filerimo in Rhodes.

The order *Rubiales* contains, besides the *Caprifoliaceae*, three other families which have a contribution, if not a very notable one, to make to British gardens. The best of the *Rubiaceae* themselves is probably the Greek *Asperula suberosa*, a woolly white carpeter for the rock garden which smothers itself in summer with small four-lobed tubular flowers of a very pure pink; but like so many woolly plants, including plenty from the Alps and the Mediterranean countries, it takes none too kindly to the damp of a typical English winter. The *Valerianaceae* also produce two or three species of the genus Valeriana itself, such as *V. celtica* and *V. supina*, which are sometimes grown in rock gardens for the sake of their fragrance; but their most familiar representative is the so-called red valerian, *Centranthus* (or *Kentranthus*) *ruber*, the typical form of which, being of a peculiarly dingy shade of red, is best left where it has colonised old walls and waste places. But the white form, and possibly also the deep red variety *atrococcineus*, have their uses as better cover than weeds for such inhospitable places as the narrow bed at the foot of the north-east-facing wall of our house, which we leave them to contest with *Bergenia crassifolia*. And finally the *Dipsacaceae* likewise contribute one good plant to the rock garden, the prostrate woody grey-leaved *Pterocephalus perennis* from Greece, with mauvy-pink flowers like those of a scabious on two-inch stems; and again, apart from our common native wild teasel, *Dipsacus fullonum* (another of the plants which, along with *Hesperis matronalis* and *Bupleurum falcatum*, we allow to seed itself more or less where it will in the herbaceous border), three good herbaceous members of the genus Scabiosa as well. The most popular is *S. caucasica*, the numerous named varieties of which, white, mauve and blue, are often to be seen in florists' shops; but there are also a taller and more upright pale yellow one, *S. columbaria ochroleuca*, which, though less often seen, is really a better plant for the average herbaceous border, and a rather straggling crimson relative, *Knautia macedonica*, which atones for its relatively small flowers by the abundance of them over a protracted season.

And so, positively last of the dicotyledons, we arrive at the *Caprifoliaceae*, and a worthy climax they make. But once again, like the *Oleaceae* in the last chapter, they impose, by sheer weight of numbers, the necessity of ruthless elimination. As a matter of fact we for our part, whether from ignorance or from lack of taste, find the task of selection less painful than in several other cases. We have so little liking for the colour of the flowers of the genus Weigela that the only two we are now attempting to grow, from cuttings scrounged last summer, are the purple-leaved and variegated varieties of *W. florida*, which we shall admit without much enthusiasm for the sake, primarily at least, of their foliage. And if we have no great passion for the genus Weigela nor, it appears, has the genus Abelia for us. At any rate the specimen of *A. floribunda* which we planted, in defiance of our colour scheme, in the front of the house succumbed to its first winter here, while that of *A. × grandiflora* which we have ordered, on the strength of its reputation for greater hardihood, for the more sheltered courtyard has yet to arrive. *Kolkwitzia amabilis*, a gracefully arching shrub from China, though closely related to the Abelias, seems a good deal hardier than they are; hardy enough, at any rate, to come unscathed through the severe frosts to which my mother-in-law's garden at nearly five hundred feet in Rutland is liable. And if you want a rounded shrub about six feet high which covers itself in early summer with clusters of pink bell-shaped flowers with yellow throats, this is probably the best of them all. We are more than content to leave the ugly *Leycesteria formosa* and all species of *Symphoricarpus*, or snowberry, to those who find them useful in flower arrangements. But all the yellow-leaved elders, variety Aurea of both *Sambucus canadensis* and of the ordinary *S. nigra* and Plumosa Aurea of *S. racemosa*, can be decorative and useful in the garden by providing a splash of golden sunshine in a predominantly green setting. And apart from the genera Lonicera, or honeysuckle, and Viburnum, both of which have so much to contribute to any garden of any size that they fully deserve at least two paragraphs each, the only other member of the family I know, and that only in the wild in the eastern Highlands of Scotland, is the delicate little creeping *Linnaea borealis* with its pairs of hanging pale pink bells; and that, much as I should like to grow it, is so emphatic in its demand both for shade, if only the shade afforded by a tall growth of ling, and for a peaty limefree soil that it would be futile to attempt to grow it in a dry and chalky garden.

The genus Viburnum, of which there are more than sixty species and hybrids listed in the *Dictionary of Gardening*, not to mention numerous varieties, presents problems of selection as acute as any other genus of shrubs except roses. The simplest criterion from which to start is simply this: Viburnums evergreen, Vibrunums deciduous, or both? It is not always easy in life to determine which comes first, principle or practice, but in our own choice of Viburnums at Shepreth we have followed Aristotle, Faith perhaps unconsciously, in the belief that, at the outset at least, practice produces principle rather than principle practice. We neither inherited any evergreen Viburnum nor ever since have introduced any; and subsequent experience, with the increasing knowledge it brings, has elevated our instinctive practice to the status of a principle. Admittedly that old favourite universally known as Laurustinus, pedantically as *Viburnum tinus*, has the two undeniable merits that its otherwise undistinguished foliage has a healthy gloss and that it produces its not unattractive clusters of flowers in the depths of winter. But heaven help me if I ever fail to think of a more attractive shrub to occupy its potential place. And as for two of its slightly less familiar evergreen congeners, *V. davidii* and *V. rhytidophyllum* (of the former of which the *Dictionary of Gardening* says in conclusion 'Good foliage shrub' and of the latter 'Remarkable for its wrinkled leaves'), my recent close observation of them in the garden at Ardtornish, where they must have been planted by the original designer, has served only to confirm me in my long-held view that the only place for them in Britain is on the periphery of a municipal park. And the sootier the park the better, since there can be few shrubs hardy in these islands the freshness and beauty of whose leaves would be not a jot impaired by the superimposition of a thick layer of grime. Unfortunately my acquaintance with *V.* × *burkwoodii* and *V. henryi*, to name but two more out of many, is so relatively slight as to deny me the right of censure. But from things seen I shall continue to judge things unseen, and I shall therefore, at least until I have beheld it with my own eyes, persist in turning a deaf ear to Faith's occasional suggestion that we introduce to Shepreth a specimen of the latter, to the allurements of which she fell a victim on a visit last summer to a friend's garden in Somerset. In the case of the former, however, I have been skilfully outmanoeuvred in my prejudice. Not only has Faith been recently given a strapping young rooted cutting of Park Farm, a superior variety of *V.* × *burkwoodii*, but, which is more undermining to my authority, I am compelled to admit that its leaves are of a fresh and lustrous green such as I do not at all associate with the evergreen species. But then again, it is after all not a species but a hybrid, and one of its parents is the wholly admirable deciduous *V. carlesii*, of which more very shortly. It must be thence rather than from the evergreen *V. utile*, which is otherwise unknown to me, that it derives whatever merits it proves to possess.

So to the deciduous Viburnums, which are a wholly different matter and provide us with several of the most spectacularly beautiful shrubs in our whole garden. The winter-flowering *V. farreri*, of which we grow two symmetrical pairs at strategic points in the garden, is too well known to need any description or encomium. If we had thought a little longer, one or other of these two pairs would certainly have been of *V.* × *bodnantense* instead, the flowers of which not only come in larger clusters but are of a decidedly deeper pink. Indeed since this past winter, when we saw it for the first time in the Cambridge Botanical Garden, we should unhesitatingly have chosen the variety called Dawn, the description of which in the *Dictionary of Gardening* as 'a very good fragrant winter-flowering shrub' is certainly no exaggeration. And second after the *farreri* group, in chronological order rather than in order of merit, comes the aforementioned *V. carlesii*, a shrub of relatively low and spreading habit, which is again so familiar among British gardeners as to require little introduction. In case any reader is unfamiliar with it, suffice it to say, first, that its three-inch clusters of pale pink flowers outdo even carnations in their fragrance, and second that it too, when crossed not so long ago with *V. macrocephalum*, gave rise to a hybrid called *V.* × *carlcephalum* which sacrificed only a little of its scent in evolving flower-clusters almost half as wide again. And after these two follows, in a hectic flurry, a whole complex of deciduous Viburnums at least two groups of which call for a paragraph on their own.

Of our two native Viburnums, the wayfaring tree or *V. lantana* and the guelder rose or *V. opulus* (each of which, incidentally, is only debarred from a place in our garden by its relative abundance in local hedgerows), the latter long ago gave rise to the variety Roseum, better known as the snowball tree, which can yield only to lilac and laburnum in universal popularity among English gardeners. Again it is too familiar to call for more than two observations. First, even though we inherited a fine specimen of it at Shepreth, such was our affection for it that we lost little time in acquiring a second young shrub of it and planting it cheek by jowl with an equally juvenile plant of *Cornus* Elegantissima in a key corner of the semi-wild garden; and now that they have realised our hopes and become inextricably entangled one with the other, they compose a simple symphony of colouring in the early summer which evokes as much admiration as anything in the garden. And in the second place, if what you long for is again bigger and better clusters of flowers, then go for its Chinese counterpart instead, the all-sterile form of *V. macrocephalum*. And if once more you feel like taking our advice, which we cribbed without acknowledgment from the gardens at Blickling Hall, then train it in the sunshine up any dark-coloured wall.

So to the last group of Viburnums that I have time or inclination to mention, that of the polymorphic *V. plicatum*, and here we enter once again an impenetrable jungle of confusion. Not only the nomenclature, but also the descriptions in the leading catalogues, seem deliberately designed to reduce the mere amateur to a state of helpless indecision. Happily every variety that I have ever encountered – and there are certainly no more than half a dozen to be unravelled from the nurserymen's tangled web – fully deserves its place in even a small garden; the profusion of white flower-heads on their horizontal branches serves to distinguish them all at a glance not only from every other Viburnum but from every other flowering shrub, Hydrangeas included, in any garden in Britain. But however many of them there may be, one among them is entitled on every score to pride of place, the shrub which the catalogues seem for once united in calling the Lanarth variety of *V. plicatum* itself. Our own specimen of it, which came some twelve years ago from Notcutt's and which has since given rise by cuttings to a number of offspring of the same proportions, contradicts all the descriptions in catalogues, however fulsome, including Notcutt's own. In outline it resembles a somewhat flattened umbrella, with its numerous spokes arching symmetrically down to the level of the lawn in which it was originally planted; after twelve years it measures exactly eleven feet across by slightly under four feet in height; and with its dense mass of flat white flower-heads, each fully five inches wide, sufficiently separated to reveal the fresh young leaves beneath, it is voted by all who see it, ourselves emphatically included, to be assuredly one of the finest flowering shrubs in existence. It is, of course, conceivable that Notcutt's unwittingly sold us a pup. But in that case the pup, having already given birth to a small litter and being apparently good for several others, may yet make the confusion of nomenclature worse confounded.

So at long last to a final rhapsody on the evocative theme of honeysuckle, and in defiance of convention the rhapsody shall be brief and brisk. For of all the many species and hybrids of Lonicera to be found in English gardens the great majority, ranging from the shrubby *L. nitida* at one end of the scale to the lovely 'Dutch' varieties of our native climbing *L. periclymenum* at the other, are so well known as to stand in no need of advertisement. There are, however, four among their number whose outstanding merits cannot go unsung. All four are climbers, since even the winter-flowering shrubby varieties, of which the best is the hybrid between *L. fragrantissima* and *L. standishii* called *L. × purpusii*, have relatively little appeal for me. The first is *L. japonica* Halliana, the apparent delicacy of a young plant of which is belied by its subsequent rampant vigour. All the varietes of *L. japonica* are easily distinguished by the fact that their fragrant flowers come in opposite pairs in the axils of the leaves; but the variety Halliana is, to my mind at least, raised far above the rest by the fact that its flowers, until they begin to wither, are not of the same nondescript and rather dingy yellow as the rest but of the purest white. This may in fact, I suspect, be one of those not infrequent cases where it is as well, before placing an order and subsequently suffering a sharp disappointment, to go to the trouble of first seeing the plant in flower in the nursery from which you propose to acquire it.

The next two in my short list can be taken together, since the second is the child of the first. The glory of *L. tragophylla*, a Chinese species, lies not in its scent, which is regrettably and totally lacking, but in its combination of leaves which, at least when young, are overlaid with bronze and of clusters of unusually large flowers, up to almost three inches in length, of a brilliant golden yellow. And the result of crossing it with *L. sempervirens* is a hybrid, *L. × tellmanniana* by name, which, though it too is devoid of fragrance and has lost also the coppery tinge in its leaves, produces a display of bright yellow flower-heads at least as spectacular as its parent's. Father and son have in this case so strong a family resemblance as to have been confused, for instance, in the National Trust's garden at Tintinhull, where the son has, or at any rate had until last summer when I had the impertinence as a mere tourist to point out the error, usurped its father's name. But to judge from our own experience, which is obviously limited and may well not be typical, there is another and perhaps more pertinent difference between parent and progeny than the purely visual. Whereas it took us three attempts to get *L. tragophylla* happily established, both the plants of *L. × tellmanniana* that we ordered, with an interval of perhaps five years between them, adapted themselves immediately to the strikingly different situations allocated to them and have never looked back.

The last of my quartet, which I shall follow the *Dictionary of Gardening* in calling *L.* × *brownii* but which we actually bought, under one of its several synonyms, as *L. fuchsioides*, need detain us even less long. It is not so vigorous a plant as the last three and may, to judge again from our own very limited experience, in which our original plant suddenly died when apparently in the prime of life, be by nature a short-lived beauty. But be that as it may, its clusters of long, thin, tubular flowers, not unlike those of the Fuchsia called Thalia, are of so brilliant a scarlet as invariably to elicit the astonishment and the interrogation of our many June visitors. And thereby it has prompted a final lugubrious thought in that small part of my mind which is dedicated to horticulture. Why, oh why, when every second garden throughout the British Isles sports at least one flamboyant specimen of either the early or the late Dutch honeysuckle, are any of my quartet still to be seen only in the gardens of those who are all too often contemptuously dismissed as either snobs or cranks? An Englishman's home may be his castle and his garden, the park in which he takes his industrious leisure, may well excel that of his counterpart in any other country in the world. Indeed as I write now, in a train from Cambridge to London which is just entering the suburbs, and as I look out at the exiguous rectangles on either side of the railway that are so lovingly dug, planted, watered and generally cherished, I am firmly convinced, even though I have never been to Japan, that it must be so. But when so much devoted care is palpably lavished on ensuring that the ground-plan of each plot in no way resembles that of any of its neighbours, it does seem the greatest of pities that the same old plants, by no means always the best of their kind, recur, recur, and go on recurring all along the line.

Conclusion

DURING the few months in which this book has been written much has been happening in both our gardens. At Shepreth we have, first, so far relented as to build, in a waste space of some fourteen feet by seven backed by an old brick wall, a tiny rock garden and moraine and, by means of a subterranean perforated polythene pipe, we have contrived to keep the latter tolerably moist in times of drought. And second, we have revisited Asolo, in north Italy, and returned thence with, among other good things, two real treasures for the garden in *Isopyrum thalictroides* and *Cardamine enneaphyllos*. The former is a member of the *Ranunculaceae* and looks at first sight, and indeed goes on looking until the shape of its fruit betrays it, just like an exceptionally delicate sister of the wood anemone, with leaves, as its specific name suggests, not unlike those of a Thalictrum and four or five white anemone-like flowers to a stem. The latter, on the other hand, belongs improbably to the *Cruciferae*, at the time of flowering it has no base leaves, its nine-inch stem is bare for most of its height but is topped with two or, usually, three leaves, each consisting of three lanceolate and toothed leaflets, subtending a cluster of four to ten hanging, tubular, four-petalled flowers of a soft primrose yellow. Both these two seem to have settled happily into their new environment, and beside them our other Italian imports, notably *Helleborus niger, H. multifidus* subsp. *istriacus, Aquilegia kitaibelii* and three hitherto unidentified species of Euphorbia, pale into relative insignificance. And meanwhile at Ardtornish the unceasing struggle against the jungle of brambles and wild raspberries, *Spiraea salicifolia* and *Rhododendron ponticum* ,has made such headway that not only do large new tracts of the garden look from the road round the head of the loch to be tended and cared for, but at least one long-forgotten paved path down the hillside has been cleared for the first time in my memory.

Another event of recent weeks, of more concern to myself than to others, is that I have been allowed to resume my peregrinations, and even my labours, in the garden, and I have become gradually and uncomfortably aware of a few meritorious plants I have unwittingly omitted, as I reclined in a warm bed throughout the worst of a wicked winter, from the pages of this book. That is, of course, the price to be paid for writing about gardens in the dormant season. But for all that, my omissions fall into two categories, the conscious and the unconscious, and I must try to make some amends to them both severally, starting with those whose existence I unaccountably and inexcusably forgot.

It is obviously no coincidence that all six of the plants forgotten are small; all but one of them, indeed, small enough to be grown in a sink or trough. The first genus to which an apology is due is that of Alyssum, if only for the sake of the little prostrate *A. tortuosum*. With its matted mass of intertwining stems, reddish-purple after their first year, its neat and tiny spoon-shaped grey leaves and its clusters of clear yellow flowers held well above the carpet, it is an ideal plant for trailing over and down the edge of a sink. Then next in botanical order comes *Arenaria montana*, a plant which there can be no excuse for having forgotten since it is undoubtedly the showiest of its genus. Although I grow it likewise in a sink, it is really too vigorous to be thus circumscribed, not least because it likes to sow itself freely. Admittedly, when it is not in flower it is not a particularly notable and, indeed, with its numerous sterile branches, rather a straggly plant. But in the flowering season its pairs of opposite, narrowly lanceolate, bright green leaves are topped with such a profusion of rounded pure white flowers at least as large as a shilling that it richly earns a place in any rock garden. And the same could, I suspect, be justly said of the variety Mediovariegatum of the Japanese *Sedum sieboldii*, another almost prostrate plant with pink to purple stems and fleshy leaves, in whorls of three and virtually sessile, which are round and deckle-edged in outline and in colour a soft blue-grey with a splash of pale yellow in the middle and a narrow rim of deep pink. Its umbels of pinkish flowers in the autumn are somewhat undistinguished, but it fully merits a place in the garden for its leaves alone. And as for the summary statement in the *Dictionary of Gardenng*, 'Pot-plant for greenhouse. Not hardy.', that would seem to be conclusively disproved by its unscathed survival, both at Shepreth and at Langham in Rutland, of the severe frosts of this past winter.

Next should be mentioned, and very briefly, a dwarf Hebe, again compact enough for a sink, called Carl Teschner or Youngii, the habit and leaves of which are typical of the genus but which is raised above the ruck by its abundance of bright purplish-blue flowers. Beside it in the same sink grows *Teucrium polium*, another evergreen sub-shrub whose dense and soft grey foliage, deeply crenate at the edges, makes an admirable foil to the regular, stiff, lanceolate little leaves of the Hebe, while its rounded heads of flowers can apparently be either white, purple or, as they are on our plant, yellow. And of my six forgotten plants that leaves only *Chrysanthemum haradjanii*[1] from the eastern Mediterranean, which, despite the disparaging fashion in which I earlier dismissed most of its congeners, may well be the best of the lot. Like *Sedum sieboldii*, it is a plant to be grown for the sake of its foliage rather than its flowers, but that foliage, a mass of grey feathers forming a low flat mound, makes it second only to *Artemisia nitida* as an edging plant for the rockery or for a brick or paved path. It is a pity that it was introduced into this country too late for inclusion in the *Dictionary of Gardening*.

My second group of omissions is of an altogether different order. Heaven alone knows how many whole families, thanks to my initial decision to deal only with those which are represented in the native flora of Britain, I have hitherto deliberately ignored; they may well outnumber those on which I have focused attention. But a few of them positively obtrude, and those few fall again into two categories. First come those, such as the *Magnoliaceae* or the *Theaceae*, the glamour of which is such that any normal gardener must long to grow them, but which we are firmly debarred by the nature of the soil from growing as natural constituents of the Shepreth garden. It is a mysterious and lugubrious fact that, while several species of Magnolia thrive and flower freely in Cambridge with the minimum of attention, not even the ubiquitous *M. × soulangiana*, which according to the *Dictionary of Gardening* 'is among the most accommodating of its genus', can be induced by liberal applications of Sequestrene to adapt itself to our chalky desert a mere eight miles to the south-west; and it is a fact for which the presence and health of a number of varieties at Ardtornish affords only scanty consolation, since we can never be there to see them in flower. And where a Magnolia refuses to grow, what hope is there for a Camellia? True, as I have said already, we do grow and flower one each in the lime-free soil in our troughs, and we also grow in the cool greenhouse a number of small specimens, of which the semi-double shell-pink *C. japonica* Hagoromo is almost universally adjudged the best, in pots small enough to bring indoors in the flowering season. But even though we deem such artifices a great deal better than nothing, and are at present extending them in desperation to young bushes of *Magnolia × soulangiana* and *M. stellata*, they are a poor substitute, as the favoured counties along the south coast show only too well, for the real thing.

Many another dicotyledonous family should doubtless receive at least

---

[1] [Now transferred to the genus *Tanacetum*.]

a mention in any book about gardening in Britain, but in the circumstances these two glaring examples must suffice. For there still remains the last category of all, those families which, though they unhappily have no British representative, yet can and do infiltrate as registered aliens into our garden at Shepreth. And here I can be more explicit and precise than is my wont: there are just nine such families, in the shape of the *Actidiniaceae*, the *Vitaceae*, the *Bignoniaceae*, the *Calycanthaceae*, the *Hamamelidaceae*, the *Stachyuraceae*, the *Sapindaceae*, the *Rutaceae* and the *Anacardiaceae*. And to these nine should perhaps be added a family to which, in my hasty transition in Chapter 11 from the *Scrophulariaceae* to the *Labiatae*, I did even more than my customary injustice, that of the *Verbenaceae*.

Although these few families are listed neither alphabetically nor botanically, their sequence is not entirely haphazard. The first three consist largely, if not exclusively, of vigorous climbers, the remainder range from small trees, through shrubs, to herbaceous plants. From our point of view, which is apparently endorsed by the *Dictionary of Gardening*, the most important members of the *Actinidiaceae*, all of which hail from eastern Asia, are two species of the genus Actinidia itself. *A. kolomikta*, a relatively slender climber with ovate leaves that are a random patchwork of green, white and pink, is so decidedly arresting rather than beautiful that we shed few tears when the plant we intended to train over the wall at the back of the winter garden abandoned the unequal struggle. Perhaps it resents, as its more rampageous congener *A. deliciosa* (formerly *chinensis*) certainly does, any interference with its determination to grow in the wrong direction. But in all other respects *A. deliciosa*, a small layer of which we long ago brought back from Ardtornish, where it attains to astronomical heights up the house and its lofty towers, is among the very best of rampant climbers. Its branches describe the most graceful and sinuous curves, its nearly circular leaves, which can attain a diameter of at least nine inches, are held on long, hairy, reddish-purple stalks, and its flowers, which seem usually to come in threes on diverging pedicels, are inch-wide pendant saucers of white, which turns through cream to apricot, more than half filled with a bunch of golden anthers.

The *Vitaceae*, of which we have so far planted four at Shepreth, are so much more familiar that they can be more hastily dismissed. The huge-leaved *Vitis coignetiae*, an undeniably noble plant with brilliant autumn colouring, is unfortunately on too large a scale for our restricted dimensions; but its lesser brethren serve a variety of our purposes to excellent effect. The grape-bearing vine called Buckland Sweetwater has scrambled so rapidly over the half of the Queen Anne façade that was not already wreathed in Wisteria, and twined so lustily into our upstairs windows, that it cannot be long before we pick bunches of sweet little green grapes without even getting out of bed. The dusky *Vitis vinifera* Purpurea seems to be taking longer to get under way up the highest wall of the paved courtyard, but this year for the first time it is beginning to overtop the low shrubs, such as *Cistus* x *corbariensis* and *Dorycnium hirsutum*, in the sunny bed at its foot. *Vitis heterophylla*, now properly called *Ampelopsis brevipedunculata*, the leaves of which vary from sharply three-lobed to almost circular and entire, so crowns our large tree of *Prunus subhirtella* Autumnalis at the back of the winter garden that in the autumn it sprinkles the paving stones in the courtyard behind with its pea-sized blue fruit. And last but not least *Vitis*, alias this time *Parthenocissus, henryana*, the only one of the Virginia creepers that we dare admit to the precincts, climbs delicately up the low white plastered wall beside the back door and protrudes its slender and flexuous young branches, themselves deep crimson and clothed with five-fingered leaves which are purplish-red in youth but green with red and white veins in maturity, through the stout and thorny limbs of the climbing rose Reveil Dijonnais.

The *Bigoniaceae* are a more versatile family than either of the foregoing, numbering among their ranks the climbing genus Campsis, large trees such as Catalpa, Jacaranda and Paulownia, and the herbaceous Incarvilleas. For our part, largely for reasons of space but also because of the severity of our winters, we confine ourselves to a single species in each class. *Campsis grandiflora*, which came originally from young self-layered plants in my father's last garden in Cambridge, has by now completely filled its allotted space on the tarred wooden wall of one of our encircling barns and is turning its attention horizontally, as we hoped it would, to cover the hideous leaning roof of corrugated asbestos as well; but alas, the majority of its orange and red trumpets come and go, like the flowers of our solitary Hibiscus, while we are up at Ardtornish. The controversial tree of the familiar *Catalpa bignonioides*, which I planted, while nobody was looking, in the middle of the oval lawn in the rose and iris garden, is still too young to have flowered, but has already begun to form the spreading umbrella of fresh green that I visualised there. And the deep rose-pink trumpets of *Incarvillea delavayi*, having been crowded out of the herbaceous border, will perhaps fare better in the less cut-throat competition on the sunny side of the courtyard.

Mercifully the next four families, the *Calycanthaceae*, the *Hamamelidaceae*, the *Stachyuraceae* and the *Sapindaceae*, contain few species hardy in Britain – indeed, the penultimate consists solely of the small genus Stachyurus itself, which is native only in the Far East – and can muster in the garden at Shepreth no more than a single representative apiece.

The pride of the *Calycanthaceae* is the well known winter-flowering shrub *Chimonanthus fragrans* or winter sweet, with its deliciously scented yellow and reddish-purple flowers. The *Hamamelidaceae* are represented at Shepreth not by the almost equally well known witch hazel, *Hamamelis mollis*, with its spidery golden flowers, which unaccountably lost little time in dying on us, but by the less ubiquitous and more refined *Corylopsis pauciflora*, a spreading shrub of a mere three or four feet with drooping spikes of only two or three flowers of primrose yellow.[1] And the member of the *Stachyuraceae* that we chose, rightly or wrongly, is *Stachyurus praecox*, which produces abundant slender hanging racemes, some three inches long, which, though they are actually composed of up to twenty little cup-shaped flowers, look from a distance like pale yellow hazel catkins. All these three, of course, have the distinction of producing their flowers from the bare bark while Britain is still firmly in the grip of winter, and accordingly we grow all three of them, though the last not exclusively, in our very visible and accessible winter garden. Our chosen representative of the *Sapindaceae*, on the other hand, the little known *Koelreuteria paniculata*, which I seem to remember mentioning more than once in the course of this book, flowers in July; and not only then, when large orangy-yellow spikes rise from among the elegantly pinnate leaves, but perhaps even more when those same leaves turn the most vivid colours in the autumn and are interspersed with brown Japanese lanterns containing three seeds each, do we rejoice at our selection of this particular representative of this particular family. There is probably no plant in the whole garden that so little deserves its general neglect.

The *Rutaceae*, although we can boast only four representatives of the family, are so polymorphic as to demand a paragraph to themselves. The said four consist of two woody shrubs in *Choisya ternata* and *Skimmia reevesiana*, a semi-woody sub-shrub in *Ruta graveolens*, and a herbaceous perennial in *Dictamnus fraxinella*, alias *D. albus purpurens*. Personally I regard *Choisya ternata* as being no less overrated than *Koelreuteria paniculata* is under, and I shall bear Faith a lasting grudge that she introduced a plant of it on either side of the gap in the old brick wall that leads to the latest acquired part of the garden while I was confined to bed. As for the Skimmia, which has recently been moved to the back of the new-made rock garden just through the same gap, neither of us has the faintest notion why or whence a young and

---

[1] As I mentioned in Chapter 6, we also grow, in the middle rank of the winter garden, the taller, showier, but for all that less aristocratic *C. spicata*. But by a grave error of judgment we planted it in a situation where, though it is still alive and kicking, its taller neighbours render it so nearly invisible that even at this late stage I contrived practically to forget its existence.

healthy plant of it suddenly materialised in the border under the greenhouse; we only know that we could not and would not have bought it. The rue, on the other hand, and especially in the variety justly called Jackman's Blue, we would both regard as being among the most indispensable plants in the garden. Its yellow flowers, though admittedly not very conspicuous, reveal a certain subtlety of design, while its little pinnately compound leaves, being nearer a genuine blue than those of any other plant in the garden except perhaps *Hosta sieboldiana* Elegans, are the perfect foil, both in shape and colour, to half the plants you care to think of. And though I would hesitate to lavish such extravagant praise on the Dictamnus, it can obviously be in no way due to the fact that we came unexpectedly on a quantity of its pink form in one of our favourite picnic places in the north of Italy that we already cherished a group of three white-flowered plants of it in the herbaceous border. I wish that I could testify to the veracity of the oft-repeated statement that, in the words of the *Dictionary of Gardening*, 'on a hot still day the volatile oil may often be ignited by bringing a lighted match near the base of the inflorescence, flaming up for a short time and leaving the plant uninjured.' But despite repeated failure in this evidently harmless experiment, I find it still makes a good talking point among sticky visitors to the garden.

So, last among the nine families which the deliberate plan of this book constrained me to omit, we arrive at the *Anacardiaceae*; and I have left them till last advisedly for the simple reason that they provide two of the most invaluable shrubs in the whole garden. The only two genera in the family with which we concern ourselves, as a matter of fact, are those of the sumachs, the genera Rhus and Cotinus, and, as is so often the case, we do not actually grow the most popular member of these genera, the so-called stag's horn sumach or *Rhus typhina*, but prefer instead to see it in countless other people's gardens. For even in its undeniably attractive laciniate variety, it manages in late autumn and winter, despite its prominent crimson fruiting spikes, to assume a forlorn and bedraggled appearance which I for one find decidedly depressing. In its stead we grow, if only for the sake of its dazzling and varied autumn colouring, a specimen of the much less familiar *Cotinus obovatus*, which, in close proximity to *Berberis thunbergii*, makes it well worth while to visit the semi-wild garden even as late in the year as November. But the glory of the family, even if it is not acknowledged as such by the *Dictionary of Gardening*, is unquestionably to our untutored eyes *Cotinus coggygria*, better known as the wig or smoke tree. Besides the type, which we grow as a specimen bush in the wild garden and which, from July onwards, is smothered in soft feathery plumes, we long ago planted also a young sample of Notcutt's version of the purple-leaved variety, which has by now grown to such dimensions that it is up to the level of the roof of the Elizabethan wing of the house and its 'dark maroon foliage', to borrow from Notcutt's own description of it, blends to perfection with the various shades of the original tiles. In all honesty, however, we have to admit that this is one of our occasional wholly unpremeditated strokes of horticultural inspiration.

Now that we are at last back to the *Verbenaceae*, the end is in sight. Apart from the sweet-scented Verbena itself, *Aloysia triphylla*, which Faith optimistically planted last year immediately outside the back door, which looked as dead as mutton after this last long and hard winter, but which, some weeks ago now, broke from below ground into new and vigorous growth, there are two other members of the family which amply justify inclusion, since neither of them requires much space, in even the smallest garden. *Caryopteris* × *clandonensis* is a spreading but tidy shrub some four feet tall and about as much in width. Its opposite leaves, which are variable in outline but on our specimen are narrowly lanceolate and deeply and sharply toothed, are soft grey-green above and pale grey beneath, and in late summer the whole bush is covered with compact clusters of pure powder-blue flowers somewhat suggestive of a fluffy Ceanothus. (Incidentally, at least two species of Ceanothus, *C. dentatus* and *C. rigidus*, would have found their way into the pages of this book under the shield of the *Rhamnaceae* had they not succumbed, as they did, I believe, throughout the whole of this part of the country, to the horrific winter of 1962–3; but since the loss of wall covering is, to our minds, the most grievous and painfully repaired of all losses that a gardener can sustain, they were sadly replaced by more reliably hardy substitutes.) And then there is *Callicarpa bodinieri giraldii*, a taller and more erect shrub than the Caryopteris, whose sharp-pointed ovate leaves and tight clusters of little violet flowers would probably attract the attention of none but the connoisseur. But when the leaves have dropped and those same clusters of little flowers have turned to bunches of brilliant purple berries, no small shrub could be so richly entitled to the uniquely prominent position that we have allocated to it in the middle of the front row of the winter garden.

And after all that I have come within an inch or two of forgetting one of the most prominent families of all, the *Moraceae*, which include not only the mulberry, whose immemorial relic is still the main feature of the south-east corner of our front garden and the support for the lusty climbing rose Silver Moon, but the fig as well. Whichever of our predecessors it was who introduced the fig tree that was already well established by the time of our arrival at Shepreth, he was guilty of an inexplicable error of judgment in planting it at the foot of a wall which faces slightly north of east. The result is, of course, that though it always sets fruit as doggedly as the gallant old mulberry, only once in sixteen years has it ripened a few of them rather than dropping them in defection to the ground. Maybe, in view of the children's present propensity to nudism, it will yet find a good use for its leaves. And maybe also, before many more years have elapsed, we shall find ourselves under pressure to add to the inhabitants of our garden, and not for the worthy purpose of making rope, an annual from a family which was until lately subsumed under the *Moraceae*, the stately adornment, I am told, of many an urban window-box, *Cannabis sativa*.

Index of Scientific Names

Index of Scientific Names

Index of Common Names

Index of Common Names